Sydney Omarr's

DAY-BY-DAY ASTROLOGICAL GUIDE FOR

CANCER

June 21–July 22

2002

A SIGNET BOOK

SIGNET
Published by New American Library, a division of
Penguin Putnam Inc., 375 Hudson Street,
New York, New York 10014, U.S.A.
Penguin Books Ltd, 27 Wrights Lane,
London W8 5TZ, England
Penguin Books Australia Ltd, Ringwood,
Victoria, Australia
Penguin Books Canada Ltd, 10 Alcorn Avenue,
Toronto, Ontario, Canada M4V 3B2
Penguin Books (N.Z.) Ltd, 182–190 Wairau Road,
Auckland 10, New Zealand

Penguin Books Ltd, Registered Offices:
Harmondsworth, Middlesex, England

First published by Signet, an imprint of New American Library,
a division of Penguin Putnam Inc.

First Printing, June 2001
10 9 8 7 6 5 4 3 2 1

Sydney Omarr is syndicated worldwide by
Los Angeles Times Syndicate.

 REGISTERED TRADEMARK—MARCA REGISTRADA

Printed in the United States of America

2002
A BRAND-NEW YEAR—
A PROMISING NEW START

Enter Sydney Omarr's star-studded world of accurate day-by-day predictions for every aspect of your life. With expert readings and forecasts, you can chart a course to romance, adventure, good health, or career opportunities while gaining valuable insight into yourself and others. Offering a daily outlook for 18 full months, this fascinating guide shows you:

- The important dates in your life
- What to expect from an astrological reading
- How the stars can help you stay healthy and fit
- Your lucky lottery numbers
  And more!

Let this expert's sound advice guide you through a year of heavenly possibilities—for today and for every day of 2002!

SYDNEY OMARR'S DAY-BY-DAY
ASTROLOGICAL GUIDE FOR

ARIES—March 21–April 19
TAURUS—April 20–May 20
GEMINI—May 21–June 20
CANCER—June 21–July 22
LEO—July 23–August 22
VIRGO—August 23–September 22
LIBRA—September 23–October 22
SCORPIO—October 23–November 21
SAGITTARIUS—November 22–December 21
CAPRICORN—December 22–January 19
AQUARIUS—January 20–February 18
PISCES—February 19–March 20

IN 2002

CHANCE TO WIN A PERSONALIZED HOROSCOPE FOR A FULL YEAR!

Enter the Sydney Omarr Horoscope Sweepstakes!

No purchase necessary. Details below. Open only to U.S. residents age 18 and up

Name _____

Address_____

City_____ State_____ Zip_____

Mail to:

Sydney Omarr Horoscope Sweepstakes
c/o Penguin Putnam Inc.
375 Hudson St., 5th floor
New York, NY 10014
All entries must be postmarked by August 31, 2001 and received by September 8, 2001.

1. NO PURCHASE NECESSARY TO ENTER OR WIN A PRIZE. To enter the Sydney Omarr Horoscope Sweepstakes, complete this official entry form or, on a 3" x 5" piece of paper, write your name and complete address. Mail your entry to: Sydney Omarr Horoscope Sweepstakes; c/o Penguin Putnam Inc.; 375 Hudson St., 5th floor; New York, NY 10014. Enter as often as you wish, but mail each entry in a separate envelope. No mechanically reproduced or computer generated entries allowed. All entries must be postmarked by 8/31/2001 and received by 9/8/2001 to be eligible. Not responsible for late, lost, damaged, incomplete, illegible, postage due or misdirected mail entries.

2. Winners will be selected from all eligible entries in a random drawing on or about 9/14/01, by Penguin Putnam Inc., whose decisions are final and binding. Odds of winning are dependent upon the number of entries received. Winners will be notified by mail and may be required to execute an affidavit of eligibility and release which must be returned within 14 days of notification or an alternate winner will be selected.

3. One (1) Grand Prize winner will receive a personalized one-year horoscope from an astrologer chosen by Sydney Omarr or Penguin Putnam Inc. One (1) Second Prize winner will receive a personalized one-month horoscope from an astrologer chosen by Sydney Omarr or Penguin Putnam Inc. Estimated aggregate value of Grand Prize and Second Prize: $250. If there is an insufficient number of entries, Penguin Putnam Inc. reserves the right not to award the prizes.

4. Sweepstakes open to residents of the U.S. 18 years of age or older, except employees and the immediate families of Penguin Putnam Inc., its affiliated companies, advertising and promotion agencies. Void in Puerto Rico, and wherever else prohibited by law. No cash substitutions, transfers or assignments of prizes are allowed. In event of unavailability, sponsor may substitute a prize of equal or greater value. Limit one prize per person, household or family. All Federal, State, and Local laws apply. Taxes, if any, are the sole responsibility of the prize winners. Winners consent to the use of their name and/or photos or likenesses for advertising purposes without additional compensation (except where prohibited). By accepting this prize, winners release Penguin Putnam Inc., its affiliated companies, advertising and promotion agencies from any and all liability for any loss, harm, injuries, damages, cost or expense arising out of participation in this Sweepstakes or the acceptance, use or misuse of the prize.

5. For the names of the prize-winners, send a self-addressed, stamped envelope after 9/28/01 to : SYDNEY OMARR HOROSCOPE SWEEPSTAKES WINNERS, Penguin Putnam Inc., 375 Hudson St., 5th floor, New York, NY 10014.

CONTENTS

INTRODUCTION

Your Cosmic Code

Are you ready for the excitement and challenges of the year 2002? We've cracked the mystery of the human genome, but there's another code that's been used to map the human personality since ancient times. Like your genetic imprint, your astrology chart is uniquely "you." It is a map of your moment in time, which has its own code, based on the position of the sun, moon, and planets at the time and place you were born. What is especially intriguing is that this system can offer specific, practical guidance, even when using only *one* of the elements of the code, your *sun sign.* Though you share that sun sign with others, there are many ways to use it every day to find a more fulfilling lifestyle. Your sun sign "map" can help you find success, attract love, look for a better job, have a healthier body, and even take the vacation of your dreams or decorate your home.

Just knowing the other person's sun sign can give you many clues to how to make your relationship a happy one. You can troubleshoot problems in advance and, if they crop up, find a way to make them work for you. In this year's edition of *Sydney Omarr's Guides,* you'll learn what's best for you and how your sign relates, positively and negatively, with every other sign under the sun.

"For every thing there is a season" could be the theme song of astrology. Will 2002 be the time to charge forward or proceed with caution, to change

1

careers or stick with the job at hand, to fall in love? We'll deal in many ways with the question of timing—when are the potentially difficult times (which also present positive challenges), when can you expect delays and potential misunderstandings, when are the best times to take risks? You'll be able to get your life "on track" and chart your course with full knowledge of the shoals ahead.

For those who are new to astrology or would like to know more about it, there is basic information to give you an inside look at how astrology works. Then you can look up the other planets in your horoscope to find out how each contributes to your unique personality.

Astrologers have been quick to embrace the new technology of the twenty-first century, especially since sophisticated astrological computer programs have eliminated the tedious work of casting a chart and deliver beautiful chart printouts. Now anyone with access to the Internet can view their astrology chart at a free Internet site or buy the same programs professional astrologers use. We'll show you where to do this in chapters devoted especially to Internet resources. We'll also give you Sydney Omarr's updated "Yellow Pages" of the best places for books, tapes, and further astrological studies.

As we explore our inner cosmos via astrology, we are still searching for the same things that always have made life worth living: love, meaningful work, and fulfilling relationships. With Sydney Omarr's astonishingly accurate day-by-day forecasts, you can use your cosmic link to the universe to enhance every aspect of your life. So here's hoping you use your star power wisely and well for a productive and happy 2002!

CHAPTER 1

The Coming Trends of 2002!

We're at the beginning of a decisive decade, when many issues are coming to the forefront simultaneously: global expansion, territorial disputes, space travel, biotechnology breakthroughs, overpopulation, dangers of nuclear warfare, and environmental crises. Here are the key planets calling the shots and the trends to watch in 2002.

This year is a "bridge" year, when there are no dramatic shifts in the atmosphere (that comes next year). So it is more a time of consolidation, of taking stock and making plans for the future. The slow-moving planet Pluto is our guide to the hottest trends. Pluto brings about a heightened consciousness and transformation of matters related to the sign it is passing through. Now in Sagittarius, Pluto is emphasizing everything associated with this sign to prepare us philosophically and spiritually for things to come.

Perhaps the most pervasive sign of Pluto in Sagittarius is globalization in all its forms, which has become a main theme of the past few years. We are re-forming boundaries, creating new forms of travel that will definitely include space travel. At this writing, the $60 billion space station is under way, a joint venture between the United States, Russia, Japan, Europe, and Canada. It is scheduled for completion in 2006 and will be one of the brightest objects in the sky.

In true Sagittarius fashion, Pluto will shift our emphasis away from acquiring wealth to a quest for the

3

meaning of it all, as upward strivers discover that money and power are not enough. Sagittarius is the sign of linking everything together; therefore the trend will be to find ways to interconnect on spiritual, philosophical, and intellectual levels.

Pluto in Sagittarius's spiritual emphasis has already filtered down to our home lives. Home altars and private sanctuaries are becoming a part of our personal environment. The oriental art of feng shui has moved westward, giving rise to a more harmonious, spiritual atmosphere in offices and homes, which also promotes luck and prosperity.

Sagittarians are known for their love of animals, and we have never been more pet-happy. Look for extremes related to animal welfare, such as vegetarianism, which will become even more popular and widespread as a lifestyle. As habitats are destroyed, the care, feeding, and control of wild animals will become a larger issue, especially where there are deer, bears, and coyotes in the back yard.

The Sagittarian love of the outdoors combined with Pluto's power has already promoted extreme sports, especially those that require strong legs, like rock climbing, trekking, or snowboarding. Rugged, sporty all-terrain vehicles continue to be popular, as are zippy little scooters which help us get around in a fun way. Expect the trend toward more adventurous travel and fitness or sports-oriented vacations to accelerate: exotic hiking trips to unexplored territories, mountain-climbing expeditions, spa vacations, and sports-associated resorts are part of this trend.

Publishing, which is associated with Sagittarius, has been transformed by the new electronic media, with an enormous variety of books available in print. The Internet bookstore will continue to prosper under Pluto in Sagittarius. It is fascinating that the online bookstore Amazon.com took the Sagittarius-influenced name of the fierce female tribe of archer-warriors who went to the extreme of removing their right breasts to better shoot their arrows.

4

Who's Lucky? Make Hay, Cancer and Leo!

Good fortune, expansion, and big money opportunities are associated with the movement of Jupiter, the planet that embodies the principle of expansion. Jupiter has a twelve-year cycle, staying in each sign for approximately one year.

When Jupiter enters a sign, the fields associated with that sign usually provide excellent opportunities. Areas of speculation associated with the sign Jupiter is passing through will have the hottest market potential—the ones that currently arouse excitement and enthusiasm.

The flip side of Jupiter is that there are no limits . . . you can expand off the planet under a Jupiter transit, which is why the planet is often called the "Gateway to Heaven." If something is going to burst—such as an artery—or overextend or go over the top in some way, it could happen under a supposedly "lucky" Jupiter transit . . . so be aware.

This year, Jupiter will finish its journey through Cancer in August, when it moves into Leo. So sun sign Cancers and Leos and those with strong Cancer or Leo influence in their horoscopes should have abundant growth opportunities during the year. On the other hand, those born under Capricorn and Aquarius, the signs which occur at the opposite time of year, may have to work harder for success.

Jupiter in Cancer should bring opportunities in home-related industries, child care, the food and shelter industries, cruises, maternal issues, shipping and boating, and water sports. Look for further expansion in home-based business and telecommuting. Combining mothering with an active career will be a key issue for Gen-X women, who'll have a tug of war between family and career.

After Jupiter moves into Leo in August, people will

be looking for more fun in life, more joy, and more opportunities to play. We'll all want to be young again, and chances are that plastic surgery will enjoy a big boom time. Bring on the divas, as larger-than-life personalities take center stage. Look for more self-aggrandizement and self-adornment in flamboyant fashions with plenty of color, style, and piles of gold jewelry. This is an influence which encourages extravagance, showing off, and enjoying the best things in life. On a more serious note, child-raising will very much be on our minds, since the sign of Leo rules children. How will we raise children in a workaholic era? Since this Jupiter encourages love affairs and casual sex, the pull of family ties and responsibilities could be one of the biggest challenges this year.

Saturn Puts on the Brakes in Gemini

Saturn keywords are focus, time, commitment, accomplishment, discipline, and restriction. If Jupiter gives you a handout, then Saturn hands you the bill. With Saturn, nothing's free; you work for what you get, so it's always a good idea to find the areas (or houses) of your horoscope where Saturn is passing through, to learn where to focus your energy on lasting value. With Saturn, you must be sure to finish what you start, be responsible, put in the hard work, and stick with it.

This year, Saturn finishes up its two-year transit of Gemini. The normally light-spirited Geminis have had to deal with the serious, sobering influence of Saturn, just after they enjoyed the expansive period of Jupiter in Gemini in 2000 and 2001. Geminis have to back up the risks they took then and will be required to deliver on promises made. It'll be a powerful challenge for changeable Geminis, who must now pay the piper.

In the world at large, Saturn in Gemini is sure to affect communications. Talk must be followed up by action now. We'll be concerned with Gemini issues of lower education and literacy, reforming the lower educational system. Since Gemini is an air sign, which rules the lungs, there will be further controversy and restriction surrounding smoking and the tobacco industry.

Uranus and Neptune in Aquarius— The High-Tech Signs

Uranus and Neptune are pushing us into the future as they continue their long stays in Aquarius. Uranus overthrows the worn-out status quo and points us toward the future. It rules the sign of Aquarius, so it has been in its most powerful position since 1995, and has created radical breakthroughs in technology, as well as a concern with issues that involve all humanity. It is now preparing to move into Pisces, a sign associated with spirituality, imagination, and creativity. Its coming influence should begin to show up this year, with some dramatic changes in the arts beginning this summer.

Our lust for techno-toys should make this a gadget-crazed time, especially as Jupiter enters playful Leo, reinforcing this trend. Interactive forms of amusement and communication will rival television for our leisure. In fact, television may be on its way out as we opt for more exciting forms of entertainment.

While Jupiter remains in Cancer, the first half of the year, look for more Cancer-related products and events in the news: home furnishings, housing, child care, food products and merchandising, and a surge in restaurants, futuristic cruise ships, and new concepts in living quarters. After Jupiter moves into Leo, it forms an uneasy relationship with Neptune and Uranus on the opposite side of the zodiac, which could engender conflicts between individuals and society at large, between what "I" want and what "they" want.

7

There will be concern about how technology is negatively affecting personal lives and creativity.

Where there is Neptune, look for imagination and creativity, and since this is the planet of deception and illusion, scams and scandals continue, especially in the high-tech area associated with Aquarius. Neptune is also associated with hospitals, which are acquiring a Neptunian glamour, as well as cutting-edge technology. The atmosphere of many hospitals is already changing from the intimidating sterile surgical environment of the past to that of a health-promoting spa, with alternative therapies such as massage, diet counseling, and aromatherapy available. New procedures in plastic surgery, also a Neptunian glamour field, and antiaging therapies should restore the bloom and the body of youth, as Jupiter in Leo glorifies the everyoung.

CHAPTER 2

Planning Ahead in 2002— Timing Your Life for Luck, Prosperity, and Love!

It's no secret that some of the most powerful and famous people, from Julius Caesar to financier J. P. Morgan, from Ronald Reagan to Cher, have consulted astrologers before they made their moves. If astrology helps the rich and famous stay on course through life's ups and downs, why not put it to work for you?

Take control of your life by coordinating your schedule with the cosmos. For instance, if you know the dates that the mischievous planet Mercury will be creating havoc with communications, you'll back up that vital fax with a duplicate by Express Mail; you'll read between the lines of contracts and put off closing that deal until you have double-checked all the information. When Venus is in your sign, making you the romantic flavor of the month, you'll be at your most attractive. That would be a great time to update your wardrobe, revamp your image, or ask someone you'd like to know better to dinner. Venus helps you make that sales pitch and win over the competition.

To find out for yourself if there's truth to the saying "Timing is everything," mark your own calendar for love, career moves, vacations, and important events, using the following information and the tables in this chapter and the one titled "Look Up Your Planets," as well as the moon sign listings under your daily forecast. Here are the happenings to note on your agenda:

- Dates of your sun sign (high-energy period)
- The month previous to your sun sign (low-energy period)
- Dates of planets in your sign this year
- Full and new moons
  (Pay special attention when these fall in your sun sign.)
- Eclipses
- Moon in your sun sign every month, as well as moon in the opposite sign (listed in daily forecast)
- Mercury retrogrades
- Other retrograde periods

Your Personal Power Time

Every birthday starts a cycle of solar energy for you. You should feel a new surge of vitality as the powerful sun enters your sign. This is the time when predominant energies are most favorable to you. So go for it! Start new projects; make your big moves. You'll get the recognition you deserve now, when everyone is attuned to your sun sign. Look in the tables in this book to see if other planets will also be passing through your sun sign at this time. Venus (love, beauty), Mars (energy, drive), or Mercury (communication, mental sharpness) reinforce the sun and give an extra boost to your life in the areas they affect. Venus will rev up your social and love life, making you seem especially attractive. Mars gives you extra energy and drive. Mercury fuels your brain power and helps you communicate. Jupiter signals an especially lucky period of expansion.

There are two "down" times related to the sun. During the month before your birthday period, when you are winding up your annual cycle, you could be feeling especially vulnerable and depleted, so get extra rest, watch your diet, and don't overstress yourself. Use this time to gear up for a big "push" when the sun enters your sign.

Another "down" time is when the sun is in the opposite sign from your sun sign (six months from your birthday) and the prevailing energies are very different from yours. You may feel at odds with the world, and things might not come easily. You'll have to work harder for recognition, because people are not on your wavelength. However, this could be a good time to work on a team, in cooperation with others or behind the scenes.

How to Use the Moon's Phase and Sign

Working with the phases of the moon is as easy as looking up at the night sky. During the new moon, when both the sun and the moon are in the same sign, it's the best time to begin new ventures, especially the activities that are favored by that sign. You'll have powerful energies pulling you in the same direction. You'll be focused outward, toward action and doing. Postpone breaking off, terminating, deliberating, or reflecting, activities that require introspection and passive work.

Get your project under way during the first quarter, then go public at the full moon, a time of high intensity, when feelings come out into the open. This is your time to shine—to express yourself. Be aware, however, that because pressures are being released, other people are also letting off steam and confrontations are possible. So try to avoid arguments. Traditionally, astrologers often advise against surgery at this time, which could produce heavier bleeding.

During the last quarter of the new moon, you'll be most controlled. This is a winding-down phase, a time to cut off unproductive relationships and do serious thinking and inward-directed activities.

You'll feel some new and full moons more strongly than others, especially those new moons that fall in your sun sign and full moons in your opposite sign. Because that full moon happens at your low-energy time of year, it is likely to be an especially stressful time in a relationship, when any hidden problems or unexpressed emotions could surface.

Full and New Moons in 2002

New Moon in Capricorn—January 13
Full Moon in Leo—January 28
New Moon in Aquarius—February 12
Full Moon in Virgo—February 27
New Moon in Pisces—March 13
Full Moon in Libra—March 28
New Moon in Aries—April 12
Full Moon in Scorpio—April 27
New Moon in Taurus—May 12
Full Moon in Sagittarius (lunar eclipse)—May 26
New Moon in Gemini (solar eclipse)—June 10
Full Moon in Capricorn (lunar eclipse)—June 24
New Moon in Cancer—July 10
Full Moon in Aquarius—July 24
New Moon in Leo—August 8
Full Moon in Aquarius (second time)—August 22
New Moon in Virgo—September 6
Full Moon in Pisces—September 21
New Moon in Libra—October 6
Full Moon in Aries—October 21
New Moon in Scorpio—November 4
Full Moon in Taurus (lunar eclipse)—November 19
New Moon in Sagittarius (solar eclipse)—December 4
Full Moon in Gemini—December 19

Moon Sign Timing

To forecast the daily emotional "weather," to determine your monthly high and low days, or to synchronize your activities with the cycles and the sign of the moon, take note of the moon's daily sign under your daily forecast at the end of the book. Here are some of the activities favored and moods you are likely to encounter under each sign.

Moon in Aries

Get moving! The new moon in Aries is an ideal time to start new projects. Everyone is pushy, raring to go, and rather impatient and short-tempered. Leave details and follow-up for later. Competitive sports or martial arts are great ways to let off steam. Quiet types could use some assertiveness, but it's a great day for dynamos. Be careful not to step on too many toes.

Moon in Taurus

It's time to do solid, methodical tasks. This is the time to tackle follow-through or backup work. Lay the foundations for success. Make investments, buy real estate, do appraisals, and do some hard bargaining. Attend to your property—get out in the country. Spend some time in your garden. Enjoy creature comforts, music, a good dinner, and sensual lovemaking. Forget starting a diet.

Moon in Gemini

Talk means action today. Telephone, write a letter, fax! Make new contacts; stay in touch with steady customers. You can handle lots of tasks at once. A great day for mental activity of any kind. Don't try to pin people down—they, too, are feeling restless. Keep it light. Flirtations and socializing are good. Watch gossip—and don't give away secrets.

Moon in Cancer

This is a moody, sensitive, emotional time. People respond to personal attention and mothering. Stay at home; have a family dinner; call your mother. Nostalgia, memories, and psychic powers are heightened. You'll want to hang on to people and things (don't clean out your closets now). You could have some shrewd insights into what others really need and want now. Pay attention to dreams, intuition, and gut reactions.

Moon in Leo

Everybody is in a much more confident, warm, generous mood. It's a good day to ask for a raise, show what you can do, or dress like a star. People will respond to flattery; enjoy a bit of drama and theater. You may be extravagant—treat yourself royally, and show off a bit (but don't break the bank!). Be careful that you don't promise more than you can deliver!

Moon in Virgo

Do practical, down-to-earth chores. Review your budget. Make repairs. Be an efficiency expert. Not a day to ask for a raise. Have a health checkup. Revamp your diet. Buy vitamins or health food. Make your home spotless. Take care of details and piled-up chores. Reorganize your work and life so they run more smoothly and efficiently. Save money. Be prepared for others to be in a critical, faultfinding mood.

Moon in Libra

Attend to legal matters. Negotiate contracts. Arbitrate. Do things with your favorite partner. Socialize.

Be romantic. Buy a special gift, a beautiful object. Decorate yourself or your surroundings. Buy new clothes. Throw a party. Have an elegant, romantic evening. Smooth over any ruffled feathers. Avoid confrontations. Stick to civilized discussions.

Moon in Scorpio

This is a day to do things with passion. You'll have excellent concentration and focus. Try not to get too intense emotionally, however, and avoid sharp exchanges with loved ones. Others may tend to go to extremes, get jealous, and overreact. Great for troubleshooting, problem-solving, research, scientific work—and making love. Pay attention to psychic vibes.

Moon in Sagittarius

A great time for travel. Have philosophical discussions. Set long-range career goals. Work out, do sports, or buy athletic equipment. Others will be feeling upbeat, exuberant, and adventurous. Risk taking is favored—you may feel like taking a gamble, betting on the horses, visiting a local casino, or buying a lottery ticket. Teaching, writing, and spiritual activities also get the green light. Relax outdoors. Take care of animals.

Moon in Capricorn

You can accomplish a lot today, so get on the ball! Issues concerning your basic responsibilities, duties, family and parents could crop up. You'll be expected to deliver on promises now. Weed out the dead wood from your life. Get a dental checkup.

Moon in Aquarius

A great day for doing things with groups—clubs, meetings, outings, politics, and parties. Campaign for your candidate. Work for a worthy cause. Deal with larger issues that affect humanity: the environment and metaphysical questions. Buy a computer or an electronic gadget. Watch TV. Wear something outrageous. Try something you've never done before. Present an original idea. Don't stick to a rigid schedule—go with the flow. Take a class in meditation, mind control, or yoga.

Moon in Pisces

This can be a very creative day, so let your imagination work overtime. Film, theater, music, or ballet could inspire you. Spend some time alone, resting and reflecting, reading or writing poetry. Daydreams can also be profitable. Help those less fortunate or lend a listening ear to someone who may be feeling blue. Don't overindulge in self-pity or escapism, however. People are especially vulnerable to substance abuse now. Turn your thoughts to romance and someone special.

When the Planets Go Backward

All the planets, except for the sun and moon, have times when they appear to move backward—or retrograde—in the sky, or so it seems from our point of view on earth. At these times, planets do not work as they normally do, so it's best to "take a break" from that planet's energies in our life and do some work on an inner level.

Mercury Retrograde

Mercury goes retrograde most often, and its effects can be especially irritating. When it reaches a short distance ahead of the sun three times a year, it seems to move backward from our point of view. Astrologers often compare retrograde motion to the optical illusion that occurs when we ride on a train that passes another train traveling at a different speed—the second train appears to be moving in reverse.

What this means to you is that the Mercury-ruled areas of your life—analytical thought processes, communications, and scheduling—are subject to all kinds of confusion. Be prepared. People will change their minds, or renege on commitments. Communications equipment can break down. Schedules must be changed on short notice. People are late for appointments or don't show up at all. Traffic is terrible. Major purchases malfunction, don't work out, or get delivered in the wrong color. Letters don't arrive or are delivered to the wrong address. Employees will make errors that have to be corrected later. Contracts don't work out or must be renegotiated.

Since most of us can't put our lives on "hold" for nine weeks every year (three Mercury retrograde periods), we should learn to tame the trickster and make it work for us. The key is in the prefix "re-." This is the time to go back over things in your life. Reflect on what you've done during the previous months. Look for deeper insights, spot errors you've missed, and take time to review and reevaluate what has happened. This time is very good for inner spiritual work and meditations. *Re*st and *re*ward yourself—it's a good time to take a vacation, especially if you revisit a favorite place. *Re*organize your work and finish up projects that are backed up. Clean out your desk and closets. Throw away what you can't *re*cycle. If you must sign contracts or agreements, do so with a contingency clause that lets you *re*evaluate the terms later.

Postpone major purchases or commitments. Don't get married (unless you're *re*marrying the same person). Try not to rely on other people keeping appointments, contracts, or agreements to the letter—have several alternatives. Double-check and read between the lines. Don't buy anything connected with communications or transportation (if you must, be sure to

17

cover yourself). Mercury retrograding through your sun sign will intensify its effect on your life.

If Mercury was retrograde when you were born, you may be one of the lucky people who don't suffer the frustrations of this period. If so, your mind probably works in a very intuitive, insightful way.

The sign Mercury is retrograding through can give you an idea of what's in store—as well as the sun signs that will be especially challenged.

MERCURY RETROGRADE PERIODS IN 2002
Mercury has three retrograde periods this year: from January 18 to February 8, from May 15 to June 8, and from September 14 to October 6.

Venus Retrograde

Retrograding Venus can cause your relationships to take a backward step, or it can make you extravagant and impractical. Shopping till you drop and buying what you cannot afford are trip-ups at this time. It's *not* a good time to redecorate—you'll hate the color of the walls later. Postpone getting a new hairstyle and try not to fall in love either. But if you wish to make amends in an already troubled relationship, make peaceful overtures at this time. (Note: there is no Mars retrograde period this year.)

VENUS RETROGRADE PERIOD IN 2002
Venus retrogrades from October 10 to November 21.

When Other Planets Retrograde

The slower-moving planets stay retrograde for months at a time (Saturn, Jupiter, Neptune, Uranus, and Pluto). When Saturn is retrograde, it's an uphill battle with self-discipline. You may feel more like hanging out at the beach than getting things done. Neptune retrograde promotes a dreamy escapism from reality, whereas Uranus retrograde may mean setbacks in areas where there have been sudden changes. Think of this as an adjustment period, a time to think things over and allow new ideas to develop. Pluto retrograde is a time to work on establishing proportion and balance in areas where there have been recent dramatic transformations.

When the planets start moving forward again, there's a shift in the atmosphere. Activities connected with each planet start moving ahead, and plans that were stalled get rolling. Make a special note of those days on your calendar and proceed accordingly.

Other Retrogrades in 2002

Jupiter is retrograde from November 2, 2001, until March 1, 2002. It turns retrograde again on December 4, 2002.

Saturn retrogrades from February 7 to October 11.
Uranus retrogrades from June 6 to November 3.
Neptune retrogrades from May 13 to October 20.
Pluto retrogrades from March 20 to August 16.

CHAPTER 3

Teach Yourself Astrology

Astrology is a powerful tool of inner transformation that can help you access your personal potential, to understand others, and to interpret events in your life and in the world at large. You don't have to be an expert in astrology to put it to work for you. In this chapter, we'll demystify the horoscope chart and walk you through the basic concepts, so you'll know a sign from a house and what the planets mean. Perhaps from here, you'll upgrade your knowledge with a computer program that calculates charts for everyone you know in a nanosecond, or you'll join an astrology class in your city, or you'll want to explore different techniques of astrology and go on to the asteroids and the fixed stars. The sky's the limit, literally. So let's take off!

The Basics: Signs, Houses, Constellations, and the Zodiac

Everyone knows what a sign is . . . or do they? A *sign* is literally a 30-degree portion of the zodiac, a circular belt of the sky. That is what is meant by a "sign of the zodiac." Things happen within a sign, but a sign does not *do* anything itself—that's the job of the planets. Each sign is simply a portion of celestial real estate and has certain unique characteristics described by four things: an *element* (earth, air, fire, water), a *quality* or mode (cardinal (active), fixed, mutable), by a *polarity* (masculine/feminine, yin/yang) and finally by a *position* in the sequence of zodiac signs.

The *signs* are named after *constellations,* patterns of stars on the zodiac which originally lit up the twelve divisions, like billboards. However, over the centuries, the constellations have shifted from our point of view here on earth. So the constellation which once marked a particular sign may now be in the territory of another sign. (Most Western astrologers use the twelve-equal-part division of the zodiac; however, there are some methods of astrology that still do use the constellations instead of the signs.) However, the *names* of the signs remain the same as their original place-markers.

Most people think of themselves in terms of their *sun sign,* which refers to the sign the sun seems to be passing through at a given moment, from our point of view here on earth. (Of course, we are the ones that are traveling around the sun.) For instance, "I'm an Aries" means that the sun was passing through Aries territory at your birth. However, there are nine other planets (plus asteroids, fixed stars, and sensitive points) which also form our total astrological personality, and some or many of these will be located in other signs. No one is completely "Aries," with all their astrological components in one sign! (Please note that, in astrology, the sun and moon are usually referred to as "planets," though of course they're not.)

Defining the Signs

What makes Aries the sign of go-getters and Taureans savvy with money? And Geminis talk a blue streak and Sagittarians footloose? Descriptions of the signs are not accidental; they are characterized by different combinations of four concepts we have already men-

21

tioned: the sign's element, quality, polarity, and position in the sequence of the zodiac.

Take the element of fire: it's associated with passion, heat. Then have it work in an active, energetic way. Give it a jolt of positive energy and place it first in line. And doesn't that sound like the active, me-first, driving, hotheaded, energetic Aries?

Then take the element of earth: it's practical, sensual, where things grow. Make it work in a fixed, stable way or mode. Give it the kind of energy that reacts to its surroundings, that settles in. Make it the consolidating force, coming right after the passionate beginning of Aries. Now you've got a good idea of how sensual, earthy Taurus operates.

Another way to grasp the idea is to pretend you're doing a magical puzzle based on the numbers that can divide into 12 (the total number of signs): 4, 3, and 2. There are 4 "building blocks" or elements, 3 ways a sign operates (qualities or modes), and 2 polarities. These alternate, in turn, around the zodiac, with a different combination coming up for each sign.

THE FOUR ELEMENTS

Here's how they add up. The *four elements* describe the physical concept of the sign. Is it fiery (dynamic), earthy (practical), airy (mental), or watery (emotional)? Divide the 12 signs by the 4 elements and you get 3 zodiac signs of each element: fire (Aries, Leo, Sagittarius); earth (Taurus, Virgo, Capricorn); air (Gemini, Libra, Aquarius); and water (Cancer, Scorpio, Pisces). These are the same elements that make up our planet: earth, air, fire, and water. But astrology uses the elements as *symbols* which link your body and psyche to the rhythms of the cosmos. If major planets in a horoscope are passing through fire signs, the person will be likely to have a warm, enthusiastic personality, able to fire up or motivate others. These are people who make ideas catch fire and spring into existence, but they also have hot tempers. Those with major planets in earth signs are the builders of the zodiac who follow through after the initiative of fire signs to make things happen. These people are solid, practical realists who enjoy material things and sensual pleasures. They are interested in ideas that can be used to achieve concrete results. With major planets in air signs, a person will be more mental, a good communicator. Following the consolidating earth signs, air people reach out to inspire others through the use of words, social contacts, discussion, and debate. Water sign people complete each four-element series, adding the ingredients of emotion, compassion, and imagination. These people are nonverbal communicators who attune themselves to their surroundings and react through the medium of feelings.

THE THREE QUALITIES

The second consideration when defining a sign is how it will operate. Will it take the initiative, or move slowly and deliberately, or adapt easily? Its *quality* (or modality) will tell. There are 3 qualities; therefore, after dividing 3 into 12 signs, it follows that there will be 4 signs of each quality: cardinal, fixed, and mutable.

Cardinal signs begin each season (Aries, Cancer, Libra, Capricorn). People with major planets in cardinal signs tend to be doers. They're active, always involved in projects. They are usually on the fast track to success, impatient to get things under way. Those with major planets in *fixed signs* (Taurus, Leo, Scorpio, Aquarius) move steadily and are always in control. Since these signs happen in the middle of a season, after the initial character of the season is established, it follows that people with major planets in fixed signs would tend to be more centered; they move more deliberately and do things more slowly but thoroughly. The fixed signs fall in parts of your horoscope where you take root and integrate your experiences. *Mutable signs* (Gemini, Virgo, Sagittarius, Pisces) embody the principle of distribution. Planets in these signs will break up the cycle, preparing the way for a change by distributing the energy to the next group. People with predominantly mutable planets are likely to be flexible, adaptable, and communicative. They can move in many directions easily, darting around obstacles.

THE TWO POLARITIES
In addition to an element and a quality, each sign has a *polarity,* either a positive or negative electrical charge that generates energy around the zodiac, like a giant battery. Polarity refers to opposites, which you could also define as masculine/feminine, yin/yang, active/reactive. In their zodiac positions, the six fire and air signs are positive, active, masculine, and yang in polarity. Therefore, planets in these signs will express their energy openly, expanding outward. The six earth and water signs are reactive, negative, and yin—in other words, nurturing and receptive in polarity, which allows the energy to develop and take shape.

All positive energy would be like a car without brakes. All negative energy would be like a stalled vehicle, going nowhere. So both polarities are needed in balanced proportion, to keep the zodiac in a state of equilibrium.

THE ORDER OF THE SIGNS
The specific order of the signs is vital to the balance of the zodiac and the transmission of energy around the cycle. Though each sign is quite different from its neighbors on either side, each seems to grow out of its predecessor like links in a chain, transmitting a synthesis of energy accumulated along the chain to the following sign, beginning with the fire-powered, active, positive, cardinal sign of Aries and ending with watery, mutable, reactive Pisces.

Houses of the Horoscope—
Where the Action Is

We come to the concept of *houses* as we set up a specific horoscope, which is a map of the heavens at a given moment in time. Picture the horoscope chart as a wheel with twelve spokes. In between each of the "spokes" is a section called a *house*. The wheel is stationary, however . . . the houses are always in the same place. Each house represents a different area of life and is influenced or "ruled" by a sign and a planet that are associated with that house. But besides the house's given "rulers," it is colored by the sign which is passing over the spoke (or cusp) at the moment when the horoscope chart is cast. In other words, the first house is naturally ruled by Aries and Mars; however, if Capricorn was the sign passing over the house at the time the chart was cast, it would have a Capricorn influence.

Numerically, the house order begins at the left center spoke (or the 9 position if you were reading a clock) and is read counterclockwise around the chart.

The First House—Home of Aries
and the Planet Mars

This is the house of "firsts"—the first impression you make, how you initiate matters, the image you choose to project. This is where you advertise yourself, where you project your personality. Planets that fall here will intensify the way you come across to others. Often the first house will project an entirely different type of energy from the sun sign. For instance, a Capricorn with Leo in the first house will come across as much more flamboyant than the average Capricorn. The sign on the cusp of this house is known as your *ascendant,* or *rising sign.*

The Second House—Home of Taurus and Venus

Here is your contact with the material world. In this house are your attitudes about money, possessions, finances, whatever belongs to you, and what you own, as well as your earning and spending capacity. On a deeper level, this house reveals your sense of self-worth, the inner values that draw wealth in various forms.

The Third House—Home of Gemini and Mercury

This house describes how you communicate with others—are you understood? Here you reach out to others nearby and interact with the immediate environment. This is how your thinking process works, the way you express your thoughts. In relationships, here are your first experiences with brothers and sisters, and how you handle people close to you, such as your neighbors or pals. It's also where you take short trips, write letters, or use the telephone. It shows how your mind works in terms of left-brain logical and analytical functions.

The Fourth House—Home of Cancer and the Moon

This house shows how you are nurtured and made to feel secure—your roots! Located at the bottom of the chart, the fourth house, like the home, shows the foundation of life, your deepest psychological underpinnings. Here is where you have the deepest confrontation with who you are, and how you make yourself feel secure. It shows your early home environment and the circumstances at the end of your life—your final "home"—as well as the place you call home now. Astrologers look here for information about the primary nurturers in your life.

The Fifth House—Home of Leo and the Sun

This is how you express yourself creatively—your idea of play. The Leo house is where the creative potential develops, where you show off your talents. It is also where you procreate, in the sense that your children are outgrowths of your creative ability. It most represents your inner childlike self, the part of you which finds joy in play. If inner security has been established by the time you reach this house, you are now free to have fun, romance, and love affairs—to give of yourself. This is also the place astrologers look for the playful kind of love affairs, flirtations, and brief romantic encounters (rather than long-term commitments).

The Sixth House—Home of Virgo and Mercury

Here is your "care and maintenance" department. It shows how you function in daily life, where you get things done, and where you determine how you look after others and fulfill service duties, such as taking care of pets. Here are your daily survival, your "job" (as opposed to your career, which is the domain of the tenth house), your diet, and your health and fitness regimens. Here is where you take care of your body and organize yourself to perform efficiently.

The Seventh House—Home of Libra and Venus

This house shows your attitude toward partners and those with whom you enter commitments, contracts, or agreements. This house has to do with your relationships—your close, intimate, one-on-one relationships (even your open enemies—those you "face off" with). Open hostilities, lawsuits, divorces, and marriages happen here. If the first house represents the "I," the seventh or opposite house represents the "not-I"—the complementary partner you attract by the way you come across. If you are having trouble with partnerships, consider what you are attracting by the interaction of your first and seventh house.

The Eighth House—Home of Scorpio and Pluto (also Mars)

This refers to how you merge with something or someone, and how you handle power and control. This is one of the most mysterious and powerful houses, where your energy transforms itself from "I" to "we." As you give up your personal power and control by uniting with something or someone, two kinds of energies merge and become something greater, leading to a regeneration of the self on a higher level. Here are your attitudes toward sex, shared resources, and taxes (what you share with the government). Because this house involves what belongs to others, you face issues of control and power struggles, or undergo a deep psychological transformation as you bond with another. Here you transcend yourself with dreams, drugs, and occult or psychic experiences that reflect the collective unconscious.

The Ninth House—Home of Sagittarius and Jupiter

Here is where you search for wisdom and higher knowledge—your belief system. While the third house represents the "lower mind," its opposite on the wheel, the ninth house, is the "higher mind." This is where you ask the "big" questions like "Why are we here?" The ninth house shows what you believe in. After the third house has explored what was close at hand, the ninth stretches out to broaden you with higher education and travel. Here you stretch spiritually with religious activity. Since you are concerned with how everything is related, you tend to take risks, break rules, and push boundaries. Here is where you express your ideas in a book or extensive thesis, where you pontificate, philosophize, or preach.

The Tenth House—Home of Capricorn and Saturn

Here is your public image and how you handle authority. Located directly overhead at the "high noon" position on the horoscope wheel, this house is associated with high-profile activities, where the world sees you. It deals with your career (but not your routine "job"), and your reputation. Here is where you go public and take on responsibilities (as opposed to the fourth house, where you stay home). This will affect the career you choose and your "public relations." This house is also associated with your father or the main authority figure in your life.

The Eleventh House—Home of Aquarius and Uranus

Here is your support system, how you relate to society and your goals. In this house, you extend your identity to belong to a group, a team, a club, a goal, or a belief system. You worry about being popular, winning the election, or making the team; you define what you really want, the kinds of friends you have, your political affiliations, and the kinds of groups you'll belong to. Here is where you become concerned with "what other people think," or you rebel against society. Here is where you could become a socially conscious humanitarian—or a party-going social butterfly. It's where you look to others to stimulate you and discover your kinship to the rest of humanity. The sign on the cusp of this house can help you understand what you gain and lose from friendships.

The Twelfth House—Home of Pisces and Neptune

Here is where the boundaries between yourself and others become blurred, where you become self-less. In your trip around the zodiac, you've gone from the "I" of self-assertion in the first house to the final house, symbolizing the dissolution that happens before rebirth. It's where accumulated experiences are processed in the unconscious. Spiritually oriented astrologers look to this house for evidence of past lives and karma. Places where we go for solitude or to do spiritual or reparatory work belong here, such as retreats, religious institutions, or hospitals. Here are also institutions such as prisons where we withdraw from society or are forced to withdraw because of antisocial behavior. Selfless giving through charitable acts is part of this house, as is helpless receiving or dependence on charity.

In your daily life, the twelfth house reveals your deepest intimacies, your best-kept secrets, especially those you hide from yourself, repressed deep in the unconscious. It is where we surrender a sense of a separate self to a deep feeling of wholeness, such as selfless service in religion or any activity that involves merging with the greater whole. Many sports stars have important planets in the twelfth house that enable them to play in the "zone," finding an inner, almost mystical, strength that transcends their limits.

The Planets Power Up Your Houses

Houses are stronger or weaker depending on how many planets are inhabiting them. If there are many planets occupying a given house, it follows that the activities of that house will be emphasized in your life. If the planet that rules the house naturally is also located there, this too adds power to the house.

Mapping Your Planets

The ten major planets (including the sun and moon) are the doers in your chart. The planets cause things to happen. They will play starring or supporting roles, depending on their positions in your horoscope. A planet in the first house, particularly one that's close to your rising sign, is sure to be a featured player. Planets that are grouped together usually operate together like a team, playing off each other, rather than expressing their energy singularly. A planet that stands alone, away from the others, is usually outstanding and sometimes calls the shots.

The best place for a planet is in the sign or signs it rules; the next best is in a sign where it is *exalted*, or especially harmonious. On the other hand, there are signs where a planet has to work harder to play its role. These are called the planet's *detriment* and *fall*. The sign opposite a planet's rulership, which embodies the opposite area of life, is its *detriment*. The sign opposite its exaltation is its *fall*. Though these terms may suggest unfortunate circumstances for the planet, that is not always true. In fact, a planet that is debilitated can actually be more complete, because it must stretch itself to meet the challenges of living in a more difficult sign. Like world leaders who've had to struggle for greatness, this planet may actually develop more strength and character.

Here's a list of the best places for each planet to be. Note that, as Uranus, Neptune, and Pluto were discovered, they replaced the traditional rulers of signs which best complemented their energies.

ARIES—Mars.
TAURUS—Venus, in its most sensual form.
GEMINI—Mercury in its communicative role.
CANCER—the moon.
LEO—the sun.

VIRGO—Also Mercury, this time in its more critical capacity.

LIBRA—Also Venus, in its more aesthetic, judgmental form.

SCORPIO—Pluto, replacing the sign's original ruler, Mars.

SAGITTARIUS—Jupiter.

CAPRICORN—Saturn.

AQUARIUS—Uranus, replacing Saturn, its original ruler.

PISCES—Neptune, replacing Jupiter, its original ruler.

A person who has many planets in exalted signs is lucky indeed, for here is where the planet can accomplish the most and be its most influential and creative.

SUN—Exalted in Aries, where its energy creates action.

MOON—Exalted in Taurus, where instincts and reactions operate on a highly creative level.

MERCURY—Exalted in Aquarius, where it can reach analytical heights.

VENUS—Exalted in Pisces, a sign whose sensitivity encourages love and creativity.

MARS—Exalted in Capricorn, a sign that puts energy to work productively.

JUPITER—Exalted in Cancer, where it encourages nurturing and growth.

SATURN—At home in Libra, where it steadies the scales of justice and promotes balanced, responsible judgment.

URANUS—Powerful in Scorpio, where it promotes transformation.

NEPTUNE—Especially favored in Cancer, where it gains the security to transcend to a higher state.

PLUTO—Exalted in Pisces, where it dissolves the old cycle, to make way for transition to the new.

The Sun and the Moon

Since the sun is always the first consideration, it is important to treat it as the star of the show. It is your conscious ego and it is always center stage, even when sharing a house or a sign with several other planets. This is why sun sign astrology works for so many people.

The sun rules the sign of Leo, gaining strength through the pride, dignity, and confidence of the fixed-fire personality. It is exalted in "me-first" Aries. In its detriment, Aquarius, the sun-ego is strengthened through group participation and social consciousness, rather than through self-centeredness. (Note how many Aquarius people are involved in politics, social work, and public life. They are following the demands of their sun sign to be spokesperson for a group.) In its fall, Libra, the sun needs the strength of a partner—an "other"—to enhance its own balance and self-expression.

As the sun represents your outer light, the moon represents the inner "you," your deep emotional nature. We go into more detail about the moon and its influence in your life and moods in a separate chapter in this book. Read it for details about this all-important planet.

Each of the other eight planets is colored by the sign it is passing through. For example, Mercury, the planet that rules the way you communicate, will express itself in a dynamic, headstrong way if it was passing through the sign of Aries when you were born. You will speak differently if it was passing through the slower, more patient sign of Taurus. And so on through the list. Here's a rundown of the planets and how they behave in every sign.

The Personal Planets—Mercury, Venus, and Mars

These planets work in your immediate personal life.

Mercury affects how you communicate and how your mental processes work. Are you a quick study who grasps information rapidly, or do you learn more slowly and thoroughly? How is your concentration? Can you express yourself easily? Are you a good writer? All these questions can be answered by your Mercury placement.

Venus shows what you react to. What turns you on? What appeals to you aesthetically? Are you charming to others? Are you attractive to look at? Your taste, your refinement, your sense of balance and proportion are all Venus-ruled.

Mars is your outgoing energy, your drive and ambition. Do you reach out for new adventures? Are you assertive? Are you motivated? Self-confident? Hot-tempered? How you channel your energy and drive is revealed by your Mars placement.

Mercury Communicates

Since Mercury never travels far from the sun, read Mercury in your sun sign, then the signs preceding and following it. Then decide which reflects the way your mind works.

Mercury in Aries

Your mind is very active and assertive. You never hesitate to say what you think or shy away from a battle. In fact, you may relish a verbal confrontation. Tact is not your strong point, so you may have to learn not to trip over your tongue.

Mercury in Taurus

Though you may be a slow learner, you have good concentration and mental stamina. You want to make your ideas really happen. You'll attack a problem methodically and consider every angle thoroughly, never jumping to conclusions. You'll stick with a subject until you master it.

Mercury in Gemini

A wonderful communicator with great facility for expressing yourself both verbally and in writing. You talk and talk, love gathering all kinds of information. You probably finish other people's sentences and talk with hand gestures. You can talk to anybody anytime and probably have phone and e-mail bills to prove it. You read anything from sci-fi to Shakespeare and might need an extra room just for your book collection. Though you learn fast, you may lack focus and discipline. Watch a tendency to jump from subject to subject.

Mercury in Cancer

You rely on intuition more than logic. Your mental processes are usually colored by your emotions, so you may seem shy or hesitant to voice your opinions. However, this placement gives you the advantage of great imagination and empathy in the way you communicate with others.

Mercury in Leo

You are enthusiastic and very dramatic in the way you express yourself. You like to hold the attention of groups and could be a great public speaker. Your mind thinks big, so you'd prefer to deal with the overall picture rather than with the details.

Mercury in Virgo

This is one of the best places for Mercury. It should give you critical ability, attention to details, and thorough analysis. Your mind focuses on the practical side of things. This type of thinking is very well suited to being a teacher or an editor.

Mercury in Libra

You're either a born diplomat who smoothes over ruffled feathers or a talented debater. However, since you're forever weighing the pros and cons of a situation, you may vacillate when making decisions.

Mercury in Scorpio

This is an investigative mind which stops at nothing to get the answers. You may have a sarcastic, stinging wit or a gift for the cutting remark. There's always a grain of truth to your verbal sallies, thanks to your penetrating insight.

Mercury in Sagittarius

You're a super salesman with a tendency to expound. Though you are very broad-minded, you can be dogmatic when it comes to telling others what's good for them. You won't hesitate to tell the truth as you see it, so watch a tendency toward tactlessness. On the plus side, you have a great sense of humor. This position of Mercury is often considered by astrologers to be at a disadvantage because Sagittarius opposes Gemini, the sign Mercury rules, and squares off with Virgo, another Mercury-ruled sign. What often happens is that Mercury in Sagittarius oversteps its bounds and loses sight of the facts in a situation. Do a reality check before making promises that you may not be able to keep.

Mercury in Capricorn

This placement endows good mental discipline. You have a love of learning and a very orderly approach to your subjects. You will patiently plod through the facts and figures until you have mastered the tasks. You grasp structured situations easily, but may be short on creativity.

Mercury in Aquarius

With Uranus and Neptune in Aquarius now energizing your Mercury, you're sure to be on the cutting edge of new ideas. An independent, original thinker, you'll have more far-out ideas than the average person and be quick to check out any unusual opportunities. Your opinions are so well researched and grounded, in fact, that once your mind is made up, it is difficult to change.

Mercury in Pisces

You have the psychic intuitive mind of a natural poet. Learn to make use of your creative imagination. You may think in terms of helping others, but check a tendency to be vague and forgetful of details.

Venus Relates

Venus tells how you relate to others and to your environment. It shows where you receive pleasure, what you love to do. Find your Venus placement on the chart on pages 68–75 by looking for the year of your birth in the left-hand column. Then follow the line of that year across the page until you reach the time period of your birthday. The sign heading that column will be your Venus. If you were born on a day when Venus was changing signs, check the signs preceding or following that day to determine if that feels more like your Venus nature.

Venus in Aries

You can't stand to be bored, confined, or ordered around. But a good challenge, maybe even a rousing row, turns you on. Don't you pick a fight now and then just to get someone stirred up? You're attracted by the chase, not the catch, which could cause some problems in your love life, if the object of your affection becomes too attainable. You love someone who keeps you on your toes. You like to wear red and be first with the latest fashion. You'll spot a trend before anyone else.

Venus in Taurus

All your senses work in high gear. You love to be surrounded by glorious tastes, smells, textures, sounds, and visuals. Austere minimalism is not your style. Neither is being rushed. You like time to enjoy your pleasures. Soothing surroundings with plenty of creature comforts are your cup of tea. You like to feel secure in your nest, with no sudden jolts or surprises. You like familiar objects—in fact, you may hate to let anything or anyone go.

Venus in Gemini

You are a lively, sparkling personality who thrives in a situation that affords a constant variety and a frequent change of scenery. A varied social life is important to you, with plenty of stimulation and a chance to engage in some light flirtation. Commitment may be difficult, because playing the field is so much fun.

Venus in Cancer

An atmosphere where you feel protected, coddled, and mothered is best for you. You love to be surrounded by children in a cozy, homelike situation. You are attracted to those who are tender and nurturing, who make you feel secure and well provided for. You may be quite secretive about your emotional life or attracted to clandestine relationships.

Venus in Leo

First-class attention in large doses turns you on, and so do the glitter of real gold and the flash of mirrors. You like to feel like a star at all times, surrounded by your admiring audience. The side effect is that you may be attracted to flatterers and tinsel, while the real gold requires some digging.

Venus in Virgo

Everything neatly in its place? On the surface, you are attracted to an atmosphere where everything is in perfect order, but underneath are some basic, earthy urges. You are attracted to those who appeal to your need to teach, be of service, or play out a Pygmalion fantasy. You are at your best when you are busy doing something useful, helping someone improve.

Venus in Libra

"Elegance" and "harmony" are your key words. You can't abide an atmosphere of contention. Your taste tends toward the classic, with light harmonies of color— nothing clashing, trendy, or outrageous. You love doing things with a partner and should be careful to pick one who is decisive, but patient enough to let you weigh the pros and cons. And steer clear of argumentative types. It helps a lot if your partner is attractive and stylish, as well as charming, and appreciates the finer things in life.

Venus in Scorpio

Hidden mysteries intrigue you. In fact, anything that is too open and aboveboard is a bit of a bore. You surely have a stack of whodunits by the bed, along with an erotic magazine or two. You like to solve puzzles, and may also be fascinated with the occult, crime, or scientific research. Intense, all-or-nothing situations add spice to your life, and you love to ferret out the secrets of others. But you could get burned by your flair for living dangerously. The color black, spicy food, dark wood furniture, and heady perfume all get you in the right mood.

Venus in Sagittarius

If you are not actually a world traveler, your surroundings are sure to reflect your love of faraway places. You like a casual outdoor atmosphere and a dog or two to pet. There should be plenty of room for athletic equipment and suitcases. You're attracted to kindred souls who love to travel and who share your freedom-loving philosophy of life. Athletics, spiritual, or New Age pursuits could be other interests.

Venus in Capricorn

No fly-by-night relationships for you! You want substance in life and you are attracted to whatever will help you get where you are going. Status objects turn you on. And so do those who have a serious, responsible, businesslike approach, or who remind you of a beloved parent. It is characteristic of this placement to be attracted to someone of a different generation. Antiques, traditional clothing, and dignified behavior favor you.

Venus in Aquarius

This Venus wants to make friends more than to make love. You like to be in a group, particularly one pushing a worthy cause. In fact, fame of one sort or another is fascinating to you. You feel quite at home surrounded by people, but may remain detached from any intense commitment. Original ideas and unpredictable people attract you. You don't like everything to be planned out in advance, preferring spontaneity and delightful surprises.

Venus in Pisces

Venus is exalted in Pisces, which makes this one of the more desirable Venuses to have. This Venus loves to give of the self, and you'll find plenty of takers. Stray animals and people appeal to your heart and your pocketbook, but be careful to look at their motives realistically once in a while. You are extremely vulnerable to sob stories of all kinds. Fantasy, theater, and psychic or spiritual activities also speak to you.

Mars Moves and Shakes

Mars shows how you pursue your goals, whether you have energy to burn or proceed at a slow, steady pace. Or are you nervous, restless, unable to sit still? Mars will also show how you get angry. Will you explode, do a slow burn, or hold everything inside, then get revenge later?

To find your Mars, turn to the chart on pages 76–87. Then find your birth year in the left-hand column and trace the line across horizontally until you come to the column headed by the month of your birth. There you will find an abbreviation of your Mars sign. If the description of your Mars sign doesn't ring true, read the description of the signs preceding and following it. You may have been born on a day when Mars was changing signs, and your Mars would then be in the adjacent sign.

Mars in Aries

In the sign it rules, Mars shows its brilliant fiery nature. You have an explosive temper and can be quite impatient, but on the other hand, you possess tremendous courage, energy, and drive. You'll let nothing stand in your way as you race to be first! Obstacles are met head-on and broken through by force. However, situations that require patience and persistence could make you explode in rage. You're a great starter, but not necessarily there at the finish.

Mars in Taurus

Slow, steady, concentrated energy gives you staying power. You've got great stamina and you never give up. Your tactic is to wear away obstacles with your persistence. Often you come out a winner because you've had the patience to hang in there. When angered, you do a slow burn.

Mars in Gemini

You can't sit still for long. This Mars craves variety. You often have two or more things going on at once. It's all an amusing game to you. Your life can get very complicated, which only adds spice and stimulation. What drives you into a nervous, hyper state? Boredom, sameness, routine, and confinement. You can do wonderful things with your hands, and you have a way with words.

Mars in Cancer

You rarely attack head-on. Instead, you'll keep things to yourself, make plans in secret, and always cover your actions. This might be interpreted by some as manipulative, but it's really your method of self-protection. You get furious when anyone knows too much about you, though you do like to know all about others. Your mothering and feeding instincts can be put to good use, if you work in food, hotel, or child-care-related businesses. You may have to overcome your fragile sense of security, which prompts you not to take risks and to get physically upset when criticized. Don't take things so personally!

Mars in Leo

You have a very dominant personality that takes center stage. Modesty is not one of your stellar traits, nor is taking a back seat, ever. You prefer giving the orders and have been known to make a dramatic scene if they are not obeyed. Properly used, this Mars confers leadership ability, endurance, and courage.

Mars in Virgo

You are the faultfinder of the zodiac, who notices every detail. Mistakes of any kind make you nervous, and you are sure you can do the job better than anyone else. You may worry, even if everything is going smoothly. Though you might not express anger directly, you sure can nag. You have definite likes and dislikes. You are certainly more industrious and detail-oriented than other signs. Your Mars energy is often most positively expressed in some kind of teaching role.

Mars in Libra

This Mars will have a passion for beauty, justice, and art. Generally, you will avoid confrontations at all costs. You prefer to spend your energy finding diplomatic solutions or weighing pros and cons. Your other techniques are passive aggression or exercising your well-known charm to get people to do what you want.

Mars in Scorpio

This is a powerful placement, so intense that it demands careful channeling into worthwhile activities. Otherwise, you could become obsessed with your sexuality or might use your need for power and control to manipulate others. You are strong-willed, shrewd, and very private about your affairs, and you'll usually have a secret agenda behind your actions. Your great stamina, focus, and discipline would be excellent assets for careers in the military or medical fields, especially research or surgery. When angry, you don't get mad—you get even!

Mars in Sagittarius

This expansive Mars often propels people into sales, travel, athletics, or philosophy. Your energies function well when you are on the move. You have a hot temper and are inclined to say what you think before you consider the consequences. You shoot for high goals and talk endlessly about them, but you may be weak on groundwork. This Mars needs a solid foundation. Watch a tendency to take unnecessary risks.

Mars in Capricorn

This is an ambitious Mars with an excellent sense of timing. You have an eye for those who can be useful to you, and you may dismiss people ruthlessly when you're angry. But you drive yourself hard and deliver full value. This is a good placement for an executive. You'll aim for status and a high material position in life, and keep climbing despite the odds. A great Mars to have!

Mars in Aquarius

This is the most rebellious Mars. You seem to have a drive to assert yourself against the status quo. You may enjoy provoking people, shocking them out of traditional views. Or this placement could express itself in an offbeat sex life. Somehow you often find yourself in unconventional situations. You enjoy being a leader of an active avant-garde group, which pursues forward-looking studies, politics, or goals.

Mars in Pisces

This Mars is a good actor who knows just how to appeal to the sympathies of others. You create and project wonderful fantasies or use your sensitive antennae to crusade for those less fortunate. You get what you want through creating a veil of illusion and glamour. This is a good Mars for someone in the creative fields—a dancer, performer, or photographer—or for someone in motion pictures. Many famous film stars have this placement. Watch a tendency to manipulate by making others feel sorry for you.

Jupiter Expands

Jupiter is the planet in your horoscope that makes you want *more.* This big, bright, swirling mass of gases is associated with abundance, prosperity, and the kind of windfall you get without too much hard work. You're optimistic under Jupiter's influence, when anything seems possible. You'll travel, expand your mind with higher education, and publish to share your knowledge widely. But a strong Jupiter has its downside, too, because Jupiter's influence is neither discriminating nor disciplined. It represents the principle of growth without judgment, and could result in extravagance, weight gain, laziness, and carelessness, if not kept in check.

Be sure to look up your Jupiter in the tables in this book. When the current position of Jupiter is favorable, you may get that lucky break. This is a great time to try new things, take risks, travel, or get more education. Opportunities seem to open up easily, so take advantage of them.

Once a year, Jupiter changes signs. That means you are due for an expansive time every twelve years, when Jupiter travels through your sun sign. You'll also have "up" periods every four years, when Jupiter is in the same element as your sun sign.

Jupiter in Aries

You are the soul of enthusiasm and optimism. Your luckiest times are when you are getting started on an exciting project or selling an ideal that you really believe in. You may have to watch a tendency to be arrogant with those who do not share your enthusiasm. You follow your impulses, often ignoring budget or other commonsense limitations. To produce real, solid benefits, you'll need patience and follow-through wherever this Jupiter falls in your horoscope.

Jupiter in Taurus

You'll spend on beautiful material things, especially those that come from nature—items made of rare woods, natural fabrics, or precious gems, for instance. You can't have too much comfort or too many sensual pleasures. Watch a tendency to overindulge in good food, or to overpamper yourself with nothing but the best. Spartan living is not for you! You may be especially lucky in matters of real estate.

Jupiter in Gemini

You are the great talker of the zodiac, and you may be a great writer, too. But restlessness could be your weak point. You jump around, talk too much, and could be a jack-of-all-trades. Keeping a secret is especially difficult, so you'll also have to watch a tendency to spill the beans. Since you love to be at the center of a beehive of activity, you'll have a vibrant social life. Your best opportunities will come through your talent for language—speaking, writing, communicating, and selling.

Jupiter in Cancer

You are luckiest in situations where you can find emotional closeness or deal with basic security needs, such as food, nurturing, or shelter. You may be a great collector and you may simply love to accumulate things—you are the one who stashes things away for a rainy day. You probably have a very good memory and love children—in fact, you may have many children to care for. The food, hotel, child-care, and shipping businesses hold good opportunities for you.

Jupiter in Leo

You are a natural showman who loves to live in a larger-than-life way. Yours is a personality full of color that always finds its way into the limelight. You can't have too much attention or applause. Show biz is a natural place for you, and so is any area where you can play to a crowd. Exercising your flair for drama, your natural playfulness, and your romantic nature brings you good fortune. But watch a tendency to be overly extravagant or to monopolize center stage.

Jupiter in Virgo

You actually love those minute details others find boring. To you, they make all the difference between the perfect and the ordinary. You are the fine craftsman who spots every flaw. You expand your awareness by finding the most efficient methods and by being of service to others. Many will be drawn to medical or teaching fields. You'll also have luck in publishing, crafts, nutrition, and service professions. Watch out for a tendency to overwork.

Jupiter in Libra

This is an other-directed Jupiter that develops best with a partner, for the stimulation of others helps you grow. You are also most comfortable in harmonious, beautiful situations, and you work well with artistic people. You have a great sense of fair play and an ability to evaluate the pros and cons of a situation. You usually prefer to play the role of diplomat rather than adversary.

Jupiter in Scorpio

You love the feeling of power and control, of taking things to their limit. You can't resist a mystery, and your shrewd, penetrating mind sees right through to the heart of most situations and people. You have luck in work that provides for solutions to matters of life and death. You may be drawn to undercover work, behind-the-scenes intrigue, psychotherapy, the occult, and sex-related ventures. Your challenge will be to develop a sense of moderation and tolerance for other beliefs. This Jupiter can be fanatical. You may have luck in handling other people's money—insurance, taxes, and inheritance can bring you a windfall.

Jupiter in Sagittarius

Independent, outgoing, and idealistic, you'll shoot for the stars. This Jupiter compels you to travel far and wide, both physically and mentally, via higher education. You may have luck while traveling in an exotic place. You also have luck with outdoor ventures, exercise, and animals, particularly horses. Since you tend to be very open about your opinions, watch a tendency to be tactless and to exaggerate. Instead, use your wonderful sense of humor to make your point.

Jupiter in Capricorn

Jupiter is much more restrained in Capricorn, the sign of rules and authority. Here, Jupiter can make you overwork and heighten any ambition or sense of duty you may have. You'll expand in areas that advance your position, putting you farther up the social or corporate ladder. You are lucky working within the establishment in a very structured situation, where you can show off your ability to organize and reap rewards for your hard work.

Jupiter in Aquarius

This is another freedom-loving Jupiter, with great tolerance and originality. You are at your best when you are working for a humanitarian cause and in the company of many supporters. This is a good Jupiter for a political career. You'll relate to all kinds of people on all social levels. You have an abundance of original ideas, but you are best off away from routine and any situation that imposes rigid rules. You need mental stimulation!

Jupiter in Pisces

You are a giver whose feelings and pocketbook are easily touched by others, so choose your companions with care. You could be the original sucker for a hard-luck story. Better find a worthy hospital or charity to appreciate your selfless support. You have a great creative imagination and may attract good fortune in fields related to oil, perfume, pharmaceuticals, petroleum, dance, footwear, and alcohol. But beware of overindulgence in alcohol—focus on a creative outlet instead.

Saturn Brakes

Jupiter speeds you up with *lucky breaks,* then along comes Saturn to slow you down with the *disciplinary brakes.* Saturn has unfairly been called a malefic planet, one of the bad guys of the zodiac. On the contrary, Saturn is one of our best friends, the kind who tells you what you need to hear, even if it's not good news. Under a Saturn transit, we grow up, take responsibility for our lives, and emerge from whatever test this planet has in store, far wiser, more capable, and more mature.

When Saturn hits a critical point in your horoscope, you can count on an experience that will make you slow up, pull back, and reexamine your life. It is a call to eliminate what is not working and to shape up. By the end of its twenty-eight-year trip around the zodiac,

Saturn will have tested you in all areas of your life. The major tests happen in seven-year cycles, when Saturn passes over the *angles* of your chart—your rising sign, midheaven, descendant, and nadir. This is when the real life-changing experiences happen. But you are also in for a testing period whenever Saturn passes a *planet* in your chart or stresses that planet from a distance. Therefore, it is useful to check your planetary positions with the timetable of Saturn to prepare in advance, or at least to brace yourself.

When Saturn returns to its location at the time of your birth, at approximately age twenty-eight, you'll have your first Saturn return. At this time, a person usually takes stock or settles down to find his mission in life and assumes full adult duties and responsibilities.

Another way Saturn helps us is to reveal the karmic lessons from previous lives and give us the chance to overcome them. So look at Saturn's challenges as much-needed opportunities for self-improvement. Under a Jupiter influence, you'll have more fun, but Saturn gives you solid, long-lasting results.

Look up your natal Saturn in the tables in this book for clues on where you need work.

Saturn in Aries

Saturn here puts the brakes on Aries's natural drive and enthusiasm. You don't let anyone push you around and you know what's best for yourself. Following orders is not your strong point, and neither is diplomacy. You tend to be quick to go on the offensive in relationships, attacking first, before anyone attacks you. Because no one quite lives up to your standards, you often wind up doing everything yourself. You'll have to learn to cooperate and tone down self-centeredness.

Saturn in Taurus

A big issue is taking control of your cash flow. There will be lean periods that can be frightening, but you have the patience and endurance to stick them out and the methodical drive to prosper in the end. Learn to take a philosophical attitude like Ben Franklin, who had this placement and who said, "A penny saved is a penny earned."

Saturn in Gemini

You are a serious student of life, who may have difficulty communicating or sharing your knowledge. You may be shy, speak slowly, or have fears about communicating, like Eleanor Roosevelt. You dwell in the realms of science, theory, or abstract analysis, even when you are dealing with the emotions, like Sigmund Freud, who also had this placement.

Saturn in Cancer

Your tests come with establishing a secure emotional base. In doing so, you may have to deal with some very basic fears centering on your early home environment. Most of your Saturn tests will have emotional roots in those early childhood experiences. You may have difficulty remaining objective in terms of what you try to achieve, so it will be especially important for you to deal with negative feelings such as guilt, paranoia, jealousy, resentment, and suspicion. Galileo and Michaelangelo also navigated these murky waters.

Saturn in Leo

This is an authoritarian Saturn, a strict, demanding parent who may deny the pleasure principle in your zeal to see that rules are followed. Though you may feel guilty about taking the spotlight, you are very ambitious and loyal. You have to watch a tendency toward rigidity, also toward overwork and holding back affection. Joseph Kennedy and Billy Graham share this placement.

Saturn in Virgo

This is a cautious, exacting Saturn, intensely hard on yourself. Most of all, you give yourself the roughest time with your constant worries about every little detail, often making yourself sick. You may have difficulties setting priorities and getting the job done. Your tests will come in learning tolerance and understanding of others. Charles de Gaulle, Mae West, and Nathaniel Hawthorne had this meticulous Saturn.

Saturn in Libra

Saturn is exalted here, which makes this planet an ally. However, there are very likely to be commitment issues. You must learn to stand solidly on your own before you can have a successful relationship. You may choose very serious, older partners in life. You are extremely cautious as you deliberate every involvement—with good reason. It is best that you find an occupation that makes good use of your sense of duty and honor. Steer clear of fly-by-night situations. Both Khrushchev and Mao Tse-tung had this placement, too.

Saturn in Scorpio

You have great staying power. This Saturn tests you in situations involving control of others. You may feel drawn to some kind of intrigue or undercover work, like J. Edgar Hoover. Or there may be an air of mystery surrounding your life and death, like Marilyn Monroe and Robert Kennedy, who had this placement. There are lessons to be learned from your sexual involvements. Often sex is used for manipulation or is somehow out of the ordinary. The Roman emperor Caligula and the transvestite Christine Jorgensen are extreme cases.

Saturn in Sagittarius

Your challenges and lessons will come from tests of your spiritual and philosophical values, as happened to Martin Luther King and Gandhi. You are high-minded and sincere with this reflective, moral placement. Uncompromising in your ethical standards, you could become a benevolent despot.

Saturn in Capricorn

With the help of Saturn at maximum strength, your judgment will improve with age. And like Spencer Tracy's screen image, you'll be the gray-haired hero with a strong sense of responsibility. You advance in life slowly but steadily, always with a strong hand at the helm and an eye for the advantageous situation. Like Pat Robertson, you're likely to stand for conservative values. Negatively, you may be a loner, prone to periods of melancholy.

Saturn in Aquarius

Your tests come from relationships with groups. Do you care too much about what others think? Do you feel like an outsider, as Greta Garbo did? You may fear being different from others and therefore demean your own unique, forward-looking gifts, or like Lord Byron and Howard Hughes, take the opposite tack and rebel in the extreme. However, others with this placement have been able to apply discipline to accomplish great humanitarian goals, as Albert Schweitzer did.

Saturn in Pisces

Your fear of the unknown and the irrational may lead you to the safety and protection of an institution. You may go on the run like Jesse James, who had this placement, to avoid looking too deeply inside. Or you might go in the opposite, more positive direction and develop a disciplined psychoanalytic approach, which puts you more in control of your feelings. Some of you will take refuge in work with hospitals, charities, or religious institutions. Queen Victoria, who had this placement, symbolized an era when institutions of all kinds were sustained. Discipline applied to artistic work, especially poetry and dance, or spiritual work, such as yoga or meditation, might be helpful.

Uranus, Neptune, and Pluto Affect Your Whole Generation

These three planets remain in signs such a long time that a whole generation bears the imprint of the sign. Mass movements, great sweeping changes, fads that characterize a generation, even the issues of the conflicts and wars of the time are influenced by the "outer three." When one of these distant planets changes signs, there is a definite shift in the atmosphere, the feeling of the end of an era.

Since these planets are so far away from the sun—too distant to be seen by the naked eye—they pick up signals from the universe at large. These planetary receivers literally link the sun with distant energies, and then perform a similar function in your horoscope by linking your central character with intuitive, spiritual, transformative forces from the cosmos. Each planet has a special domain and will reflect this in the area of your chart where it falls.

Uranus Wakes You Up

There is nothing ordinary about this quirky green planet that seems to be traveling on its side, surrounded by a swarm of moons. Is it any wonder that astrologers assigned it to Aquarius, the most eccentric and gregarious sign? Uranus seems to wend its way around the sun, marching to its own tune.

Uranus's energy is electrical, happening in sudden flashes. It is not influenced by karma or past events, nor does it regard tradition, sex, or sentiment. The Uranian key words are "surprise" and "awakening." Uranus wakes you up, jolts you out of your comfortable rut. Suddenly, there's that flash of inspiration, that bright idea, a totally new approach that revolutionizes whatever you're doing. A Uranus event takes you by surprise, happens from out of the blue, for better or for worse. The Uranus place in your life is where you wake up to your own special qualities and become your own person, leaving the structures of Saturn behind.

Look up the sign of Uranus at the time of your birth. Then place it in the appropriate house in your chart and see where you follow your own tune.

Uranus in Aries

BIRTH DATES:
    March 31, 1927–November 4, 1927
    January 13, 1928—June 6, 1934
    October 10, 1934—March 28, 1935

Your generation is original, creative, pioneering. It developed the computer, the airplane, and the cyclotron. You let nothing hold you back from exploring the unknown and have a powerful mixture of fire and electricity behind you. Women of your generation were among the first to be liberated. You were the unforgettable style setters. You have a surprise in store for everyone. Like Yoko Ono, Grace Kelly, and Jacqueline Onassis, your life may be jolted by sudden and violent changes.

Uranus in Taurus

BIRTH DATES:
    June 6, 1934–October 10, 1934
    March 28, 1935–August 7, 1941
    October 5, 1941–May 15, 1942

World War II began during your generation. You are probably self-employed or would like to be. You have original ideas about making money, and you brace yourself for sudden changes of fortune. This Uranus can cause shakeups, particularly in finances, but it can also make you a born entrepreneur.

Uranus in Gemini

BIRTH DATES:
  August 7, 1941–October 5, 1941
  May 15, 1942–August 30, 1948
  November 12, 1948–June 10, 1949

You were the first children to be influenced by television. Now, in your adult years, your generation stocks up on answering machines, cordless phones, car phones, computers, and fax machines—any new way you can communicate. You have an inquiring mind, but your interests may be rather short-lived. This Uranus can be easily fragmented if there is no structure and focus.

Uranus in Cancer

BIRTH DATES:
  August 30, 1948–November 12, 1948
  June 10, 1949–August 24, 1955
  January 28, 1956–June 10, 1956

This generation came at a time when divorce was becoming commonplace, so your home image is unconventional. You may have an unusual relationship with your parents; you may have come from a broken home or an unconventional one. You'll have unorthodox ideas about parenting, intimacy, food, and shelter. You may also be interested in dreams, psychic phenomena, and memory work.

Uranus in Leo

BIRTH DATES:
   August 24, 1955–January 28, 1956
   June 10, 1956–November 1, 1961
   January 10, 1962–August 10, 1962

This generation understands how to use electronic media. Many of your group are now leaders in the high-tech industries, and you also understand how to use the new media to promote yourself. Like Isadora Duncan, you may have a very eccentric kind of charisma and a life that is sparked by unusual love affairs. Your children, too, may have traits that are out of the ordinary. Where this planet falls in your chart, you'll have a love of freedom, be a bit of an egomaniac, and show the full force of your personality in a unique way, like tennis great Martina Navratilova.

Uranus in Virgo

BIRTH DATES:
   November 1, 1961–January 10, 1962
   August 10, 1962–September 28, 1968
   May 20, 1969–June 24, 1969

You'll have highly individual work methods, and many will be finding newer, more practical ways to use computers. Like Einstein, who had this placement, you'll break the rules brilliantly. Your generation came at a time of student rebellions, the civil rights movement, and the general acceptance of health foods. Chances are, you're concerned about pollution and cleaning up the environment. You may also be involved with non-traditional healing methods. Heavyweight champ Mike Tyson has this placement.

Uranus in Libra

BIRTH DATES:
  September 28, 1968–May 20, 1969
  June 24, 1969–November 21, 1974
  May 1, 1975–September 8, 1975

Your generation will be always changing partners. Born during the era of women's liberation, you may have come from a broken home and have no clear image of what a marriage entails. There will be many sudden splits and experiments before you settle down. Your generation will be much involved in legal and political reforms and in changing artistic and fashion looks.

Uranus in Scorpio

BIRTH DATES:
  November 21, 1974–May 1, 1975
  September 8, 1975–February 17, 1981
  March 20, 1981–November 16, 1981

Interest in transformation, meditation, and life after death signaled the beginning of New Age consciousness. Your generation recognizes no boundaries, no limits, and no external controls. You'll have new attitudes toward death and dying, psychic phenomena, and the occult. Like Mae West and Casanova, you'll shock 'em sexually, too.

Uranus in Sagittarius

BIRTH DATES:
  February 17, 1981–March 20, 1981
  November 16, 1981–February 15, 1988
  May 27, 1988–December 2, 1988

Could this generation be the first to travel in outer space? An earlier generation with this placement included Charles Lindbergh—at that time, the first Zeppelins and the Wright Brothers were conquering the skies. Uranus here forecasts great discoveries, mind expansion, and long-distance travel. Like Galileo and Martin Luther, this generation will formulate new theories about the cosmos and man's relation to it.

Uranus in Capricorn

BIRTH DATES:
December 20, 1904–January 30, 1912
September 4, 1912–November 12, 1912
February 15, 1988–May 27, 1988
December 2, 1988–April 1, 1995
June 9, 1995–January 12, 1996

This generation will challenge traditions with the help of electronic gadgets. During the mid-1990s, we got organized with the help of technology put to practical use. Home computers and handheld devices became widely used. Great leaders, who were movers and shakers of history, like Julius Caesar and Henry VIII, were born under this placement.

Uranus in Aquarius

BIRTH DATES:
January 30, 1912–September 4, 1912
November 12, 1912–April 1, 1919
August 16, 1919–January 22, 1920
April 1, 1995–June 9, 1995
January 12, 1996–March 10, 2003

The last generation with this placement produced great innovative minds such as Leonard Bernstein and Orson Welles. Babies who are born now will become another radical breakthrough generation, much concerned with global issues that involve all humanity. Intuition, innovation, and sudden changes will continue to surprise everyone while Uranus is in its home sign.

Uranus in Pisces

BIRTH DATES:
  April 1, 1919–August 16, 1919
  January 22, 1920–March 31, 1927
  November 4, 1927–January 12, 1928
  March 10, 2003–May 28, 2010

Uranus in Pisces previously focused attention on the rise of electronic entertainment—radio and the cinema—and the secretiveness of Prohibition. This produced a generation of idealists exemplified by Judy Garland's theme, "Somewhere Over the Rainbow." Coming up next year will be the dramatic return of Uranus to Pisces, which should spark a wonderful spurt of creativity and innovation in the arts.

Neptune Takes You out of This World

Under Neptune's influence, you see what you want to see. But Neptune also encourages you to create, letting your fantasies and daydreams run free. Neptune is often maligned as the planet of illusions, drugs, and alcohol, where you can't bear to face reality. But it also embodies the energy of glamour, subtlety, mystery, and mysticism, and governs anything that takes you beyond the mundane world, including out-of-body experiences.

Neptune acts to break through your ordinary perceptions and take you to another level of reality, where you experience either confusion or ecstasy. Neptune's force can pull you off-course, the way this planet affects its neighbor, Uranus, but only if you allow this to happen. Those who use Neptune wisely can translate their daydreams into poetry, theater, design, or inspired moves in the business world, avoiding the tricky "con artist" side of this planet.

Find your Neptune listed below:

Neptune in Cancer

BIRTH DATES:
   July 19, 1901–December 25, 1901
   May 21, 1902–September 23, 1914
   December 14, 1914–July 19, 1915
   March 1916–May 2, 1916

Dreams of the homeland, idealistic patriotism, and glamorization of the nurturing assets of women characterized this time. You who were born here have unusual psychic ability and deep insights into the basic needs of others.

Neptune in Leo

BIRTH DATES:
   September 23, 1914–December 14, 1914
   July 19, 1915–March 19, 1916
   May 2, 1916–September 21, 1928
   February 19, 1929–July 24, 1929

Neptune here brought us the glamour and high living of the 1920s and the big spenders of that time. The Neptunian temptations of gambling, seduction, theater, and lavish entertaining distracted us from the realities of the age. Those born in this generation also made great advances in the arts.

Neptune in Virgo

BIRTH DATES:
September 21, 1928–February 19, 1929
July 24, 1929–October 3, 1942
April 17, 1943–August 2, 1943

Neptune in Virgo encompassed the Great Depression and World War II, while those born at this time later spread the gospel of health and fitness. This generation's devotion to spending hours at the office inspired the term "workaholic."

Neptune in Libra

BIRTH DATES:
October 3, 1942–April 17, 1943
August 2, 1943–December 24, 1955
March 12, 1956–October 19, 1956
June 15, 1957–August 6, 1957

Neptune in Libra produced the romantic generation who would later be extremely concerned with relating. As this generation matured, there was a new trend toward marriage and commitment. Racial and sexual equality become important issues, as they redesigned traditional relationship roles to suit modern times.

Neptune in Scorpio

BIRTH DATES:
December 24, 1955–March 12, 1956
October 19, 1956–June 15, 1957
August 6, 1957–January 4, 1970
May 3, 1970–November 6, 1970

Neptune in Scorpio ushered in a generation that would become interested in transformative power. Born in an era that glamorized sex, drugs, rock and roll, and Eastern religion, they matured in a more sobering time of AIDS, cocaine abuse, and New Age spirituality. As they evolve, they will become active in healing the planet from the results of the abuse of power.

Neptune in Sagittarius

BIRTH DATES:
   January 4, 1970–May 3, 1970
   November 6, 1970–January 19, 1984
   June 23, 1984–November 21, 1984

Neptune in Sagittarius was the time when space and astronaut travel became a reality. The Neptune influence glamorized new approaches to mysticism, religion, and mind expansion. This generation will take a new approach to spiritual life, with emphasis on visions, mysticism, and clairvoyance.

Neptune in Capricorn

BIRTH DATES:
   January 19, 1984–June 23, 1984
   November 21, 1984–January 29, 1998

Neptune in Capricorn brought a time when delusions about material power were first glamorized, then dashed on the rocks of reality. It was also a time when the psychic and occult worlds spawned a new category of business enterprise, and sold services on television.

Neptune in Aquarius

BIRTH DATES:
   January 29, 1998–April 4, 2111

This should continue to be a time of breakthroughs, when the creative influence of Neptune reaches a universal audience. This is a time of dissolving barriers, of globalization, when we truly become one world. Computer technology used for the creative arts, innovative drug therapies, and high-tech "highs" such as trance music are recent manifestations.

Pluto Transforms You

Pluto is a mysterious little planet with a strange elliptical orbit that occasionally runs inside the orbit of its neighbor Neptune. Because of its eccentric path, the length of time Pluto stays in any given sign can vary from thirteen to thirty-two years. It has covered only seven signs in the past century. Though it is a tiny planet, its influence is great. When Pluto zaps a strategic point in your horoscope, your life changes dramatically.

This little planet is the power behind the scenes; it affects you at deep levels of consciousness, causing events to come to the surface that will transform you and your generation. Nothing escapes, or is sacred, with this probing planet. The Pluto place in your horoscope is where you have invisible power (Mars governs the visible power), where you can transform, heal, and affect the unconscious needs of the masses. Pluto tells how your generation projects power, what makes it seem "cool" to others. And when Pluto changes signs, there's a whole new concept of what's cool.

Pluto in Gemini

BIRTH DATES:
Late 1800s–May 26, 1914

This was a time of mass suggestion and breakthroughs in communications, when many brilliant writers, such as Ernest Hemingway and F. Scott Fitzgerald, were born. Henry Miller, D. H. Lawrence, and James Joyce scandalized society by using explicit sexual images and language in their literature. "Muckraking" journalists exposed corruption. Pluto-ruled Scorpio President Theodore Roosevelt said, "Speak softly, but carry a big stick." This generation had an intense need to communicate and made major breakthroughs in knowledge. A compulsive restlessness and a thirst for a variety of experiences characterizes many of this generation.

Pluto in Cancer

BIRTH DATES:
  May 26, 1914–June 14, 1939

Dictators and mass media rose up to wield emotional power over the masses. Women's rights was a popular issue. Deep sentimental feelings, acquisitiveness, and possessiveness characterized these times and people. The great Hollywood stars who embodied the American image were born during this period: Grace Kelly, Esther Williams, Frank Sinatra, Lana Turner, etc.

Pluto in Leo

BIRTH DATES:
  June 14, 1939–August 19, 1957

The performing arts played on the emotions of the masses. Mick Jagger, John Lennon, and rock and roll were born at this time. So were "baby boomers" like Bill and Hillary Clinton. Those born here tend to be self-centered, powerful, and boisterous. This generation does its own thing, for better or for worse.

Pluto in Virgo

BIRTH DATES:
  August 19, 1957–October 5, 1971
  April 17, 1972–July 30, 1972

This is the "yuppie" generation that sparked a mass movement toward fitness, health, and career. A much more sober, serious, driven generation than the fun-loving Pluto in Leos. During this time, machines were invented to process detail work efficiently. Inventions took a practical turn, as answering machines, fax machines, car phones, and home office equipment contributed to transform the workplace.

Pluto in Libra

BIRTH DATES:
  October 5, 1971–April 17, 1972
  July 30, 1972–August 28, 1984

A mellower generation concerned with partnerships, working together, and finding diplomatic solutions to problems. Marriage is important to this generation, who will redefine it, combining traditional values with equal partnership. This was a time of women's liberation, gay rights, ERA, and legal battles over abortion, all of which transformed our ideas about relationships.

Pluto in Scorpio

BIRTH DATES:
  August 28, 1984–January 17, 1995

Pluto was in its ruling sign for a comparatively short period of time. In 1989, it was at its perihelion, or closest point to the sun and Earth. We have all felt the transforming power somewhere in our lives. This was a time of record achievements, destructive sexually transmitted diseases, nuclear power controversies, and explosive political issues. Pluto destroys in order to create new understanding—the phoenix rising from the ashes, which should be some consolation for those of you who felt Pluto's force before 1995. Sexual shockers were par for the course during these intense years, when black clothing, transvestites, body piercing, tattoos, and sexually explicit advertising pushed the boundaries of good taste.

Pluto in Sagittarius

BIRTH DATES:
  January 17, 1995–January 27, 2008

During our current Pluto transit, we are being pushed to expand our horizons. For many of us, this will mean rolling down the information superhighway into the future. Another trend is to find deeper spiritual meaning in life. This is a time when spiritual emphasis will become pervasive, when religious convictions will exert more power in our political life as well.

Since Sagittarius is the sign that rules travel, there's a good possibility that Pluto, the planet of extremes, will make space travel a reality for some of us. Discovery of life on Mars, which traveled here on meteors, could transform our ideas about where we came from.

New dimensions in electronic publishing, concern with animal rights and the environment, and an increasing emphasis on extreme forms of religion are other signs of these times. Look for charismatic religious leaders to arise now. We'll also be developing far-reaching philosophies designed to elevate our lives with a new sense of purpose.

VENUS SIGNS 1901–2002

	Aries	Taurus	Gemini	Cancer	Leo	Virgo
1901	3/29–4/22	4/22–5/17	5/17–6/10	6/10–7/5	7/5–7/29	7/29–8/23
1902	5/7–6/3	6/3–6/30	6/30–7/25	7/25–8/19	8/19–9/13	9/13–10/7
1903	2/28–3/24	3/24–4/18	4/18–5/13	5/13–6/9	6/9–7/7	7/7–8/17
						9/6–11/8
1904	3/13–5/7	5/7–6/1	6/1–6/25	6/25–7/19	7/19–8/13	8/13–9/6
1905	2/3–3/6	3/6–4/9	7/8–8/6	8/6–9/1	9/1–9/27	9/27–10/21
	4/9–5/28	5/28–7/8				
1906	3/1–4/7	4/7–5/2	5/2–5/26	5/26–6/20	6/20–7/16	7/16–8/11
1907	4/27–5/22	5/22–6/16	6/16–7/11	7/11–8/4	8/4–8/29	8/29–9/22
1908	2/14–3/10	3/10–4/5	4/5–5/5	5/5–9/8	9/8–10/8	10/8–11/3
1909	3/29–4/22	4/22–5/16	5/16–6/10	6/10–7/4	7/4–7/29	7/29–8/23
1910	5/7–6/3	6/4–6/29	6/30–7/24	7/25–8/18	8/19–9/12	9/13–10/6
1911	2/28–3/23	3/24–4/17	4/18–5/12	5/13–6/8	6/9–7/7	7/8–11/8
1912	4/13–5/6	5/7–5/31	6/1–6/24	6/24–7/18	7/19–8/12	8/13–9/5
1913	2/3–3/6	3/7–5/1	7/8–8/5	8/6–8/31	9/1–9/26	9/27–10/20
	5/2–5/30	5/31–7/7				
1914	3/14–4/6	4/7–5/1	5/2–5/25	5/26–6/19	6/20–7/15	7/16–8/10
1915	4/27–5/21	5/22–6/15	6/16–7/10	7/11–8/3	8/4–8/28	8/29–9/21
1916	2/14–3/9	3/10–4/5	4/6–5/5	5/6–9/8	9/9–10/7	10/8–11/2
1917	3/29–4/21	4/22–5/15	5/16–6/9	6/10–7/3	7/4–7/28	7/29–8/21
1918	5/7–6/2	6/3–6/28	6/29–7/24	7/25–8/18	8/19–9/11	9/12–10/5
1919	2/27–3/22	3/23–4/16	4/17–5/12	5/13–6/7	6/8–7/7	7/8–11/8
1920	4/12–5/6	5/7–5/30	5/31–6/23	6/24–7/18	7/19–8/11	8/12–9/4
1921	2/3–3/6	3/7–4/25	7/8–8/5	8/6–8/31	9/1–9/25	9/26–10/20
	4/26–6/1	6/2–7/7				
1922	3/13–4/6	4/7–4/30	5/1–5/25	5/26–6/19	6/20–7/14	7/15–8/9
1923	4/27–5/21	5/22–6/14	6/15–7/9	7/10–8/3	8/4–8/27	8/28–9/20
1924	2/13–3/8	3/9–4/4	4/5–5/5	5/6–9/8	9/9–10/7	10/8–11/12
1925	3/28–4/20	4/21–5/15	5/16–6/8	6/9–7/3	7/4–7/27	7/28–8/21

Libra	Scorpio	Sagittarius	Capricorn	Aquarius	Pisces
8/23–9/17	9/17–10/12	10/12–1/16	1/16–2/9 11/7–12/5	2/9–3/5 12/5–1/11	3/5–3/29
10/7–10/31	10/31–11/24	11/24–12/18	12/18–1/11	2/6–4/4	1/11–2/6 4/4–5/7
8/17–9/6 11/8–12/9	12/9–1/5			1/11–2/4	2/4–2/28
9/6–9/30	9/30–10/25	1/5–1/30 10/25–11/18	1/30–2/24 11/18–12/13	2/24–3/19 12/13–1/7	3/19–4/13
10/21–11/14	11/14–12/8	12/8–1/1/06			1/7–2/3
8/11–9/7	9/7–10/9 12/15–12/25	10/9–12/15 12/25–2/6	1/1–1/25	1/25–2/18	2/18–3/14
9/22–10/16	10/16–11/9	11/9–12/3	2/6–3/6 12/3–12/27	3/6–4/2 12/27–1/20	4/2–4/27
11/3–11/28	11/28–12/22	12/22–1/15			1/20–2/4
8/23–9/17	9/17–10/12	10/12–11/17	1/15–2/9 11/17–12/5	2/9–3/5 12/5–1/15	3/5–3/29
10/7–10/30	10/31–11/23	11/24–12/17	12/18–12/31	1/1–1/15 1/29–4/4	1/16–1/28 4/5–5/6
11/19–12/8	12/9–12/31		1/1–1/10	1/11–2/2	2/3–2/27
9/6–9/30	1/1–1/4 10/1–10/24	1/5–1/29 10/25–11/17	1/30–2/23 11/18–12/12	2/24–3/18 12/13–12/31	3/19–4/12
10/21–11/13	11/14–12/7	12/8–12/31		1/1–1/6	1/7–2/2
8/11–9/6	9/7–10/9 12/6–12/30	10/10–12/5 12/31	1/1–1/24	1/25–2/17	2/18–3/13
9/22–10/15	10/16–11/8	1/1–2/6 11/9–12/2	2/7–3/6 12/3–12/26	3/7–4/1 12/27–12/31	4/2–4/26
11/3–11/27	11/28–12/21	12/22–12/31		1/1–1/19	1/20–2/13
8/22–9/16	9/17–10/11	1/1–1/14 10/12–11/6	1/15–2/7 11/7–12/5	2/8–3/4 12/6–12/31	3/5–3/28
10/6–10/29	10/30–11/22	11/23–12/16	12/17–12/31	1/1–4/5	4/6–5/6
11/9–12/8	12/9–12/31		1/1–1/9	1/10–2/2	2/3–2/26
9/5–9/30	1/1–1/3 9/31–10/23	1/4–1/28 10/24–11/17	1/29–2/22 11/18–12/11	2/23–3/18 12/12–12/31	3/19–4/11
10/21–11/13	11/14–12/7	12/8–12/31		1/1–1/6	1/7–2/2
8/10–9/6	9/7–10/10 11/29–12/31	10/11–11/28	1/1–1/24	1/25–2/16	2/17–3/12
9/21–10/14	1/1 10/15–11/7	1/2–2/6 11/8–12/1	2/7–3/5 12/2–12/25	3/6–3/31 12/26–12/31	4/1–4/26
11/13–11/26	11/27–12/21	12/22–12/31		1/1–1/19	1/20–2/12
8/22–9/15	9/16–10/11	1/1–1/14 10/12–11/6	1/15–2/7 11/7–12/5	2/8–3/3 12/6–12/31	3/4–3/27

VENUS SIGNS 1901–2002

	Aries	Taurus	Gemini	Cancer	Leo	Virgo
1926	5/7–6/2	6/3–6/28	6/29–7/23	7/24–8/17	8/18–9/11	9/12–10/5
1927	2/27–3/22	3/23–4/16	4/17–5/11	5/12–6/7	6/8–7/7	7/8–11/9
1928	4/12–5/5	5/6–5/29	5/30–6/23	6/24–7/17	7/18–8/11	8/12–9/4
1929	2/3–3/7	3/8–4/19	7/8–8/4	8/5–8/30	8/31–9/25	9/26–10/19
	4/20–6/2	6/3–7/7				
1930	3/13–4/5	4/6–4/30	5/1–5/24	5/25–6/18	6/19–7/14	7/15–8/9
1931	4/26–5/20	5/21–6/13	6/14–7/8	7/9–8/2	8/3–8/26	8/27–9/19
1932	2/12–3/8	3/9–4/3	4/4–5/5	5/6–7/12	9/9–10/6	10/7–11/1
			7/13–7/27	7/28–9/8		
1933	3/27–4/19	4/20–5/28	5/29–6/8	6/9–7/2	7/3–7/26	7/27–8/20
1934	5/6–6/1	6/2–6/27	6/28–7/22	7/23–8/16	8/17–9/10	9/11–10/4
1935	2/26–3/21	3/22–4/15	4/16–5/10	5/11–6/6	6/7–7/6	7/7–11/8
1936	4/11–5/4	5/5–5/28	5/29–6/22	6/23–7/16	7/17–8/10	8/11–9/4
1937	2/2–3/8	3/9–4/13	7/7–8/3	8/4–8/29	8/30–9/24	9/25–10/18
	4/14–6/3	6/4–7/6				
1938	3/12–4/4	4/5–4/28	4/29–5/23	5/24–6/18	6/19–7/13	7/14–8/8
1939	4/25–5/19	5/20–6/13	6/14–7/8	7/9–8/1	8/2–8/25	8/26–9/19
1940	2/12–3/7	3/8–4/3	4/4–5/5	5/6–7/4	9/9–10/5	10/6–10/31
			7/5–7/31	8/1–9/8		
1941	3/27–4/19	4/20–5/13	5/14–6/6	6/7–7/1	7/2–7/26	7/27–8/20
1942	5/6–6/1	6/2–6/26	6/27–7/22	7/23–8/16	8/17–9/9	9/10–10/3
1943	2/25–3/20	3/21–4/14	4/15–5/10	5/11–6/6	6/7–7/6	7/7–11/8
1944	4/10–5/3	5/4–5/28	5/29–6/21	6/22–7/16	7/17–8/9	8/10–9/2
1945	2/2–3/10	3/11–4/6	7/7–8/3	8/4–8/29	8/30–9/23	9/24–10/18
	4/7–6/3	6/4–7/6				
1946	3/11–4/4	4/5–4/28	4/29–5/23	5/24–6/17	6/18–7/12	7/13–8/8
1947	4/25–5/19	5/20–6/12	6/13–7/7	7/8–8/1	8/2–8/25	8/26–9/18
1948	2/11–3/7	3/8–4/3	4/4–5/6	5/7–6/28	9/8–10/5	10/6–10/31
			6/29–8/2	8/3–9/7		
1949	3/26–4/19	4/20–5/13	5/14–6/6	6/7–6/30	7/1–7/25	7/26–8/19
1950	5/5–5/31	6/1–6/26	6/27–7/21	7/22–8/15	8/16–9/9	9/10–10/3
1951	2/25–3/21	3/22–4/15	4/16–5/10	5/11–6/6	6/7–7/7	7/8–11/9

Libra	Scorpio	Sagittarius	Capricorn	Aquarius	Pisces
10/6–10/29	10/30–11/22	11/23–12/16	12/17–12/31	1/1–4/5	4/6–5/6
11/10–12/8	12/9–12/31	1/1–1/7	1/8	1/9–2/1	2/2–2/26
9/5–9/28	1/1–1/3	1/4–1/28	1/29–2/22	2/23–3/17	3/18–4/11
	9/29–10/23	10/24–11/16	11/17–12/11	12/12–12/31	
10/20–11/12	11/13–12/6	12/7–12/30	12/31	1/1–1/5	1/6–2/2
8/10–9/6	9/7–10/11	10/12–11/21	1/1–1/23	1/24–2/16	2/17–3/12
	11/22–12/31				
9/20–10/13	1/1–1/3	1/4–2/6	2/7–3/4	3/5–3/31	4/1–4/25
	10/14–11/6	11/7–11/30	12/1–12/24	12/25–12/31	
11/2–11/25	11/26–12/20	12/21–12/31		1/1–1/18	1/19–2/11
8/21–9/14	9/15–10/10	1/1–1/13	1/14–2/6	2/7–3/2	3/3–3/26
		10/11–11/5	11/6–12/4	12/5–12/31	
10/5–10/28	10/29–11/21	11/22–12/15	12/16–12/31	1/1–4/5	4/6–5/5
11/9–12/7	12/8–12/31		1/1–1/7	1/8–1/31	2/1–2/25
9/5–9/27	1/1–1/2	1/3–1/27	1/28–2/21	2/22–3/16	3/17–4/10
	9/28–10/22	10/23–11/15	11/16–12/10	12/11–12/31	
10/19–11/11	11/12–12/5	12/6–12/29	12/30–12/31	1/1–1/5	1/6–2/1
8/9–9/6	9/7–10/13	10/14–11/14	1/1–1/22	1/23–2/15	2/16–3/11
	11/15–12/31				
9/20–10/13	1/1–1/3	1/4–2/5	2/6–3/4	3/5–3/30	3/31–4/24
	10/14–11/6	11/7–11/30	12/1–12/24	12/25–12/31	
11/1–11/25	11/26–12/19	12/20–12/31		1/1–1/18	1/19–2/11
8/21–9/14	9/15–10/9	1/1–1/12	1/13–2/5	2/6–3/1	3/2–3/26
		10/10–11/5	11/6–12/4	12/5–12/31	
10/4–10/27	10/28–11/20	11/21–12/14	12/15–12/31	1/1–4/4	4/6–5/5
11/9–12/7	12/8–12/31		1/1–1/7	1/8–1/31	2/1–2/24
9/3–9/27	1/1–1/2	1/3–1/27	1/28–2/20	2/21–3/16	3/17–4/9
	9/28–10/21	10/22–11/15	11/16–12/10	12/11–12/31	
10/19–11/11	11/12–12/5	12/6–12/29	12/30–12/31	1/1–1/4	1/5–2/1
8/9–9/6	9/7–10/15	10/16–11/7	1/1–1/21	1/22–2/14	2/15–3/10
	11/8–12/31				
9/19–10/12	1/1–1/4	1/5–2/5	2/6–3/4	3/5–3/29	3/30–4/24
	10/13–11/5	11/6–11/29	11/30–12/23	12/24–12/31	
11/1–11/25	11/26–12/19	12/20–12/31		1/1–1/17	1/18–2/10
8/20–9/14	9/15–10/9	1/1–1/12	1/13–2/5	2/6–3/1	3/2–3/25
		10/10–11/5	11/6–12/5	12/6–12/31	
10/4–10/27	10/28–11/20	11/21–12/13	12/14–12/31	1/1–4/5	4/6–5/4
11/10–12/7	12/8–12/31		1/1–1/7	1/8–1/31	2/1–2/24

VENUS SIGNS 1901–2002

	Aries	Taurus	Gemini	Cancer	Leo	Virgo
1952	4/10–5/4	5/5–5/28	5/29–6/21	6/22–7/16	7/17–8/9	8/10–9/3
1953	2/2–3/3	3/4–3/31	7/8–8/3	8/4–8/29	8/30–9/24	9/25–10/18
	4/1–6/5	6/6–7/7				
1954	3/12–4/4	4/5–4/28	4/29–5/23	5/24–6/17	6/18–7/13	7/14–8/8
1955	4/25–5/19	5/20–6/13	6/14–7/7	7/8–8/1	8/2–8/25	8/26–9/18
1956	2/12–3/7	3/8–4/4	4/5–5/7	5/8–6/23	9/9–10/5	10/6–10/31
			6/24–8/4	8/5–9/8		
1957	3/26–4/19	4/20–5/13	5/14–6/6	6/7–7/1	7/2–7/26	7/27–8/19
1958	5/6–5/31	6/1–6/26	6/27–7/22	7/23–8/15	8/16–9/9	9/10–10/3
1959	2/25–3/20	3/21–4/14	4/15–5/10	5/11–6/6	6/7–7/8	7/9–9/20
					9/21–9/24	9/25–11/9
1960	4/10–5/3	5/4–5/28	5/29–6/21	6/22–7/15	7/16–8/9	8/10–9/2
1961	2/3–6/5	6/6–7/7	7/8–8/3	8/4–8/29	8/30–9/23	9/24–10/17
1962	3/11–4/3	4/4–4/28	4/29–5/22	5/23–6/17	6/18–7/12	7/13–8/8
1963	4/24–5/18	5/19–6/12	6/13–7/7	7/8–7/31	8/1–8/25	8/26–9/18
1964	2/11–3/7	3/8–4/4	4/5–5/9	5/10–6/17	9/9–10/5	10/6–10/31
			6/18–8/5	8/6–9/8		
1965	3/26–4/18	4/19–5/12	5/13–6/6	6/7–6/30	7/1–7/25	7/26–8/19
1966	5/6–6/31	6/1–6/26	6/27–7/21	7/22–8/15	8/16–9/8	9/9–10/2
1967	2/24–3/20	3/21–4/14	4/15–5/10	5/11–6/6	6/7–7/8	7/9–9/9
					9/10–10/1	10/2–11/9
1968	4/9–5/3	5/4–5/27	5/28–6/20	6/21–7/15	7/16–8/8	8/9–9/2
1969	2/3–6/6	6/7–7/6	7/7–8/3	8/4–8/28	8/29–9/22	9/23–10/17
1970	3/11–4/3	4/4–4/27	4/28–5/22	5/23–6/16	6/17–7/12	7/13–8/8
1971	4/24–5/18	5/19–6/12	6/13–7/6	7/7–7/31	8/1–8/24	8/25–9/17
1972	2/11–3/7	3/8–4/3	4/4–5/10	5/11–6/11		
			6/12–8/6	8/7–9/8	9/9–10/5	10/6–10/30
1973	3/25–4/18	4/18–5/12	5/13–6/5	6/6–6/29	7/1–7/25	7/26–8/19
1974						
	5/5–5/31	6/1–6/25	6/26–7/21	7/22–8/14	8/15–9/8	9/9–10/2
1975	2/24–3/20	3/21–4/13	4/14–5/9	5/10–6/6	6/7–7/9	7/10–9/2
					9/3–10/4	10/5–11/9

Libra	Scorpio	Sagittarius	Capricorn	Aquarius	Pisces
9/4–9/27		1/3–1/27	1/28–2/20	2/21–3/16	3/17–4/9
	9/28–10/21	10/22–11/15	11/16–12/10	12/11–12/31	
10/19–11/11	11/12–12/5	12/6–12/29	12/30–12/31	1/1–1/5	1/6–2/1
8/9–9/6	9/7–10/22	10/23–10/27	1/1–1/22	1/23–2/15	2/16–3/11
	10/28–12/31				
9/19–10/13		1/7–2/5	2/6–3/4	3/5–3/30	3/31–4/24
	10/14–11/5	11/6–11/30	12/1–12/24	12/25–12/31	
11/1–11/25	11/26–12/19	12/20–12/31		1/1–1/17	1/18–2/11
8/20–9/14	9/15–10/9	1/1–1/12	1/13–2/5	2/6–3/1	3/2–3/25
		10/10–11/5	11/6–12/6	12/7–12/31	
10/4–10/27	10/28–11/20	11/21–12/14	12/15–12/31	1/1–4/6	4/7–5/5
11/10–12/7	12/8–12/31		1/1–1/7	1/8–1/31	2/1–2/24
9/3–9/26	1/1–1/2	1/3–1/27	1/28–2/20	2/21–3/15	3/16–4/9
	9/27–10/21	10/22–11/15	11/16–12/10	12/11–12/31	
10/18–11/11	11/12–12/4	12/5–12/28	12/29–12/31	1/1–1/5	1/6–2/2
8/9–9/6	9/7–12/31		1/1–1/21	1/22–2/14	2/15–3/10
9/19–10/12	1/1–1/6	1/7–2/5	2/6–3/4	3/5–3/29	3/30–4/23
	10/13–11/5	11/6–11/29	11/30–12/23	12/24–12/31	
11/1–11/24	11/25–12/19	12/20–12/31		1/1–1/16	1/17–2/10
8/20–9/13	9/14–10/9	1/1–1/12	1/13–2/5	2/6–3/1	3/2–3/25
		10/10–11/5	11/6–12/7	12/8–12/31	
10/3–10/26	10/27–11/19	11/20–12/13	2/7–2/25	1/1–2/6	4/7–5/5
			12/14–12/31	2/26–4/6	
11/10–12/7	12/8–12/31		1/1–1/6	1/7–1/30	1/31–2/23
9/3–9/26	1/1	1/2–1/26	1/27–2/20	2/21–3/15	3/16–4/8
	9/27–10/21	10/22–11/14	11/15–12/9	12/10–12/31	
10/18–11/10	11/11–12/4	12/5–12/28	12/29–12/31	1/1–1/4	1/5–2/2
8/9–9/7	9/8–12/31		1/1–1/21	1/22–2/14	2/15–3/10
9/18–10/11	1/1–1/7	1/8–2/5	2/6–3/4	3/5–3/29	3/30–4/23
	10/12–11/5	11/6–11/29	11/30–12/23	12/24–12/31	
	11/25–12/18	12/19–12/31		1/1–1/16	1/17–2/10
10/31–11/24					
8/20–9/13	9/14–10/8	1/1–1/12	1/13–2/4	2/5–2/28	3/1–3/24
		10/9–11/5	11/6–12/7	12/8–12/31	
			1/30–2/28	1/1–1/29	
10/3–10/26	10/27–11/19	11/20–12/13	12/14–12/31	3/1–4/6	4/7–5/4
			1/1–1/6	1/7–1/30	1/31–2/23
11/10–12/7	12/8–12/31				

VENUS SIGNS 1901–2002

	Aries	Taurus	Gemini	Cancer	Leo	Virgo
1976	4/8–5/2	5/2–5/27	5/27—6/20	6/20–7/14	7/14–8/8	8/8–9/1
1977	2/2–6/6	6/6–7/6	7/6–8/2	8/2–8/28	8/28–9/22	9/22–10/17
1978	3/9–4/2	4/2–4/27	4/27–5/22	5/22–6/16	6/16–7/12	7/12–8/6
1979	4/23–5/18	5/18–6/11	6/11–7/6	7/6–7/30	7/30–8/24	8/24–9/17
1980	2/9–3/6	3/6–4/3	4/3–5/12	5/12–6/5	9/7–10/4	10/4–10/30
			6/5–8/6	8/6–9/7		
1981	3/24–4/17	4/17–5/11	5/11–6/5	6/5–6/29	6/29–7/24	7/24–8/18
1982	5/4–5/30	5/30–6/25	6/25–7/20	7/20–8/14	8/14–9/7	9/7–10/2
1983	2/22–3/19	3/19–4/13	4/13–5/9	5/9–6/6	6/6–7/10	7/10–8/27
					8/27–10/5	10/5–11/9
1984	4/7–5/2	5/2–5/26	5/26–6/20	6/20–7/14	7/14–8/7	8/7–9/1
1985	2/2–6/6	6/7–7/6	7/6–8/2	8/2–8/28	8/28–9/22	9/22–10/16
1986	3/9–4/2	4/2–4/26	4/26–5/21	5/21–6/15	6/15–7/11	7/11–8/7
1987	4/22–5/17	5/17–6/11	6/11–7/5	7/5–7/30	7/30–8/23	8/23–9/16
1988	2/9–3/6	3/6–4/3	4/3–5/17	5/17–5/27	9/7–10/4	10/4–10/29
			5/27–8/6	8/28–9/22	9/22–10/16	
1989	3/23–4/16	4/16–5/11	5/11–6/4	6/4–6/29	6/29–7/24	7/24–8/18
1990	5/4–5/30	5/30–6/25	6/25–7/20	7/20–8/13	8/13–9/7	9/7–10/1
1991	2/22–3/18	3/18–4/13	4/13–5/9	5/9–6/6	6/6–7/11	7/11–8/21
					8/21–10/6	10/6–11/9
1992	4/7–5/1	5/1–5/26	5/26–6/19	6/19–7/13	7/13–8/7	8/7–8/31
1993	2/2–6/6	6/6–7/6	7/6–8/1	8/1–8/27	8/27–9/21	9/21–10/16
1994	3/8–4/1	4/1–4/26	4/26–5/21	5/21–6/15	6/15–7/11	7/11–8/7
1995	4/22–5/16	5/16–6/10	6/10–7/5	7/5–7/29	7/29–8/23	8/23–9/16
1996	2/9–3/6	3/6–4/3	4/3–8/7	8/7–9/7	9/7–10/4	10/4–10/29
1997	3/23–4/16	4/16–5/10	5/10–6/4	6/4–6/28	6/28–7/23	7/23–8/17
1998	5/3–5/29	5/29–6/24	6/24–7/19	7/19–8/13	8/13–9/6	9/6–9/30
1999	2/21–3/18	3/18–4/12	4/12–5/8	5/8–6/5	6/5–7/12	7/12–8/15
					8/15–10/7	10/7–11/9
2000	4/6–5/1	5/1–5/25	5/25–6/13	6/13–7/13	7/13–8/6	8/6–8/31
2001	2/2–6/6	6/6–7/5	7/5–8/1	8/1–8/26	8/26–9/20	9/20–10/15
2002	3/7–4/1	4/1–4/25	4/25–5/20	5/20–6/14	6/14–7/10	7/10–8/7

Libra	Scorpio	Sagittarius	Capricorn	Aquarius	Pisces
9/1–9/26	9/26–10/20	1/1–1/26	1/26–2/19	2/19–3/15	3/15–4/8
		10/20–11/14	11/14–12/8	12/9–1/4	
10/17–11/10	11/10–12/4	12/4–12/27	12/27–1/20/78		1/4–2/2
8/6–9/7	9/7–1/7			1/20–2/13	2/13–3/9
9/17–10/11	10/11–11/4	1/7–2/5	2/5–3/3	3/3–3/29	3/29–4/23
		11/4–11/28	11/28–12/22	12/22–1/16/80	
10/30–11/24	11/24–12/18	12/18–1/11/81			1/16–2/9
8/18–9/12	9/12–10/9	10/9–11/5	1/11–2/4	2/4–2/28	2/28–3/24
			11/5–12/8	12/8–1/23/82	
10/2–10/26	10/26–11/18	11/18–12/12	1/23–3/2	3/2–4/6	4/6–5/4
			12/12–1/5/83		
11/9–12/6	12/6–1/1/84			1/5–1/29	1/29–2/22
9/1–9/25	9/25–10/20	1/1–1/25	1/25–2/19	2/19–3/14	3/14–4/7
		10/20–11/13	11/13–12/9	12/10–1/4	
10/16–11/9	11/9–12/3	12/3–12/27	12/28–1/19		1/4–2/2
8/7–9/7	9/7–1/7			1/20–2/13	2/13–3/9
9/16–10/10	10/10–11/3	1/7–2/5	2/5–3/3	3/3–3/28	3/28–4/22
		11/3–11/28	11/28–12/22	12/22–1/15	
10/29–11/23	11/23–12/17	12/17–1/10			1/15–2/9
8/18–9/12	9/12–10/8	10/8–11/5	1/10–2/3	2/3–2/27	2/27–3/23
			11/5–12/10	12/10–1/16/90	
10/1–10/25	10/25–11/18	11/18–12/12	1/16–3/3	3/3–4/6	4/6–5/4
			12/12–1/5		
11/9–12/6	12/6–12/31	12/31–1/25/92		1/5–1/29	1/29–2/22
8/31–9/25	9/25–10/19	10/19–11/13	1/25–2/18	2/18–3/13	3/13–4/7
			11/13–12/8	12/8–1/3/93	
10/16–11/9	11/9–12/2	12/2–12/26	12/26–1/19		1/3–2/2
8/7–9/7	9/7–1/7			1/19–2/12	2/12–3/8
9/16–10/10	10/10–11/13	1/7–2/4	2/4–3/2	3/2–3/28	3/28–4/22
		11/3–11/27	11/27–12/21	12/21–1/15	
10/29–11/23	11/23–12/17	12/17–1/10/97			1/15–2/9
8/17–9/12	9/12–10/8	10/8–11/5	1/10–2/3	2/3–2/27	2/27–3/23
			11/5–12/12	12/12–1/9	
9/30–10/24	10/24–11/17	11/17–12/11	1/9–3/4	3/4–4/6	4/6–5/3
11/9–12/5	12/5–12/31	12/31–1/24		1/4–1/28	1/28–2/21
8/31–9/24	9/24–10/19	10/19–11/13	1/24–2/18	2/18–3/12	3/13–4/6
			11/13–12/8	12/8	
10/15–11/8	11/8–12/2	12/2–12/26	12/26/01–1/19/02	12/8/00–1/3/01	1/3–2/2
8/7–9/7	9/7–1/7/03		1/26/01–1/18	1/18–2/11	2/11–3/7

How to Use the Mars, Jupiter, and Saturn Tables

Find the year of your birth on the left side of each column. The dates when the planet entered each sign are listed on the right side of each column. (Signs are abbreviated to three letters.) Your birthday should fall on or between each date listed, and your planetary placement should correspond to the earlier sign of that period.

MARS SIGNS 1901–2002

Year	Month	Day	Sign	Year	Month	Day	Sign
1901	MAR	1	Leo	1905	JAN	13	Scp
	MAY	11	Vir		AUG	21	Sag
	JUL	13	Lib		OCT	8	Cap
	AUG	31	Scp		NOV	18	Aqu
	OCT	14	Sag		DEC	27	Pic
	NOV	24	Cap	1906	FEB	4	Ari
1902	JAN	1	Aqu		MAR	17	Tau
	FEB	8	Pic		APR	28	Gem
	MAR	19	Ari		JUN	11	Can
	APR	27	Tau		JUL	27	Leo
	JUN	7	Gem		SEP	12	Vir
	JUL	20	Can		OCT	30	Lib
	SEP	4	Leo		DEC	17	Scp
	OCT	23	Vir	1907	FEB	5	Sag
	DEC	20	Lib		APR	1	Cap
1903	APR	19	Vir		OCT	13	Aqu
	MAY	30	Lib		NOV	29	Pic
	AUG	6	Scp	1908	JAN	11	Ari
	SEP	22	Sag		FEB	23	Tau
	NOV	3	Cap		APR	7	Gem
	DEC	12	Aqu		MAY	22	Can
1904	JAN	19	Pic		JUL	8	Leo
	FEB	27	Ari		AUG	24	Vir
	APR	6	Tau		OCT	10	Lib
	MAY	18	Gem		NOV	25	Scp
	JUN	30	Can	1909	JAN	10	Sag
	AUG	15	Leo		FEB	24	Cap
	OCT	1	Vir		APR	9	Aqu
	NOV	20	Lib		MAY	25	Pic

76

	JUL	21	Ari	AUG	19	Can
	SEP	26	Pic	OCT	7	Leo
	NOV	20	Ari	1916 MAY	28	Vir
1910	JAN	23	Tau	JUL	23	Lib
	MAR	14	Gem	SEP	8	Scp
	MAY	1	Can	OCT	22	Sag
	JUN	19	Leo	DEC	1	Cap
	AUG	6	Vir	1917 JAN	9	Aqu
	SEP	22	Lib	FEB	16	Pic
	NOV	6	Scp	MAR	26	Ari
	DEC	20	Sag	MAY	4	Tau
1911	JAN	31	Cap	JUN	14	Gem
	MAR	14	Aqu	JUL	28	Can
	APR	23	Pic	SEP	12	Leo
	JUN	2	Ari	NOV	2	Vir
	JUL	15	Tau	1918 JAN	11	Lib
	SEP	5	Gem	FEB	25	Vir
	NOV	30	Tau	JUN	23	Lib
1912	JAN	30	Gem	AUG	17	Scp
	APR	5	Can	OCT	1	Sag
	MAY	28	Leo	NOV	11	Cap
	JUL	17	Vir	DEC	20	Aqu
	SEP	2	Lib	1919 JAN	27	Pic
	OCT	18	Scp	MAR	6	Ari
	NOV	30	Sag	APR	15	Tau
1913	JAN	10	Cap	MAY	26	Gem
	FEB	19	Aqu	JUL	8	Can
	MAR	30	Pic	AUG	23	Leo
	MAY	8	Ari	OCT	10	Vir
	JUN	17	Tau	NOV	30	Lib
	JUL	29	Gem	1920 JAN	31	Scp
	SEP	15	Can	APR	23	Lib
1914	MAY	1	Leo	JUL	10	Scp
	JUN	26	Vir	SEP	4	Sag
	AUG	14	Lib	OCT	18	Cap
	SEP	29	Scp	NOV	27	Aqu
	NOV	11	Sag	1921 JAN	5	Pic
	DEC	22	Cap	FEB	13	Ari
1915	JAN	30	Aqu	MAR	25	Tau
	MAR	9	Pic	MAY	6	Gem
	APR	16	Ari	JUN	18	Can
	MAY	26	Tau	AUG	3	Leo
	JUL	6	Gem	SEP	19	Vir

	NOV	6	Lib		APR	7	Pic
	DEC	26	Scp		MAY	16	Ari
1922	FEB	18	Sag		JUN	26	Tau
	SEP	13	Cap		AUG	9	Gem
	OCT	30	Aqu		OCT	3	Can
	DEC	11	Pic		DEC	20	Gem
1923	JAN	21	Ari	1929	MAR	10	Can
	MAR	4	Tau		MAY	13	Leo
	APR	16	Gem		JUL	4	Vir
	MAY	30	Can		AUG	21	Lib
	JUL	16	Leo		OCT	6	Scp
	SEP	1	Vir		NOV	18	Sag
	OCT	18	Lib		DEC	29	Cap
	DEC	4	Scp	1930	FEB	6	Aqu
1924	JAN	19	Sag		MAR	17	Pic
	MAR	6	Cap		APR	24	Ari
	APR	24	Aqu		JUN	3	Tau
	JUN	24	Pic		JUL	14	Gem
	AUG	24	Aqu		AUG	28	Can
	OCT	19	Pic		OCT	20	Leo
	DEC	19	Ari	1931	FEB	16	Can
1925	FEB	5	Tau		MAR	30	Leo
	MAR	24	Gem		JUN	10	Vir
	MAY	9	Can		AUG	1	Lib
	JUN	26	Leo		SEP	17	Scp
	AUG	12	Vir		OCT	30	Sag
	SEP	28	Lib		DEC	10	Cap
	NOV	13	Scp	1932	JAN	18	Aqu
	DEC	28	Sag		FEB	25	Pic
1926	FEB	9	Cap		APR	3	Ari
	MAR	23	Aqu		MAY	12	Tau
	MAY	3	Pic		JUN	22	Gem
	JUN	15	Ari		AUG	4	Can
	AUG	1	Tau		SEP	20	Leo
1927	FEB	22	Gem		NOV	13	Vir
	APR	17	Can	1933	JUL	6	Lib
	JUN	6	Leo		AUG	26	Scp
	JUL	25	Vir		OCT	9	Sag
	SEP	10	Lib		NOV	19	Cap
	OCT	26	Scp		DEC	28	Aqu
	DEC	8	Sag	1934	FEB	4	Pio
1928	JAN	19	Cap		MAR	14	Ari
	FEB	28	Aqu		APR	22	Tau

	JUN	2	Gem		AUG	19	Vir
	JUL	15	Can		OCT	5	Lib
	AUG	30	Leo		NOV	20	Scp
	OCT	18	Vir	1941	JAN	4	Sag
	DEC	11	Lib		FEB	17	Cap
1935	JUL	29	Scp		APR	2	Aqu
	SEP	16	Sag		MAY	16	Pic
	OCT	28	Cap		JUL	2	Ari
	DEC	7	Aqu	1942	JAN	11	Tau
1936	JAN	14	Pic		MAR	7	Gem
	FEB	22	Ari		APR	26	Can
	APR	1	Tau		JUN	14	Leo
	MAY	13	Gem		AUG	1	Vir
	JUN	25	Can		SEP	17	Lib
	AUG	10	Leo		NOV	1	Scp
	SEP	26	Vir		DEC	15	Sag
	NOV	14	Lib	1943	JAN	26	Cap
1937	JAN	5	Scp		MAR	8	Aqu
	MAR	13	Sag		APR	17	Pic
	MAY	14	Scp		MAY	27	Ari
	AUG	8	Sag		JUL	7	Tau
	SEP	30	Cap		AUG	23	Gem
	NOV	11	Aqu	1944	MAR	28	Can
	DEC	21	Pic		MAY	22	Leo
1938	JAN	30	Ari		JUL	12	Vir
	MAR	12	Tau		AUG	29	Lib
	APR	23	Gem		OCT	13	Scp
	JUN	7	Can		NOV	25	Sag
	JUL	22	Leo	1945	JAN	5	Cap
	SEP	7	Vir		FEB	14	Aqu
	OCT	25	Lib		MAR	25	Pic
	DEC	11	Scp		MAY	2	Ari
1939	JAN	29	Sag		JUN	11	Tau
	MAR	21	Cap		JUL	23	Gem
	MAY	25	Aqu		SEP	7	Can
	JUL	21	Cap		NOV	11	Leo
	SEP	24	Aqu		DEC	26	Can
	NOV	19	Pic	1946	APR	22	Leo
1940	JAN	4	Ari		JUN	20	Vir
	FEB	17	Tau		AUG	9	Lib
	APR	1	Gem		SEP	24	Scp
	MAY	17	Can		NOV	6	Sag
	JUL	3	Leo		DEC	17	Cap

1947	JAN	25	Aqu	MAR	20	Tau
	MAR	4	Pic	MAY	1	Gem
	APR	11	Ari	JUN	14	Can
	MAY	21	Tau	JUL	29	Leo
	JUL	1	Gem	SEP	14	Vir
	AUG	13	Can	NOV	1	Lib
	OCT	1	Leo	DEC	20	Scp
	DEC	1	Vir	1954	FEB	9	Sag
1948	FEB	12	Leo	APR	12	Cap
	MAY	18	Vir	JUL	3	Sag
	JUL	17	Lib	AUG	24	Cap
	SEP	3	Scp	OCT	21	Aqu
	OCT	17	Sag	DEC	4	Pic
	NOV	26	Cap	1955	JAN	15	Ari
1949	JAN	4	Aqu	FEB	26	Tau
	FEB	11	Pic	APR	10	Gem
	MAR	21	Ari	MAY	26	Can
	APR	30	Tau	JUL	11	Leo
	JUN	10	Gem	AUG	27	Vir
	JUL	23	Can	OCT	13	Lib
	SEP	7	Leo	NOV	29	Scp
	OCT	27	Vir	1956	JAN	14	Sag
	DEC	26	Lib	FEB	28	Cap
1950	MAR	28	Vir	APR	14	Aqu
	JUN	11	Lib	JUN	3	Pic
	AUG	10	Scp	DEC	6	Ari
	SEP	25	Sag	1957	JAN	28	Tau
	NOV	6	Cap	MAR	17	Gem
	DEC	15	Aqu	MAY	4	Can
1951	JAN	22	Pic	JUN	21	Leo
	MAR	1	Ari	AUG	8	Vir
	APR	10	Tau	SEP	24	Lib
	MAY	21	Gem	NOV	8	Scp
	JUL	3	Can	DEC	23	Sag
	AUG	18	Leo	1958	FEB	3	Cap
	OCT	5	Vir	MAR	17	Aqu
	NOV	24	Lib	APR	27	Pic
1952	JAN	20	Scp	JUN	7	Ari
	AUG	27	Sag	JUL	21	Tau
	OCT	12	Cap	SEP	21	Gem
	NOV	21	Aqu	OCT	29	Tau
	DEC	30	Pic	1959	FEB	10	Gem
1953	FEB	8	Ari	APR	10	Can

	JUN	1	Leo		NOV	14	Cap
	JUL	20	Vir		DEC	23	Aqu
	SEP	5	Lib	1966	JAN	30	Pic
	OCT	21	Scp		MAR	9	Ari
	DEC	3	Sag		APR	17	Tau
1960	JAN	14	Cap		MAY	28	Gem
	FEB	23	Aqu		JUL	11	Can
	APR	2	Pic		AUG	25	Leo
	MAY	11	Ari		OCT	12	Vir
	JUN	20	Tau		DEC	4	Lib
	AUG	2	Gem	1967	FEB	12	Scp
	SEP	21	Can		MAR	31	Lib
1961	FEB	5	Gem		JUL	19	Scp
	FEB	7	Can		SEP	10	Sag
	MAY	6	Leo		OCT	23	Cap
	JUN	28	Vir		DEC	1	Aqu
	AUG	17	Lib	1968	JAN	9	Pic
	OCT	1	Scp		FEB	17	Ari
	NOV	13	Sag		MAR	27	Tau
	DEC	24	Cap		MAY	8	Gem
1962	FEB	1	Aqu		JUN	21	Can
	MAR	12	Pic		AUG	5	Leo
	APR	19	Ari		SEP	21	Vir
	MAY	28	Tau		NOV	9	Lib
	JUL	9	Gem		DEC	29	Scp
	AUG	22	Can	1969	FEB	25	Sag
	OCT	11	Leo		SEP	21	Cap
1963	JUN	3	Vir		NOV	4	Aqu
	JUL	27	Lib		DEC	15	Pic
	SEP	12	Scp	1970	JAN	24	Ari
	OCT	25	Sag		MAR	7	Tau
	DEC	5	Cap		APR	18	Gem
1964	JAN	13	Aqu		JUN	2	Can
	FEB	20	Pic		JUL	18	Leo
	MAR	29	Ari		SEP	3	Vir
	MAY	7	Tau		OCT	20	Lib
	JUN	17	Gem		DEC	6	Scp
	JUL	30	Can	1971	JAN	23	Sag
	SEP	15	Leo		MAR	12	Cap
	NOV	6	Vir		MAY	3	Aqu
1965	JUN	29	Lib		NOV	6	Pic
	AUG	20	Scp		DEC	26	Ari
	OCT	4	Sag	1972	FEB	10	Tau

	MAR	27	Gem	1978	JAN	26	Can
	MAY	12	Can		APR	10	Leo
	JUN	28	Leo		JUN	14	Vir
	AUG	15	Vir		AUG	4	Lib
	SEP	30	Lib		SEP	19	Scp
	NOV	15	Scp		NOV	2	Sag
	DEC	30	Sag		DEC	12	Cap
1973	FEB	12	Cap	1979	JAN	20	Aqu
	MAR	26	Aqu		FEB	27	Pic
	MAY	8	Pic		APR	7	Ari
	JUN	20	Ari		MAY	16	Tau
	AUG	12	Tau		JUN	26	Gem
	OCT	29	Ari		AUG	8	Can
	DEC	24	Tau		SEP	24	Leo
1974	FEB	27	Gem		NOV	19	Vir
	APR	20	Can	1980	MAR	11	Leo
	JUN	9	Leo		MAY	4	Vir
	JUL	27	Vir		JUL	10	Lib
	SEP	12	Lib		AUG	29	Scp
	OCT	28	Scp		OCT	12	Sag
	DEC	10	Sag		NOV	22	Cap
1975	JAN	21	Cap		DEC	30	Aqu
	MAR	3	Aqu	1981	FEB	6	Pic
	APR	11	Pic		MAR	17	Ari
	MAY	21	Ari		APR	25	Tau
	JUL	1	Tau		JUN	5	Gem
	AUG	14	Gem		JUL	18	Can
	OCT	17	Can		SEP	2	Leo
	NOV	25	Gem		OCT	21	Vir
1976	MAR	18	Can		DEC	16	Lib
	MAY	16	Leo	1982	AUG	3	Scp
	JUL	6	Vir		SEP	20	Sag
	AUG	24	Lib		OCT	31	Cap
	OCT	8	Scp		DEC	10	Aqu
	NOV	20	Sag	1983	JAN	17	Pic
1977	JAN	1	Cap		FEB	25	Ari
	FEB	9	Aqu		APR	5	Tau
	MAR	20	Pic		MAY	16	Gem
	APR	27	Ari		JUN	29	Can
	JUN	6	Tau		AUG	13	Leo
	JUL	17	Gem		SEP	30	Vir
	SEP	1	Can		NOV	18	Lib
	OCT	26	Leo	1984	JAN	11	Scp

Year	Mon	Day	Sign		Year	Mon	Day	Sign
	AUG	17	Sag			JUL	12	Tau
	OCT	5	Cap			AUG	31	Gem
	NOV	15	Aqu			DEC	14	Tau
	DEC	25	Pic		1991	JAN	21	Gem
1985	FEB	2	Ari			APR	3	Can
	MAR	15	Tau			MAY	26	Leo
	APR	26	Gem			JUL	15	Vir
	JUN	9	Can			SEP	1	Lib
	JUL	25	Leo			OCT	16	Scp
	SEP	10	Vir			NOV	29	Sag
	OCT	27	Lib		1992	JAN	9	Cap
	DEC	14	Scp			FEB	18	Aqu
1986	FEB	2	Sag			MAR	28	Pic
	MAR	28	Cap			MAY	5	Ari
	OCT	9	Aqu			JUN	14	Tau
	NOV	26	Pic			JUL	26	Gem
1987	JAN	8	Ari			SEP	12	Can
	FEB	20	Tau		1993	APR	27	Leo
	APR	5	Gem			JUN	23	Vir
	MAY	21	Can			AUG	12	Lib
	JUL	6	Leo			SEP	27	Scp
	AUG	22	Vir			NOV	9	Sag
	OCT	8	Lib			DEC	20	Cap
	NOV	24	Scp		1994	JAN	28	Aqu
1988	JAN	8	Sag			MAR	7	Pic
	FEB	22	Cap			APR	14	Ari
	APR	6	Aqu			MAY	23	Tau
	MAY	22	Pic			JUL	3	Gem
	JUL	13	Ari			AUG	16	Can
	OCT	23	Pic			OCT	4	Leo
	NOV	1	Ari			DEC	12	Vir
1989	JAN	19	Tau		1995	JAN	22	Leo
	MAR	11	Gem			MAY	25	Vir
	APR	29	Can			JUL	21	Lib
	JUN	16	Leo			SEP	7	Scp
	AUG	3	Vir			OCT	20	Sag
	SEP	19	Lib			NOV	30	Cap
	NOV	4	Scp		1996	JAN	8	Aqu
	DEC	18	Sag			FEB	15	Pic
1990	JAN	29	Cap			MAR	24	Ari
	MAR	11	Aqu			MAY	2	Tau
	APR	20	Pic			JUN	12	Gem
	MAY	31	Ari			JUL	25	Can

	SEP	9	Leo		NOV	26	Aqu
	OCT	30	Vir	2000	JAN	4	Pic
1997	JAN	3	Lib		FEB	12	Ari
	MAR	8	Vir		MAR	23	Tau
	JUN	19	Lib		MAY	3	Gem
	AUG	14	Scp		JUN	16	Can
	SEP	28	Sag		AUG	1	Leo
	NOV	9	Cap		SEP	17	Vir
	DEC	18	Aqu		NOV	4	Lib
1998	JAN	25	Pic		DEC	23	Scp
	MAR	4	Ari	2001	FEB	14	Sag
	APR	13	Tau		SEP	8	Cap
	MAY	24	Gem		OCT	27	Aqu
	JUL	6	Can		DEC	8	Pic
	AUG	20	Leo	2002	JAN	18	Ari
	OCT	7	Vir		MAR	1	Tau
	NOV	27	Lib		APR	13	Gem
1999	JAN	26	Scp		MAY	28	Can
	MAY	5	Lib		JUL	13	Leo
	JUL	5	Scp		AUG	29	Vir
	SEP	2	Sag		OCT	15	Lib
	OCT	17	Cap		DEC	1	Scp

JUPITER SIGNS 1901–2002

1901	JAN	19	Cap	1911	DEC	10	Sag
1902	FEB	6	Aqu	1913	JAN	2	Cap
1903	FEB	20	Pic	1914	JAN	21	Aqu
1904	MAR	1	Ari	1915	FEB	4	Pic
	AUG	8	Tau	1916	FEB	12	Ari
	AUG	31	Ari		JUN	26	Tau
1905	MAR	7	Tau		OCT	26	Ari
	JUL	21	Gem	1917	FEB	12	Tau
	DEC	4	Tau		JUN	29	Gem
1906	MAR	9	Gem	1918	JUL	13	Can
	JUL	30	Can	1919	AUG	2	Leo
1907	AUG	18	Leo	1920	AUG	27	Vir
1908	SEP	12	Vir	1921	SEP	25	Lib
1909	OCT	11	Lib	1922	OCT	26	Scp
1910	NOV	11	Scp	1923	NOV	24	Sag

1924	DEC	18	Cap	1955	JUN	13	Leo
1926	JAN	6	Aqu		NOV	17	Vir
1927	JAN	18	Pic	1956	JAN	18	Leo
	JUN	6	Ari		JUL	7	Vir
	SEP	11	Pic		DEC	13	Lib
1928	JAN	23	Ari	1957	FEB	19	Vir
	JUN	4	Tau		AUG	7	Lib
1929	JUN	12	Gem	1958	JAN	13	Scp
1930	JUN	26	Can		MAR	20	Lib
1931	JUL	17	Leo		SEP	7	Scp
1932	AUG	11	Vir	1959	FEB	10	Sag
1933	SEP	10	Lib		APR	24	Scp
1934	OCT	11	Scp		OCT	5	Sag
1935	NOV	9	Sag	1960	MAR	1	Cap
1936	DEC	2	Cap		JUN	10	Sag
1937	DEC	20	Aqu		OCT	26	Cap
1938	MAY	14	Pic	1961	MAR	15	Aqu
	JUL	30	Aqu		AUG	12	Cap
	DEC	29	Pic		NOV	4	Aqu
1939	MAY	11	Ari	1962	MAR	25	Pic
	OCT	30	Pic	1963	APR	4	Ari
	DEC	20	Ari	1964	APR	12	Tau
1940	MAY	16	Tau	1965	APR	22	Gem
1941	MAY	26	Gem		SEP	21	Can
1942	JUN	10	Can		NOV	17	Gem
1943	JUN	30	Leo	1966	MAY	5	Can
1944	JUL	26	Vir		SEP	27	Leo
1945	AUG	25	Lib	1967	JAN	16	Can
1946	SEP.	25	Scp		MAY	23	Leo
1947	OCT	24	Sag		OCT	19	Vir
1948	NOV	15	Cap	1968	FEB	27	Leo
1949	APR	12	Aqu		JUN	15	Vir
	JUN	27	Cap		NOV	15	Lib
	NOV	30	Aqu	1969	MAR	30	Vir
1950	APR	15	Pic		JUL	15	Lib
	SEP	15	Aqu		DEC	16	Scp
	DEC	1	Pic	1970	APR	30	Lib
1951	APR	21	Ari		AUG	15	Scp
1952	APR	28	Tau	1971	JAN	14	Sag
1953	MAY	9	Gem		JUN	5	Scp
1954	MAY	24	Can		SEP	11	Sag

1972	FEB	6	Cap		1986	FEB	20	Pic
	JUL	24	Sag		1987	MAR	2	Ari
	SEP	25	Cap		1988	MAR	8	Tau
1973	FEB	23	Aqu			JUL	22	Gem
1974	MAR	8	Pic			NOV	30	Tau
1975	MAR	18	Ari		1989	MAR	11	Gem
1976	MAR	26	Tau			JUL	30	Can
	AUG	23	Gem		1990	AUG	18	Leo
	OCT	16	Tau		1991	SEP	12	Vir
1977	APR	3	Gem		1992	OCT	10	Lib
	AUG	20	Can		1993	NOV	10	Scp
	DEC	30	Gem		1994	DEC	9	Sag
1978	APR	12	Can		1996	JAN	3	Cap
	SEP	5	Leo		1997	JAN	21	Aqu
1979	FEB	28	Can		1998	FEB	4	Pic
	APR	20	Leo		1999	FEB	13	Ari
	SEP	29	Vir			JUN	28	Tau
1980	OCT	27	Lib			OCT	23	Ari
1981	NOV	27	Scp		2000	FEB	14	Tau
1982	DEC	26	Sag			JUN	30	Gem
1984	JAN	19	Cap		2001	JUL	14	Can
1985	FEB	6	Aqu					

SATURN SIGNS 1903–2002

1903	JAN	19	Aqu		1916	OCT	17	Leo
1905	APR	13	Pic			DEC	7	Can
	AUG	17	Aqu		1917	JUN	24	Leo
1906	JAN	8	Pic		1919	AUG	12	Vir
1908	MAR	19	Ari		1921	OCT	7	Lib
1910	MAY	17	Tau		1923	DEC	20	Scp
	DEC	14	Ari		1924	APR	6	Lib
1911	JAN	20	Tau			SEP	13	Scp
1912	JUL	7	Gem		1926	DEC	2	Sag
	NOV	30	Tau		1929	MAR	15	Cap
1913	MAR	26	Gem			MAY	5	Sag
1914	AUG	24	Can			NOV	30	Cap
	DEC	7	Gem		1932	FEB	24	Aqu
1915	MAY	11	Can			AUG	13	Cap

	NOV	20	Aqu		FEB	21	Gem
1935	FEB	14	Pic	1973	AUG	1	Can
1937	APR	25	Ari	1974	JAN	7	Gem
	OCT	18	Pic		APR	18	Can
1938	JAN	14	Ari	1975	SEP	17	Leo
1939	JUL	6	Tau	1976	JAN	14	Can
	SEP	22	Ari				
1940	MAR	20	Tau		JUN	5	Leo
1942	MAY	8	Gem	1977	NOV	17	Vir
1944	JUN	20	Can	1978	JAN	5	Leo
1946	AUG	2	Leo		JUL	26	Vir
1948	SEP	19	Vir	1980	SEP	21	Lib
1949	APR	3	Leo	1982	NOV	29	Scp
	MAY	29	Vir	1983	MAY	6	Lib
1950	NOV	20	Lib		AUG	24	Scp
1951	MAR	7	Vir	1985	NOV	17	Sag
	AUG	13	Lib	1988	FEB	13	Cap
1953	OCT	22	Scp		JUN	10	Sag
1956	JAN	12	Sag		NOV	12	Cap
	MAY	14	Scp	1991	FEB	6	Aqu
	OCT	10	Sag	1993	MAY	21	Pic
1959	JAN	5	Cap		JUN	30	Aqu
1962	JAN	3	Aqu	1994	JAN	28	Pic
1964	MAR	24	Pic	1996	APR	7	Ari
	SEP	16	Aqu	1998	JUN	9	Tau
	DEC	16	Pic		OCT	25	Ari
1967	MAR	3	Ari	1999	MAR	1	Tau
1969	APR	29	Tau	2000	AUG	10	Gem
1971	JUN	18	Gem		OCT	16	Tau
1972	JAN	10	Tau	2001	APR	21	Gem

CHAPTER 4

Crack the Astrology Code—
Decipher Those Mysterious
Glyphs on Your Chart

The first time you look at a horoscope, you'll realize that astrology has a code all its own, written in strange-looking characters which represent the planets and signs. These symbols, or *glyphs,* are used by astrologers worldwide and by computer astrology programs. So, if you want to progress in astrology enough to read a horoscope, there's no way around it . . . you've got to know the meaning of the glyphs.

Besides enabling you to read a horoscope chart, learning the astrology code can help you interpret the meaning of the signs and planets, because each glyph contains a minilesson in what its planet or sign represents. And since there are only twelve signs and ten planets (not counting a few asteroids and other space creatures some astrologers use), they're a lot easier to learn than, say, Chinese!

Here's a code cracker for the glyphs, beginning with the glyphs for the planets. To those who already know their glyphs, don't just skim over the chapter! There are hidden meanings to discover, so test your glyph-ese.

The Glyphs for the Planets

The glyphs for the planets are easy to learn. They're simple combinations of the most basic visual elements: the circle, the semicircle or arc, and the cross. However, each component of a glyph has a special meaning in relation to the others, which adds up to create the total meaning of the symbol.

The circle, which has no beginning or end, is one of the oldest symbols of spirit or spiritual forces. All of the early diagrams of the heavens—spiritual territory—are shown in circular form. The never-ending line of the circle is the perfect symbol for eternity. The semicircle or arc is an incomplete circle, symbolizing the receptive, finite soul, which contains spiritual potential in the curving line.

The vertical line of the cross symbolizes movement from heaven to earth. The horizontal line describes temporal movement, here and now, in time and space. Combined in a cross, the vertical and horizontal planes symbolize manifestation in the material world.

The Sun Glyph ☉

The sun is always shown by this powerful solar symbol, a circle with a point in the center. The center point is you, your spiritual center, and the symbol represents your infinite personality incarnating (the point) into the finite cycles of birth and death.

The sun has been represented by a circle or disk since ancient Egyptian times, when the solar disk represented the sun god, Ra. Some archaeologists believe the great stone circles found in England were centers of sun worship. This particular version of the symbol was brought into common use in the sixteenth century, after German occultist and scholar Cornelius Agrippa (1486–1535) wrote a book called *Die Occulta Philosophia,* which became accepted as the standard work in its field. Agrippa collected many medieval astrological and magical symbols in this book, which have been used by astrologers since then.

The Moon Glyph ☽

The moon glyph is the most recognizable symbol on a chart, a left-facing arc stylized into the crescent moon. As part of a circle, the arc symbolizes the potential fulfillment of the entire circle, the life force that is still incomplete. Therefore, it is the ideal representation of the reactive, receptive, emotional nature of the moon.

The Mercury Glyph ☿

Mercury contains all three elemental symbols, the crescent, the circle, and the cross in vertical order. This is the "Venus with a hat" glyph (compare with the symbol of Venus). With another stretch of the imagination, can't you see the winged cap of Mercury the messenger? Think of the upturned crescent as antennae that tune in and transmit messages from the sun, reminding you that Mercury is the way you communicate, the way your mind works. The upturned arc is receiving energy into the spirit or solar circle, which will later be translated into action on the material plane, symbolized by the cross. All the elements are equally sized because Mercury is neutral; it doesn't play favorites! This planet symbolizes objective, detached, unemotional thinking.

The Venus Glyph ♀

Here the relationship is between two components, the circle or spirit and the cross of matter. Spirit is elevated over matter, pulling it upward. Venus asks, "What is beautiful? What do you like best? What do you love to have done to you?" Consequently,

Venus determines both your ideal of beauty and what feels good sensually. It governs your own allure and power to attract, as well as what attracts and pleases you.

The Mars Glyph ♂

In this glyph, the cross of matter is stylized into an arrowhead pointed up and outward, propelled by the circle of spirit. With a little imagination, you can visualize it as the shield and spear of Mars, the ancient god of war. You can deduce that Mars embodies your spiritual energy projected into the outer world. It's your assertiveness, your initiative, your aggressive drive, what you like to do to others, your temper. If you know someone's Mars, you know whether they'll blow up when angry or do a slow burn. Your task is to use your outgoing Mars energy wisely and well.

The Jupiter Glyph ♃

Jupiter is the basic cross of matter, with a large stylized crescent perched on the left side of the horizontal, temporal plane. You might think of the crescent as an open hand, because one meaning of Jupiter is "luck," what's handed to you. You don't work for what you get from Jupiter; it comes to you, if you're open to it.

The Jupiter glyph might also remind you of a jumbo jet plane with a huge tail fin, about to take off. This is the planet of travel, mental and spiritual, of expanding your horizons via new ideas, new spiritual dimensions, and new places. Jupiter embodies the optimism and enthusiasm of the traveler about to embark on an exciting adventure.

The Saturn Glyph ♄

Flip Jupiter over and you've got Saturn. (This might not be immediately apparent, because Saturn is usually stylized into an "h" form like the one shown here.) The principle it expresses is the opposite of Jupiter's expansive tendencies. Saturn pulls you back to earth—the receptive arc is pushed down underneath the cross of matter. Before there are any rewards or expansion, the duties and obligations of the material world must be considered. Saturn says, "Stop, wait, finish your chores before you take off!"

Saturn's glyph also resembles the scythe of old "Father Time." Saturn was first known as Chronos, the Greek god of time, for time brings all matter to an end. When it was the most distant planet (before the discovery of Uranus), Saturn was believed to be the place where time stopped. After the soul departed from Earth, it journeyed back to the outer reaches of the universe and finally stopped at Saturn, or at "the end of time."

The Uranus Glyph ♅

The glyph for Uranus is often stylized to form a capital "H" after Sir William Herschel, who discovered the planet. But the more esoteric version curves the two pillars of the H into crescent antennae, or "ears," like satellite disks receiving signals from space. These are perched on the horizontal material line of the cross (matter) and pushed from below by the circle of the spirit. To many sci-fi fans, Uranus looks like an orbiting satellite.

Uranus channels the highest energy of all, the white electrical light of the universal spiritual force which holds the cosmos together. This pure electrical energy is gathered from all over the universe. Because Uranian energy doesn't follow any ordinary celestial drumbeat, it can't be controlled or predicted (which is also true of those who are strongly influenced by this eccentric planet). In the symbol, this energy is manifested through the balance of polarities (the two opposite arms of the glyph) like the two polarized wires of a light bulb.

The Neptune Glyph Ψ

Neptune's glyph is usually stylized to look like a trident, the weapon of the Roman god Neptune. However, on a more esoteric level, it shows the large, upturned crescent of the soul pierced through by the cross of matter. Neptune nails down, or materializes, soul energy, bringing impulses from the soul level into manifestation. That is why Neptune is associated with imagination or "imagining in," making an image of the soul. Neptune works through feeling, sensitivity, and a mystical capacity to bring the divine into the earthly realm.

The Pluto Glyph ♀

Pluto is written two ways. One is a composite of the letters PL, the first two letters of the word "Pluto" and coincidentally the initials of Percival Lowell, one of the planet's discoverers. The other, more esoteric symbol is a small circle above a large open crescent which surmounts the cross of matter. This depicts Pluto's power to regenerate—imagine a new little spirit emerging from the sheltering cup of the soul. Pluto rules the forces of life and death—after this planet has passed a sensitive point in your chart, you are transformed, reborn in some way.

Sci-fi fans might visualize this glyph as a small satellite (the circle) being launched. It was shortly after Pluto's discovery that we learned how to harness the nuclear forces that made space exploration possible. Pluto rules the transformative power of atomic energy, which totally changed our lives and from which there is no turning back.

The Glyphs for the Signs

On an astrological chart, the glyph for the sign will appear after that of the planet. For example, when you see the moon glyph followed first by a number and then by another glyph representing the sign, this means that the moon was passing over a certain degree of that astrological sign at the time of the chart. On the dividing lines between the segments or "houses" on your chart, you'll find the symbol for the sign that rules the house.

Because sun sign symbols do not contain the same basic geometric components of the planetary glyphs, we must look elsewhere for clues to their meanings. Many have been passed down from ancient Egyptian and Chaldean civilizations with few modifications. Others have been adapted over the centuries. In deciphering many of the glyphs, you'll often find that the symbols reveal a dual nature of the sign, which is not always apparent in the usual sun sign descriptions. For instance, the Gemini glyph is similar to the Roman numeral for two, and reveals this sign's longing to discover a twin soul. The Cancer glyph may be interpreted as resembling either the nurturing breasts or the self-protective claws of the crab, both symbols associated with the contrasting qualities of this sign. Libra's glyph embodies the duality of the spirit balanced with material reality. The Sagittarius glyph shows that the aspirant must also carry along the earthly animal nature in his quest. The Capricorn sea goat is another symbol with dual emphasis. The goat climbs high, yet is always pulled back by the deep waters of the unconscious. Aquarius embodies the double waves of mental detachment, balanced by the desire for connection with others in a friendly way. And finally, the two fishes of Pisces, which are forever tied together, show the duality of the soul and the spirit that must be reconciled.

The Aries Glyph ♈

Since the symbol for Aries is the ram, this glyph is obviously associated with a ram's horns, which characterize one aspect of the Aries personality—an aggressive, me-first, leaping-headfirst attitude. But the symbol can be interpreted in other ways as well. Some astrologers liken it to a fountain of energy, which Aries people also embody. The first sign of the zodiac bursts on the scene eagerly, ready to go. Another analogy is to the eyebrows and nose of the human head, which Aries rules, and the thinking power that is initiated in the brain.

One theory of this symbol links it to the Egyptian god Amun, represented by a ram in ancient times. As Amun-Ra, this god was believed to embody the creator of the universe, the leader of all the other gods. This relates easily to the position of Aries as the leader (or first sign) of the zodiac, which begins at the spring equinox, a time of the year when nature is renewed.

The Taurus Glyph ♉

This is another easy glyph to draw and identify. It takes little imagination to decipher the bull's head with long curving horns. Like the bull, the archetypal Taurus is slow to anger, but ferocious when provoked, as well as stubborn, steady, and sensual. Another association is the larynx (and thyroid) of the throat area (ruled by Taurus) and the eustachian tubes running up to the ears, which coincide with the relationship of Taurus to the voice, song, and music. Many famous singers, musicians, and composers have prominent Taurus influences.

Many ancient religions involved a bull as the central figure in fertility rites or initiations, usually symbolizing the victory of man over his animal nature. Another possible origin is in the sacred bull of Egypt, who embodied the incarnate form of Osiris, god of death and resurrection. In early Christian imagery, the Taurean bull represented St. Luke.

The Gemini Glyph ♊

The standard glyph immediately calls to mind the Roman numeral II and the "twins" symbol for Gemini. In almost all drawings and images used for this sign, the relationship between two persons is emphasized. Usually one twin will be touching the other, which signifies communication, human contact, and the desire to share.

The top line of the Gemini glyph indicates mental communication, while the bottom line indicates shared physical space.

The most famous Gemini legend is that of the twin sons, Castor and Pollux, one of whom had a mortal father, while the other was the son of Zeus, king of the gods. When it came time for the mortal twin to die, his grief-stricken brother pleaded with Zeus, who agreed to let them spend half the year on earth in mortal form and half in immortal life, with the gods on Mt. Olympus. This reflects a basic duality of humankind, which possesses an immortal soul, yet is also subject to the limits of mortality.

The Cancer Glyph ♋

Two convenient images relate to the Cancer glyph. It is easiest to decode the curving claws of the Cancer symbol, the crab. Like the crab, Cancer's element is water. This sensitive sign also has a hard protective shell to protect its tender interior. The crab must be wily to escape predators, scampering sideways and hiding under rocks. The crab also responds to the cycles of the moon, as do all shellfish. The other image is that of two female breasts, which Cancer rules, showing that this is a sign that nurtures and protects others as well as itself.

In ancient Egypt, Cancer was also represented by

the scarab beetle, a symbol of regeneration and eternal life.

The Leo Glyph ♌

Notice that the Leo glyph seems to be an extension of Cancer's glyph, with a significant difference. In the Cancer glyph, the lines curve inward protectively, while the Leo glyph expresses energy outwardly and there is no duality in the symbol (or in Leo).

Lions have belonged to the sign of Leo since earliest times, and it is not difficult to imagine the king of beasts with his sweeping mane and curling tail from this glyph. The upward sweep of the glyph easily describes the positive energy of Leos: the flourishing tail, their flamboyant qualities. Another analogy, which is a stretch of the imagination, is that of a heart leaping up with joy and enthusiasm, very typical of Leo, which also rules the heart. In early Christian imagery, the Leo lion represented St. Mark.

The Virgo Glyph ♍

You can read much into this mysterious glyph. For instance, it could represent the initials of "Mary Virgin," or a young woman holding a stalk of wheat, or stylized female genitalia, all common interpretations. The "M" shape might also remind you that Virgo is ruled by Mercury. The cross beneath the symbol reveals the grounded, practical nature of this earth sign.

The earliest zodiacs link Virgo with the Egyptian goddess Isis, who gave birth to the god Horus after her husband Osiris had been killed, in the archetype of a miraculous conception. There are many ancient statues of Isis nursing her baby son, which are reminiscent of medieval Virgin and Child motifs. This sign has also been associated with the image of the Holy

Grail, when the Virgo symbol was substituted with a chalice.

The Libra Glyph ♎

It is not difficult to read the standard image for Libra, the scales, into this glyph. There is another meaning, however, that is equally relevant: the setting sun as it descends over the horizon. Libra's natural position on the zodiac wheel is the descendant or sunset position (as Aries's natural position is the ascendant, or rising sign). Both images relate to Libra's personality. Libra is always weighing pros and cons for a balanced decision. In the sunset image, the sun (male) hovers over the horizontal Earth (female) before setting. Libra is the space between these lines, harmonizing yin and yang, spiritual and material, male and female, ideal and real worlds. The glyph has also been linked to the kidneys, which are ruled by Libra.

The Scorpio Glyph ♏

With its barbed tail, this glyph is easy to identify with the sign of the Scorpion. It also represents the male sexual parts, over which the sign rules. However, some earlier Egyptian symbols for Scorpio represent it as an erect serpent. You can also draw the conclusion that Mars was once its ruler by the arrowhead.

Another image for Scorpio, which is not identifiable in this glyph, is the eagle. Scorpios can go to extremes, either soaring like the eagle or self-destructing like the scorpion. In early Christian imagery, which often used zodiacal symbols, the Scorpio eagle was chosen to symbolize the intense apostle St. John the Evangelist.

The Sagittarius Glyph ♐

This glyph is one of the easiest to spot and draw—an upward pointing arrow lifting up a cross. The arrow is pointing skyward, while the cross represents the four elements of the material world, which the arrow must convey. Elevating materiality into spirituality is an important Sagittarius quality, which explains why this sign is associated with higher learning, religion, philosophy, and travel—the aspiring professions. Sagittarians can also send barbed arrows of frankness in their pursuit of truth. (This is also the sign of the supersalesman.)

Sagittarius is symbolically represented by the centaur, a mythological creature who is half man, half horse, aiming his arrow toward the skies. Though Sagittarius is motivated by spiritual aspiration, it also must balance the powerful appetites of the animal nature. The centaur Chiron, a figure in Greek mythology, became a wise teacher who, after many adventures and world travels, was killed by a poisoned arrow.

The Capricorn Glyph ♑

One of the most difficult symbols to draw, this glyph may take some practice. It is a representation of the sea goat: a mythical animal that is a goat with a curving fish's tail. The goat part of Capricorn wants to leave the waters of the emotions and climb to the elevated areas of life. But the fish tail is the unconscious, the deep chaotic psychic level that draws the goat back. Capricorn is often trying to escape the deep, feeling part of life by submerging himself in work, steadily ascending to the top. To some people, the glyph represents a seated figure with a bent knee, a reminder that Capricorn governs the knee area of the body.

An interesting aspect of this glyph is the contrast of the sharp pointed horns of the symbol, which represent the penetrating, shrewd, conscious side of Capricorn, with the swishing tail, which represents its serpentine, unconscious, emotional force. One Capricorn legend, which dates from Roman times, tells of the earthy fertility god, Pan, who tried to save himself from uncontrollable sexual desires by jumping into the Nile. His upper body then turned into a goat, while the lower part became a fish. Later, Jupiter gave him a safe haven in the skies, as a constellation.

The Aquarius Glyph ≈

This ancient water symbol can be traced back to an Egyptian hieroglyph representing streams of life force. Symbolized by the water bearer, Aquarius is distributor of the waters of life—the magic liquid of regeneration. The two waves can also be linked to the positive and negative charges of the electrical energy that Aquarius rules, a sort of universal wavelength. Aquarius is tuned in intuitively to higher forces via this electrical force. The duality of the glyph could also refer to the dual nature of Aquarius, a sign that runs hot and cold, is friendly but also detached in the mental world of air signs.

In Greek legends, Aquarius is represented by Ganymede, who was carried to heaven by an eagle in order to become the cup bearer of Zeus and to supervise the annual flooding of the Nile. The sign later became associated with aviation and notions of flight.

The Pisces Glyph)(

Here is an abstraction of the familiar image of Pisces, two fishes swimming in opposite directions, yet bound together by a cord. The fishes represent the spirit, which yearns for the freedom of heaven, and the soul, which remains attached to the desires of the temporal world. During life on Earth, the spirit and the soul are bound together. When they complement each other, instead of pulling in opposite directions they facilitate the Pisces creativity. The ancient version of this glyph, taken from the Egyptians, had no connecting line, which was added in the fourteenth century.

In another interpretation, it is said that the left fish

indicates the direction of involution or the beginning of a cycle, while the right fish signifies the direction of evolution, the way to completion of a cycle. It's an appropriate grand finale for Pisces, the last sign of the zodiac.

CHAPTER 5

How Your Rising Sign Personalizes Your Horoscope

Have you ever wondered what makes your horoscope unique, how your chart could be different from that of anyone else born on your birthday? Yes, other babies who may have been born later or earlier on the same day, in the same hospital, as you were, will be sure to have most planets in the same signs as you do. Most of your high school class, in fact, will have several planets in the same signs as your planets, especially the slow-moving planets (Uranus, Neptune, Pluto) and very possibly Jupiter and Saturn, which usually spend a year or more in each sign.

What makes a horoscope truly "yours" is the rising sign (or ascendant), the sign that was coming up over the eastern horizon at the moment you were born. This sign establishes the exact horoscope of your birth time. In astrology, this is called the *rising sign,* often referred to as the ascendant. As the earth moves, a different sign rises every two hours.

If you have read the chapter in this book on houses, you'll know that the houses are twelve stationary divisions of the horoscope, which represent areas of life. The sign which is moving over the house describes that area of life. The rising sign marks the border of the first house, which represents your first presentation to the world, your physical body, and how you come across to others. It has been called your "shop window," the first impression you give to others. After the rising sign is determined, then each "house" will be influenced by the signs which follow it.

Once the rising sign is established, it becomes possible to analyze a chart accurately because the astrologer knows in which area of life (house) the planets will operate. For instance, if Mars is in Gemini and your rising sign is Taurus, then Mars will most likely be active in the second or financial house of your chart. If you were born later in the day and your rising sign is Virgo, then Mars will be positioned at the top of your chart, energizing your tenth house or career. That is why many astrologers insist on knowing the exact time of a client's birth, before they analyze a chart. The more exact your birthtime, the more accurately an astrologer can position the planets in your chart. This is important, because if you were born when the midportion of a sign was rotating over the horizon and a key planet—let's say Saturn—was in the early degrees of that sign, then it would already be over the horizon, located in the twelfth house, rather than the first. So the interpretation of your horoscope would be quite different: you would not have the serious Saturn influence in the way you come across to others, which would be the case if you were born an hour earlier. If a planet is near the ascendant, sometimes even a few minutes can make a big difference.

Your rising sign has an important relationship with your sun sign. Some will complement the sun sign; others hide it under a totally different mask, as if playing an entirely different role, so it is often difficult to guess the person's sun sign from outer appearances. For example, a Leo with a conservative Capricorn ascendant would come across as much less flamboyant than a Leo with a fiery Aries or Sagittarius ascendant. The exception is when the sun sign is reinforced by other planets; then, with other planets on its side, the sun may assert its personality much more strongly, overcoming the image of a contradictory rising sign. For example, a Leo with Venus and Jupiter also in

Leo might counteract the conservative image of the Capricorn ascendant, in the above example. However, in most cases, the ascendant is the ingredient most strongly reflected in the first impression you make.

Rising signs change every two hours with the Earth's rotation. Those born early in the morning when the sun was on the horizon will be most likely to project the image of their sun sign. These people are often called a "double Aries" or a "double Virgo," because the same sun sign and ascendant reinforce each other.

Look up your rising sign on the chart at the end of this chapter. Since rising signs change every two hours, it is important to know your birth time as close to the minute as possible. Even a few minutes' difference could change the rising sign and therefore the setup of your chart. If you are unsure about the exact time, but know within a few hours, check the following descriptions to see which is most like the personality you project.

Aries Rising—Fiery Emotions

You are the most aggressive version of your sun sign, with boundless energy which can be used productively, if it's channeled in the right direction. Watch a tendency to overreact emotionally and blow your top. You come across as openly competitive, a positive asset in business or sports. Be on guard against impatience, which could lead to head injuries. Your walk and bearing could have the telltale head-forward Aries posture. You may wear more bright colors, especially red, than others of your sign. You may also have a tendency to drive your car faster.

Taurus Rising—The Earth Mother

You'll exude a protective nurturing quality, even if you're male, which draws those in need of TLC and support. You're slow-moving, with a beautiful (or distinctive) speaking or singing voice that can be especially soothing or melodious. You probably surround yourself with comfort, good food, luxurious surroundings and sensual pleasures, and prefer welcoming others into your home to gadding about. You may have a talent for business, especially in trading, appraising, and real estate. This ascendant gives a well-padded or curvaceous physique, which gains weight easily. Women with this ascendant are naturally sexy in a bodacious way.

Gemini Rising—Expressive Talents

You're naturally sociable, with lighter, more ethereal mannerisms than others of your sign, especially if you're female. You love to communicate with people and express your ideas and feelings easily. You may have writing or public speaking talent. Like Drew Barrymore, you may thrive on a constantly changing scenario with a varied cast of characters, though you may be far more sympathetic and caring than you project. You will probably travel widely, changing partners and jobs several times (or juggling two at once). Physically, you should cultivate a calm, tranquil atmosphere, because your nerves are quite sensitive.

Cancer Rising—Sensitive Antennae

Like billionaire Bill Gates, you are naturally acquisitive, possessive, private, a moneymaker. You easily pick up others' needs and feelings, a great gift in business, the arts, and personal relationships, but guard against overreacting or taking things too personally, especially during full moon periods. Find creative outlets for your natural nurturing gifts, such as helping the less fortunate, particularly children. Your insights would be useful in psychology, your desire to feed and care for others in the restaurant, hotel, or child care industry. You may be especially fond of wearing romantic old clothes, collecting antiques, and of course, good food. Since your body may retain fluids, pay attention to your diet. To relax, escape to places near water.

Leo Rising—The Scene Player

You may come across as more poised than you really feel; however, you play it to the hilt, projecting a proud royal presence. This ascendant gives you a natural flair for drama, like Marilyn Monroe. You'll also project a much more outgoing, optimistic, sunny personality than others of your sign. You take care to please your public by always projecting your best star quality, probably tossing a luxuriant mane of hair or, if you're female, dazzling with a spectacular jewelry collection. Since you may have a strong parental nature, you could well be the regal family matriarch or patriarch.

Virgo Rising—Cool and Calculating

Virgo rising masks your inner nature with a practical, analytical outer image. You seem neat, orderly, more particular than others of your sign. Others in your life may feel they must live up to your high standards. Though at times you may be openly critical, this masks a well-meaning desire to have only the best for loved ones. Your sharp eye for details could be used in the financial world, or your literary skills could draw you to teaching or publishing. The healing arts, health care, service-oriented professions attract many with this Virgo emphasis in their chart. Like Madonna, you're likely to take good care of yourself, with great attention to health, diet, and exercise. Physically, you may have a very sensitive digestive system.

Libra Rising—The Charmer

Libra rising makes you appear as a charmer, more of a social, public person than others of your sign. Your private life will extend beyond your home and family to include an active social life. You may tend to avoid confrontations in relationships, preferring to smooth the way or negotiate diplomatically, rather than give in to an emotional reaction. Because you are interested in all aspects of a situation, you may be slow to reach decisions. Physically, you'll have good proportions and pleasing symmetry. You're likely to have pleasing, if not beautiful, facial features. You move gracefully, and you have a winning smile and good taste in your clothes and home decor. Legal, diplomatic, or public relations professions could draw your interest. Men with Libra rising, like Bill Clinton and John F. Kennedy, have charming smiles and easy social manner that charms the ladies.

Scorpio Rising—Magnetic Power

Even when you're in the public eye, like Jacqueline Kennedy Onassis, you never lose your intriguing air of mystery and sense of underlying power. You can be a master manipulator, always in control and moving comfortably in the world of power. Your physical impression comes across as intense, and many of you have remarkable eyes, with a direct, penetrating gaze. But you'll never reveal your private agenda, and you tend to keep your true feelings under wraps (watch a tendency toward paranoia). You may have an interesting romantic history with secret love affairs. Many of you heighten your air of mystery by wearing black. You're happiest near water and should provide yourself with a seaside retreat.

Sagittarius Rising—The Wanderer

You travel with this ascendant. You may also be a more outdoor, sportive type, with an athletic, casual, outgoing air. Your moods are camouflaged with cheerful optimism or a philosophical attitude. Though you don't hesitate to speak your mind, you can also laugh at your troubles or crack a joke more easily than others of your sign, like Candice Bergen, who is best known for her comedy role as the outspoken "Murphy Brown." This ascendant can also draw you to the field of higher education or to spiritual life. You'll seem to have less attachment to things and people and may travel widely. Your strong, fast legs are a physical bonus.

Capricorn Rising—Serious Business

This rising sign makes you come across as serious, goal-oriented, disciplined, and careful with cash. You are not one of the zodiac's big spenders, though you might splurge occasionally on items with good investment value. You're the traditional, conservative type in dress and environment, and you might come across as quite formal and businesslike. You'll function well in a structured or corporate environment where you can climb to the top. (You are always aware of who's the boss.) In your personal life, you could be a loner or a single parent who is "father and mother" to your children. Like Paul Newman, you're likely to prefer a quiet private life to living in the spotlight.

Aquarius Rising—One of a Kind

You come across as less concerned about what others think and could even be a bit eccentric. Your appearance is sure to be unique and memorable. You're more at ease with groups of people than others in your sign, and may be attracted to public life. Your appearance may be unique, either unconventional or unimportant to you. Those with the sun in a water sign (Cancer, Scorpio, Pisces) may exercise your nurturing qualities with a large group, an extended family, or a day care or community center. Audrey Hepburn and Princess Diana, who had this rising sign, were known for their unique charisma and work on behalf of worthy causes.

Pisces Rising—Romantic Roles

Your creative, nurturing talents are heightened and so is your ability to project emotional drama. And your dreamy eyes and poetic air bring out the protective instinct in others. You could be attracted to the arts, especially theater, dance, film, or photography, or to psychology or spiritual or charity work. You are happiest when you are using your creative ability to help others, as Robert Redford has done. Since you are vulnerable to mood swings, it is especially important for you to find interesting, creative work where you can express your talents and boost your self-esteem. Accentuate the positive and be wary of escapist tendencies, particularly involving alcohol or drugs, to which you are supersensitive.

RISING SIGNS—A.M. BIRTHS

	1 AM	2 AM	3 AM	4 AM	5 AM	6 AM	7 AM	8 AM	9 AM	10 AM	11 AM	12 NOON
Jan 1	Lib	Sc	Sc	Sc	Sag	Sag	Cap	Cap	Aq	Aq	Pis	Ar
Jan 9	Lib	Sc	Sc	Sag	Sag	Sag	Cap	Cap	Aq	Pis	Ar	Tau
Jan 17	Sc	Sc	Sc	Sag	Sag	Cap	Cap	Aq	Aq	Pis	Ar	Tau
Jan 25	Sc	Sc	Sag	Sag	Sag	Cap	Cap	Aq	Pis	Ar	Tau	Tau
Feb 2	Sc	Sc	Sag	Sag	Cap	Cap	Aq	Pis	Pis	Ar	Tau	Gem
Feb 10	Sc	Sag	Sag	Sag	Cap	Cap	Aq	Pis	Ar	Tau	Tau	Gem
Feb 18	Sc	Sag	Sag	Cap	Cap	Aq	Pis	Pis	Ar	Tau	Gem	Gem
Feb 26	Sag	Sag	Sag	Cap	Aq	Aq	Pis	Ar	Tau	Tau	Gem	Gem
Mar 6	Sag	Sag	Cap	Cap	Aq	Pis	Pis	Ar	Tau	Gem	Gem	Can
Mar 14	Sag	Cap	Cap	Aq	Aq	Pis	Ar	Tau	Tau	Gem	Gem	Can
Mar 22	Sag	Cap	Cap	Aq	Pis	Ar	Ar	Tau	Gem	Gem	Can	Can
Mar 30	Cap	Cap	Aq	Pis	Pis	Ar	Tau	Tau	Gem	Can	Can	Can
Apr 7	Cap	Cap	Aq	Pis	Ar	Ar	Tau	Gem	Gem	Can	Can	Leo
Apr 14	Cap	Aq	Aq	Pis	Ar	Tau	Tau	Gem	Gem	Can	Can	Leo
Apr 22	Cap	Aq	Pis	Ar	Ar	Tau	Gem	Gem	Gem	Can	Leo	Leo
Apr 30	Aq	Aq	Pis	Ar	Tau	Tau	Gem	Can	Can	Can	Leo	Leo
May 8	Aq	Pis	Ar	Ar	Tau	Gem	Gem	Can	Can	Leo	Leo	Leo
May 16	Aq	Pis	Ar	Tau	Gem	Gem	Can	Can	Can	Leo	Leo	Vir
May 24	Pis	Ar	Ar	Tau	Gem	Gem	Can	Can	Leo	Leo	Leo	Vir
June 1	Pis	Ar	Tau	Gem	Gem	Can	Can	Can	Leo	Leo	Vir	Vir
June 9	Ar	Ar	Tau	Gem	Gem	Can	Can	Leo	Leo	Leo	Vir	Vir
June 17	Ar	Tau	Gem	Gem	Can	Can	Can	Leo	Leo	Vir	Vir	Vir
June 25	Tau	Tau	Gem	Gem	Can	Can	Leo	Leo	Leo	Vir	Vir	Lib
July 3	Tau	Gem	Gem	Can	Can	Can	Leo	Leo	Vir	Vir	Vir	Lib
July 11	Tau	Gem	Gem	Can	Can	Leo	Leo	Leo	Vir	Vir	Lib	Lib
July 18	Gem	Gem	Can	Can	Can	Leo	Leo	Vir	Vir	Vir	Lib	Lib
July 26	Gem	Gem	Can	Can	Leo	Leo	Vir	Vir	Vir	Lib	Lib	Lib
Aug 3	Gem	Can	Can	Can	Leo	Leo	Vir	Vir	Vir	Lib	Lib	Sc
Aug 11	Gem	Can	Can	Leo	Leo	Leo	Vir	Vir	Lib	Lib	Lib	Sc
Aug 18	Can	Can	Can	Leo	Leo	Vir	Vir	Vir	Lib	Lib	Sc	Sc
Aug 27	Can	Can	Leo	Leo	Leo	Vir	Vir	Lib	Lib	Lib	Sc	Sc
Sept 4	Can	Can	Leo	Leo	Leo	Vir	Vir	Vir	Lib	Lib	Sc	Sc
Sept 12	Can	Leo	Leo	Leo	Vir	Vir	Lib	Lib	Lib	Sc	Sc	Sag
Sept 20	Leo	Leo	Leo	Vir	Vir	Vir	Lib	Lib	Sc	Sc	Sc	Sag
Sept 28	Leo	Leo	Leo	Vir	Vir	Lib	Lib	Lib	Sc	Sc	Sag	Sag
Oct 6	Leo	Leo	Vir	Vir	Vir	Lib	Lib	Sc	Sc	Sc	Sag	Sag
Oct 14	Leo	Vir	Vir	Vir	Lib	Lib	Lib	Sc	Sc	Sag	Sag	Cap
Oct 22	Leo	Vir	Vir	Lib	Lib	Lib	Sc	Sc	Sc	Sag	Sag	Cap
Oct 30	Vir	Vir	Vir	Lib	Lib	Sc	Sc	Sc	Sag	Sag	Cap	Cap
Nov 7	Vir	Vir	Lib	Lib	Lib	Sc	Sc	Sc	Sag	Sag	Cap	Cap
Nov 15	Vir	Vir	Lib	Lib	Sc	Sc	Sc	Sag	Sag	Cap	Cap	Aq
Nov 23	Vir	Lib	Lib	Lib	Sc	Sc	Sag	Sag	Sag	Cap	Cap	Aq
Dec 1	Vir	Lib	Lib	Sc	Sc	Sc	Sag	Sag	Cap	Cap	Aq	Aq
Dec 9	Lib	Lib	Lib	Sc	Sc	Sag	Sag	Sag	Cap	Cap	Aq	Pis
Dec 18	Lib	Lib	Sc	Sc	Sc	Sag	Sag	Cap	Cap	Aq	Aq	Pis
Dec 28	Lib	Lib	Sc	Sc	Sag	Sag	Sag	Cap	Aq	Aq	Pis	Ar

RISING SIGNS—P.M. BIRTHS

	1 PM	2 PM	3 PM	4 PM	5 PM	6 PM	7 PM	8 PM	9 PM	10 PM	11 PM	12 MIDNIGHT
Jan 1	Tau	Gem	Gem	Can	Can	Can	Leo	Leo	Vir	Vir	Vir	Lib
Jan 9	Tau	Gem	Gem	Can	Can	Leo	Leo	Leo	Vir	Vir	Vir	Lib
Jan 17	Gem	Gem	Gem	Can	Can	Leo	Leo	Vir	Vir	Vir	Lib	Lib
Jan 25	Gem	Gem	Can	Can	Leo	Leo	Leo	Vir	Vir	Lib	Lib	Lib
Feb 2	Gem	Can	Can	Can	Leo	Leo	Vir	Vir	Vir	Lib	Lib	Sc
Feb 10	Gem	Can	Can	Leo	Leo	Leo	Vir	Vir	Lib	Lib	Lib	Sc
Feb 18	Can	Can	Can	Leo	Leo	Vir	Vir	Vir	Lib	Lib	Sc	Sc
Feb 26	Can	Can	Leo	Leo	Leo	Vir	Vir	Lib	Lib	Lib	Sc	Sc
Mar 6	Can	Leo	Leo	Leo	Vir	Vir	Vir	Lib	Lib	Sc	Sc	Sc
Mar 14	Can	Leo	Leo	Vir	Vir	Vir	Lib	Lib	Lib	Sc	Sc	Sag
Mar 22	Leo	Leo	Leo	Vir	Vir	Lib	Lib	Lib	Sc	Sc	Sc	Sag
Mar 30	Leo	Leo	Vir	Vir	Vir	Lib	Lib	Sc	Sc	Sc	Sag	Sag
Apr 7	Leo	Leo	Vir	Vir	Lib	Lib	Lib	Sc	Sc	Sc	Sag	Sag
Apr 14	Leo	Vir	Vir	Vir	Lib	Lib	Sc	Sc	Sc	Sag	Sag	Cap
Apr 22	Leo	Vir	Vir	Lib	Lib	Lib	Sc	Sc	Sc	Sag	Sag	Cap
Apr 30	Vir	Vir	Vir	Lib	Lib	Sc	Sc	Sc	Sag	Sag	Cap	Cap
May 8	Vir	Vir	Lib	Lib	Lib	Sc	Sc	Sag	Sag	Sag	Cap	Cap
May 16	Vir	Vir	Lib	Lib	Sc	Sc	Sc	Sag	Sag	Cap	Cap	Aq
May 24	Vir	Lib	Lib	Lib	Sc	Sc	Sag	Sag	Sag	Cap	Cap	Aq
June 1	Vir	Lib	Lib	Sc	Sc	Sc	Sag	Sag	Cap	Cap	Aq	Aq
June 9	Lib	Lib	Lib	Sc	Sc	Sag	Sag	Sag	Cap	Cap	Aq	Pis
June 17	Lib	Lib	Sc	Sc	Sc	Sag	Sag	Cap	Cap	Aq	Aq	Pis
June 25	Lib	Lib	Sc	Sc	Sag	Sag	Sag	Cap	Cap	Aq	Pis	Ar
July 3	Lib	Sc	Sc	Sc	Sag	Sag	Cap	Cap	Aq	Aq	Pis	Ar
July 11	Lib	Sc	Sc	Sag	Sag	Sag	Cap	Cap	Aq	Pis	Ar	Tau
July 18	Sc	Sc	Sc	Sag	Sag	Cap	Cap	Aq	Aq	Pis	Ar	Tau
July 26	Sc	Sc	Sag	Sag	Sag	Cap	Cap	Aq	Pis	Ar	Tau	Tau
Aug 3	Sc	Sc	Sag	Sag	Cap	Cap	Aq	Aq	Pis	Ar	Tau	Gem
Aug 11	Sc	Sag	Sag	Sag	Cap	Cap	Aq	Pis	Ar	Tau	Tau	Gem
Aug 18	Sc	Sag	Sag	Cap	Cap	Aq	Pis	Pis	Ar	Tau	Gem	Gem
Aug 27	Sag	Sag	Sag	Cap	Cap	Aq	Pis	Ar	Tau	Tau	Gem	Gem
Sept 4	Sag	Sag	Cap	Cap	Aq	Pis	Pis	Ar	Tau	Gem	Gem	Can
Sept 12	Sag	Sag	Cap	Aq	Aq	Pis	Ar	Tau	Tau	Gem	Gem	Can
Sept 20	Sag	Cap	Cap	Aq	Pis	Pis	Ar	Tau	Gem	Gem	Can	Can
Sept 28	Cap	Cap	Aq	Aq	Pis	Ar	Tau	Tau	Gem	Gem	Can	Can
Oct 6	Cap	Cap	Aq	Pis	Ar	Ar	Tau	Gem	Gem	Can	Can	Leo
Oct 14	Cap	Aq	Aq	Pis	Ar	Tau	Tau	Gem	Gem	Can	Can	Leo
Oct 22	Cap	Aq	Pis	Ar	Ar	Tau	Gem	Gem	Can	Can	Leo	Leo
Oct 30	Aq	Aq	Pis	Ar	Tau	Tau	Gem	Can	Can	Can	Leo	Leo
Nov 7	Aq	Aq	Pis	Ar	Tau	Tau	Gem	Can	Can	Can	Leo	Leo
Nov 15	Aq	Pis	Ar	Tau	Gem	Gem	Can	Can	Can	Leo	Leo	Vir
Nov 23	Pis	Ar	Ar	Tau	Gem	Gem	Can	Can	Leo	Leo	Leo	Vir
Dec 1	Pis	Ar	Tau	Gem	Gem	Can	Can	Can	Leo	Leo	Vir	Vir
Dec 9	Ar	Tau	Tau	Gem	Gem	Can	Can	Leo	Leo	Leo	Vir	Vir
Dec 18	Ar	Tau	Gem	Gem	Can	Can	Can	Leo	Leo	Vir	Vir	Vir
Dec 28	Tau	Tau	Gem	Gem	Can	Can	Leo	Leo	Vir	Vir	Vir	Lib

CHAPTER 6

The Moon—Our Light Within

In some astrology-conscious lands, the moon is given as much importance in a horoscope as the sun. Astrologers often refer to these two bodies as the "lights," an apt term, since they shed the most light upon our personality in a horoscope reading. This also is a more technically appropriate description, since the sun and moon are not really planets, but a star and a satellite.

The most fascinating aspect of the moon is its connection with our emotional state. Our moods seem to wax and wane with the moon. Even the state of shellfish, animals, and planets is affected by the moon phase. Imagine what would happen if the moon were somehow caused to change its orbit, perhaps by a bombarding asteroid. What would happen to the tides, to ocean and plant life, which respond to the moon, or to our own bodies, which are mostly water? Life on earth would be impossible!

As the closest celestial body, the moon represents your receptive, reflective, female, nurturing self. And it reflects who you were nurtured by—the "mother" or mother figure in your chart. In a man's chart, the moon position also describes his receptive, emotional, "yin" side, as well as the woman in his life who will have the deepest effect, usually his mother. (Venus reveals the kind of woman who attracts him physically.)

The sign the moon was passing through at birth reveals much about your inner life, your needs and secrets, as well as those of people you'd like to know better. You can learn what appeals to a person sub-consciously by knowing their moon sign, which reflects their instinctive, emotional nature.

It's well worth having an accurate chart cast to determine your moon sign. Since accurate moon tables are too extensive for this book, check through these descriptions to find the moon sign that feels most familiar.

The moon is more at home in some signs than others. It rules maternal Cancer and is exalted in Taurus—both comforting, home-loving signs where the natural emotional energies of the moon are easily and productively expressed. But when the moon is in the opposite signs—Capricorn or Scorpio—it leaves the comfortable nest and deals with emotional issues of power and achievement in the outside world. Those of you with the moon in these signs are more likely to find your emotional role more challenging in life.

Moon in Aries

You are an idealistic, impetuous person who falls in and out of love easily. This placement makes you both independent and ardent. You love a challenge, but could cool once your quarry is captured. You should cultivate patience and tolerance—or you might tend to gravitate toward those who treat you rough, just for the sake of challenge and excitement.

Moon in Taurus

You are a sentimental soul who is very fond of the good life and gravitates toward solid, secure relationships. You like displays of affection and creature comforts—all the tangible trappings of a cozy, safe, calm atmosphere. You are sensual and steady emotionally, but very stubborn and determined. You can't be pushed and tend to dislike changes. You should make an effort to broaden your horizons and to take a risk sometimes.

Moon in Gemini

You crave mental stimulation and variety in life, which you usually get through either an ever-varied social life, the excitement of flirtation, and/or multiple professional involvements. You may marry more than once and have a rather chaotic emotional life due to your difficulty with commitment and settling down. Be sure to find a partner who is as outgoing as you are. You will have to learn at some point to focus your energies because you tend to be somewhat fragmented—to do two things at once, to have two homes or even two lovers. If you can find a creative way to express your many-faceted nature, you'll be ahead of the game.

Moon in Cancer

This is the most powerful lunar position, which is sure to make a deep imprint on your character. Your needs are very much associated with your reaction to the needs of others. You are very sensitive and self-protective, though some of you may mask this with a hard shell. This placement also gives you an excellent memory, keen intuition, and an uncanny ability to perceive the needs of others. All of the lunar phases will affect you, especially full moons and eclipses, so you would do well to mark them on your calendar. Because you're happiest at home, you may work at home or turn your office into a second home, where you can nurture and comfort people. (You may tend to "mother the world.") With natural psychic, intuitive ability, you might be drawn to occult work in some way. Or you may get professionally involved with providing food and shelter to others.

Moon in Leo

This warm, passionate moon takes everything to heart. You are attracted to all that is noble, generous, and aristocratic in life (and may be a bit of a snob). You have an innate ability to take command emotionally, but you do need strong support, loyalty, and loud applause from those you love. You are possessive of your loved ones and your turf and will roar if anyone threatens to take over your territory.

Moon in Virgo

You are rather cool until you decide if others measure up. But once someone or something meets your ideal standards, you hold up your end of the arrangement perfectly. You may, in fact, drive yourself too hard to attain some notion of perfection. Try to be a bit easier on yourself and others. Don't always act the censor! You love to be the teacher and are drawn to situations where you can change others for the better, but sometimes you must learn to accept others for what they are—enjoy what you have!

Moon in Libra

A partnership-oriented moon—you may find it difficult to be alone or to do things alone. After you have learned emotional balance by leaning on yourself first, you can have excellent relationships. It is best for you to avoid extremes, however, which set your scales swinging and can make your love life precarious. You thrive in a rather conservative, traditional, romantic relationship, where you receive attention and flattery—but not possessiveness—from your partner. You'll be your most charming in an elegant, harmonious atmosphere.

Moon in Scorpio

This is a moon that enjoys and responds to intense, passionate feelings. You may go to extremes and have a very dramatic emotional life, full of ardor, suspicion, jealousy, and obsession. It would be much healthier to channel your need for power and control into meaningful work. This is a good position for anyone in the fields of medicine, police work, research, the occult, psychoanalysis, or intuitive work, because life-and-death situations don't faze you. However, you do take personal disappointments very hard.

Moon in Sagittarius

You take life's ups and downs with good humor and the proverbial grain of salt. You'll love 'em and leave 'em, taking off on a great adventure at a moment's notice. "Born free" could be your slogan. Attracted by the exotic, you have wanderlust mentally and physically. You may be too much in search of new mental and spiritual stimulation to ever settle down.

Moon in Capricorn

Are you ever accused of being too cool and calculating? You have an earthy side, but you take prestige and position very seriously. Your strong drive to succeed extends to your romantic life, where you will be devoted to improving your lifestyle, rising to the top. A structured situation where you can advance methodically makes you feel wonderfully secure. You may be attracted to someone older or very much younger or from a different social world. It may be difficult to look at the lighter side of emotional relationships; however, the "up" side of this moon in the

sign of its detriment is that you tend to be very dutiful
and responsible to those you care for.

Moon in Aquarius

You are a people collector with many friends of all
backgrounds. You are happiest surrounded by people
and may feel uneasy when left alone. Though you usually stay friends with lovers, intense emotions and demanding one-on-one relationships turn you off. You
don't like anything to be too rigid or scheduled. Though
tolerant and understanding, you can be emotionally unpredictable and may opt for an unconventional love life.
With plenty of space, you will be able to sustain relationships with liberal, freedom-loving types.

Moon in Pisces

You are very responsive and empathetic to others,
especially if they have problems or are the underdog.
(Be on guard against attracting too many people with
sob stories.) You'll be happiest if you can express your
creative imagination in the arts or in the spiritual or
healing professions. Because you may tend to escape in
fantasies or overreact to the moods of others, you need
an emotional anchor to help you keep a firm foothold
in reality. Steer clear of too much escapism (especially
in alcohol) or reclusiveness. Places near water soothe
your moods. Working in a field that gives you emotional variety will also help you to be productive.

What Eclipses Do to Your Moods

In case we've been taking the moon for granted, the
eclipse seasons, which occur about every six months,
remind us how important the moon is for our survival.
Perhaps that is why eclipses have always had an omi-

nous reputation. Folklore all over the world blames eclipses for catastrophes such as birth defects, crop failures, and hurricanes. Villagers on the peninsula of Baja California paint their fruit trees red and wear red ribbons and underwear to deflect "evil rays." During the total eclipse of July 1991, everyone retreated safely indoors to follow the eclipse on television. In other native societies, people play drums and make loud noises to frighten off heavenly monsters believed to destroy the light of the sun and moon. Only the romantic Tahitians seem to have positive feelings about an eclipse. In this sensual tropical paradise, legend declares that the "lights" go out when the sun and moon make love and procreate the stars.

Ancient Chaldean astrologer-priests were the first to time eclipses accurately. They discovered that 6,585 days after an eclipse, another eclipse would happen. By counting ahead after all the eclipses in a given year, they could predict eclipses eighteen years into the future. This technique was practiced by navigators through the centuries, including Christopher Columbus, who used his knowledge of an upcoming lunar eclipse to extort food from the frightened inhabitants of Jamaica in 1504. In ancient Mexico, Mayan astronomer-priests also discovered that eclipses occur at regular intervals and recorded them with a hieroglyph of a serpent swallowing the sun.

What Causes an Eclipse?

A solar eclipse is the passage of the new moon directly across the face of the sun. It is a very exciting and awesome event, which causes the sky to darken suddenly. Though the effect lasts only a few minutes, it is enough to strike panic in the uninformed viewer.

A lunar eclipse happens when the full moon passes through the shadow of the Earth on the opposite side from the sun; as a result, the Earth blocks out the sun's light from reaching the moon. The moon must be in level alignment with the sun and Earth for a lunar eclipse to occur.

Conditions are ripe for an eclipse twice a year, when a full or a new moon is most likely to cross the path of the sun at two points known as the *nodes*.

What to Know About Nodes

To understand the nodes, visualize two rings, one inside the other. As you move the rings, you'll notice that the two circles intersect at opposite points. Now imagine one ring as the moon's orbit and the other as the sun's (as seen from Earth). The crossing points are called the moon's "nodes."

For an eclipse to happen, two conditions must be met. First, the path of the orbiting moon must be close enough to a node. Second, this must happen at a time when there is either a new or a full moon. (Not every new or full moon happens close enough to the nodes to create an eclipse.) The axis of the nodes is continually moving backward through the zodiac at the rate of about one and a half degrees per month; therefore, eclipses will eventually occur in every sign of the zodiac.

How Often Do Eclipses Occur?

Whenever the sun draws close to one of the nodes, any new or full moon happening near that time will create an eclipse. This "eclipse season" happens twice a year, approximately six months apart. There are at least four eclipses each year, and there can be as many as seven. In 2002, there will be five eclipses:

- Full Moon in Sagittarius (lunar eclipse)—May 26
- New Moon in Gemini (solar eclipse)—June 10
- Full Moon in Capricorn (lunar eclipse)—June 24

- Full Moon in Taurus (lunar eclipse)—November 19
- New Moon in Sagittarius (solar eclipse)—December 4

Eclipses Have Family Ties

One of the most interesting things about eclipses is that they have "families." Each eclipse is a member of a string of related eclipses that pop up regularly. As mentioned before, the ancient Chaldeans, who were the first great sky-watchers, discovered that eclipses recur in patterns, repeating themselves after approximately eighteen years plus nine to eleven days, in a cycle lasting a total of approximately 1,300 years. Much later, in the eleventh century A.D., these patterns became known as the "Saros Series." (In ancient Greek, "saros" means repetition.)

Because each Saros Series begins at a moment in time, the initial eclipse has a horoscope, and therefore a "personality" which goes through stages of development as the series of eclipses progresses over its 1,300-year lifetime. So as a Saros Series moves through your chart, it will produce an eclipse with a similar "personality" every eighteen years. In the interim, you'll experience eclipses belonging to other Saros Series, which will exhibit their own special family characteristics. Therefore, there can be no one generic interpretation for eclipses, since each affects your horoscope in a different way, according to the personality of its particular Saros Series.

What Is the Purpose of an Eclipse in My Life?

Eclipses can bring on milestone events in your life, if they aspect a key point in your horoscope. In general, they shake up the status quo, bringing hidden areas out into the open. During this time, problems you've been avoiding or have brushed aside can surface to demand your attention. A good coping strategy is to accept whatever comes up as a challenge. It could make a big difference in your life. And don't forget the power of your sense of humor. If you can laugh at something, you'll never be afraid of it.

Second-guessing the eclipses is easy if you have a copy of your horoscope calculated by a computer. (If you do not have a computer or an astrology program, there are several sites on the Internet which will calculate your chart free. See the listings in the resource chapter of this book.) This enables you to pinpoint the area of your life which will be affected. However, you can make an educated guess, by setting up a rough diagram on your own. If you'd like to find out which area of your life this year's eclipses are most likely to affect, follow these easy steps. First, you must know the time of day you were born and look up your rising sign listed in the tables in this book. Then set up an estimated horoscope by drawing a circle, then dividing it into four parts by making a cross directly through the center. Continue to divide each of the parts into thirds, as if you were dividing a cake, until you have twelve slices. Write your rising sign on the middle left-hand slice, which would be the 9 o'clock point, if you were looking at your watch. Then continue listing the signs counterclockwise, until you have listed all twelve signs of the zodiac on the "slices" of the chart.

You should now have a basic diagram of your horoscope chart (minus the planets, of course). Starting with your rising sign "slice," number each portion consecutively, working counterclockwise. Since this year's eclipses will fall in Gemini, Sagittarius, Taurus, and Capricorn, find the number of these slices or "houses" on the chart and read the following descriptions for the kinds of issues that are likely to be emphasized.

If an eclipse falls in your FIRST HOUSE—
Events cause you to examine the ways you are acting independently, pushing you to become more visible and to assert yourself. This is a time when you feel compelled to make your own decisions and do your own thing. There is an emphasis on how you are coming across to others. You may want to change your physical appearance, body image, or style of dress in some way. Under affliction, there might be illness or physical harm.

If an eclipse falls in your SECOND HOUSE—
This is the place where you consider all matters of security. You consolidate your resources, earn money, acquire property, and decide what you value and what you want to own. On a deeper level, this house reveals your sense of self-worth, the inner values that draw wealth in various forms.

If an eclipse falls in your THIRD HOUSE—
Here you communicate, reach out to others, express your ideas, and explore different courses of action. You may feel especially restless, and have confrontations with neighbors or siblings. In your search for more knowledge, you may decide to improve your skills, get more education, or sign up for a course that interests you, which could ultimately alter your lifestyle. Local transportation, especially your car, might be affected by an eclipse here.

If an eclipse falls in your FOURTH HOUSE—
Here is where you put down roots and establish your home base. You'll consider what home really means to you. Issues involving parents, the physical setup or location of your home, or your immediate family demand your attention. You may be especially concerned with parenting or relationships with your own mother. You may consider moving your home to a new location or leaving home, untying family ties.

If an eclipse falls in your FIFTH HOUSE—

Here is where you express yourself, either through your personal talents or through procreating children. You are interested in making your special talents visible. This is also the house of love affairs and the romantic aspect of life, where you flirt, have fun, and enjoy the excitement of love. Hobbies and crafts, the ways you explore the playful child within, fall in this area.

If an eclipse falls in your SIXTH HOUSE—

This is your care and maintenance department, where you take care of your health, organize your life, and set up a daily routine. It is also the place where you perfect your skills and add polish to your life. The chores you do every day, the skills you learn, and the techniques you use fall here. If something doesn't "work" in your life, an eclipse is sure to bring this to light. If you've been neglecting your health, diet, and fitness, you'll probably pay the consequences during an eclipse. Or you may be faced with work that requires much routine organization and steady effort, rather than creative ability. Or you may be required to perform services for others. (In ancient astrology, this was the place of slavery!)

If an eclipse falls in your SEVENTH HOUSE—

This is the area of committed relationships, of those which involve legal agreements, of working in a close relationship with another. Here you'll be dealing with how you relate and what you'll be willing to give up for the sake of a marriage or partnership. Eclipses here can put extra pressure on a relationship and, if it's not working, precipitate a breakup. Lawsuits and open enemies also reside here.

If an eclipse falls in your EIGHTH HOUSE—

This area is concerned with power and control. Consider what you are willing to give up in order that something might happen. Power struggles, intense relationships, and a desire to penetrate a deeper mystery belong here. Debts, loans, financial matters that involve another party, and wheeling and dealing also come into focus. So does sex, where you surrender your individual power to create a new life together. Matters involving birth and death are also involved here.

If an eclipse falls in your NINTH HOUSE—
Here is where you look at the Big Picture: how everything relates to form a pattern. You'll seek information that helps you find meaning in life: higher education, religion, travel, and global issues. Eclipses here can push you to get out of your rut, explore something you've never done before, and expand your horizons.

If an eclipse falls in your TENTH HOUSE—
This is the high-profile point in your chart. Here is where you consider how society looks at you, and what your position is in the outside world. You'll be concerned about whether you receive proper credit for your work and if you're recognized by higher-ups. Promotions, raises, and other forms of recognition can be given or denied. Your standing in your career or community can be challenged, or you'll get publicly acknowledged for achieving a goal. An eclipse here can make you famous . . . or burst your balloon if you've been too ambitious or neglecting other areas of your life.

If an eclipse falls in your ELEVENTH HOUSE—
Your relationship with groups of people comes under scrutiny during an eclipse—whom you are identified with, whom you socialize with, and how well you are accepted by other members of your team. Activities of clubs, political parties, networking, and social inter-

actions become important. You'll be concerned about what other people think: "Do they like me?" "Will I make the team, or win the election?"

If an eclipse falls in your TWELFTH HOUSE—
This is the time when the focus turns to your inner life. An especially favorable eclipse here might bring you great insight and inspiration. Or events may happen which cause you to retreat from public life. Here is where we go to be alone, or to do spiritual or reparative work in retreats, hospitals, religious institutions, or psychotherapy. Here is where you deliver selfless service, through charitable acts. Good aspects from an eclipse could promote an ability to go with the flow, to rise above the competition and find an inner, almost mystical strength that enables you to connect with the deepest needs of others.

What Is the Best Thing to Do During an Eclipse?

When the natural rhythms of the sun and moon are disturbed, it's best to postpone important activities. Be sure to mark eclipse days on your calendar, especially if the eclipse falls in your birth sign. This year, Gemini, Sagittarius, Taurus, and Capricorn should take special note of the conscious and unconscious feelings that arise or are suppressed. With lunar eclipses, some possibilities could be a break from attachments, or the healing of an illness or substance abuse which had been triggered by the subconscious. The temporary event could be a healing time, when you gain perspective. During solar eclipses, when you could be in a highly subjective state, pay attention to the hidden subconscious patterns that surface, the emotional truth that is revealed in your feelings at this time.

The effect of the eclipse can reverberate for some time, often months after the event. But it is especially important to stay cool and make no major moves during the period known as the shadow of the eclipse, which begins about a week before as the energy begins to crescendo and lasts until at least three days after the eclipse, when the emotional atmosphere simmers down. After three days, the daily rhythms should be back to normal and you can proceed with business as usual.

The most positive way to view eclipses is as very special times, when we can receive great insight through a changed perspective. By blocking out the emotional pressure of the full moon, a lunar eclipse could be a time of reason, rather than confusion, a time when we can take a break from our problems. A solar eclipse, when the new moon blocks out the sun (or ego), could be a time when the moon's most positive qualities are expressed, bringing us a feeling of oneness, nurturing, and compassion.

CHAPTER 7

Astro-Mating—An Element-ary Guide to Love

How many people turn to astrology for the light it can shed on their love life! Probably the question astrologers hear most is: What sign is best for me in love? Or: I'm a Taurus and my lover is a Gemini—what are our prospects? Each sun sign does have certain predictable characteristics in love, and by comparing the sun signs, you can reach a better understanding of the dynamics of the relationship. However, it is very easy to oversimplify. Just because someone's sun sign is said to be "incompatible" is no reason why the relationship can't work out. A true in-depth comparison involves far more than just the sun sign. An astrologer considers the interrelationships of all the planets and houses (where they fall in your respective horoscopes). There are several bonds between planets that can offset any difficulties between sun signs. It's worthwhile to analyze them to learn more about your relationship. You can do this by making a very simple chart which compares the moon, Mars, and Venus, as well as the sun signs of the partners in a relationship. You can find the signs for Mars and Venus in the tables in this book. Unfortunately the moon tables are too long for a book of this size—so it might be worth your while to consult an astrological ephemeris (a book of planetary tables) in your local library or to have a computer chart cast to find out the moon placement.

Simply look up the signs of Mars and Venus (and

the Moon, if possible) for each person and list them, with the sun sign, next to each other, then add the *element* of each sign. The Earth signs are Taurus, Virgo, Capricorn. The Air signs are Gemini, Libra, Aquarius. The Fire signs are Aries, Leo, Sagittarius. And the Water signs are Cancer, Scorpio, Pisces.

Example:

ROMEO'S PLANETS:

SUN	MOON	MARS	VENUS
Aries/Fire	Leo/Fire	Scorpio/Water	Taurus/Earth

JULIET'S PLANETS:

SUN	MOON	MARS	VENUS
Pisces/Water	Leo/Fire	Aries/Fire	Aquarius/Air

As a rule of thumb, signs of the *same element* or *complementary elements* (fire with air and earth with water) get along best. So, after comparing this couple's planets, you can see that this particular Romeo and Juliet could have some challenges ahead.

The Lunar Link—Here's the Person You *Need*

The planet in your chart which governs your emotions is the moon. (Note: the moon is not technically a planet, but is usually referred to as one by astrologers.) So you would naturally take this into consideration when evaluating a potential romantic partnership. If a person's moon is in a good relationship to your sun, moon, Venus, or Mars, preferably in the same sign or element, you should relate well on some emotional level. Your needs will be compatible: you'll understand each other's feelings without much effort. If the moon is in a compatible element, such as earth with water or fire with air, you may have a few adjustments, but you will be able to make them easily. With a water-fire or earth-air combination, you'll have to make a considerable effort to understand where the other is coming from emotionally.

It's worth having a computer chart done, just to find the position of your moon. (Since the moon changes signs every two days, the tables are too long to print in this book.)

The Venus Attraction—Here's the One You *Want*

Venus is what you respond to, so if you and your partner have a good Venus aspect, you should have much in common. You'll enjoy doing things together. The same type of lovemaking will turn you both on. You'll have no trouble pleasing each other.

Look up both partners' Venus placements in the charts on page 69. Your lover's Venus in the same sign or a sign of the *same element* as your own Venus, Mars, moon, or sun is best. Second best is a sign of a compatible element (earth with water, air with fire). Venus in water with air, or earth with fire means that you may have to make a special effort to understand what appeals to each other. And you'll have to give each other plenty of space to enjoy activities that don't particularly appeal to you. By the way, this chart can work not only for lovers, but for any relationship where compatibility of tastes is important to you.

The Mars Connection—This One Lights Your Fire!

Mars positions reveal your sexual energy . . . how often you like to make love, for instance. It also shows your temper . . . do you explode or do a slow burn? Here you'll find out if your partner is direct, aggressive, and hot-blooded or more likely to take the cool, mental approach. Mutually supportive partners have their Mars working together in the same or complementary elements. But *any* contacts between Mars and Venus in two charts can strike sexy sparks. Even the difficult aspects, such as your partner's Mars three or six signs away from your sun, Mars, or Venus, can be sexually stimulating. Who doesn't get turned on by a challenge from time to time? On the other hand, the easy-flowing Mars relationships can drift into soporific dullness.

The Solar Bond

The sun is the focus of our personality and therefore the most powerful component involved. Each pair of sun signs has special lessons to teach and learn from each other. There is a negative side to the most ideal couple and a positive side to the unlikeliest match. Each has an up- and a downside. You'll find a comparison of your sun sign with every other one in the "pairs" section of the individual sun sign chapters in this book. If the forecast for you and your beloved (or business associate) seems like an uphill struggle, take heart! Such legendary lovers as Juan and Eva Peron, Ronald and Nancy Reagan, Harry and Bess Truman, Julius Caesar and Cleopatra, Billy and Ruth Graham, and George and Martha Washington are among the many who have made successful partnerships between supposedly incompatible sun signs.

Try astro-mating these hot celebrity couples for practice. Look up their planets in the "planet" tables in this book and discover the secret of their cosmic attraction. (Some may not be an "item" by the time this is published. Maybe you can figure out what went wrong!)

ARIES Matthew Broderick (3/21/62) and ARIES Sarah Jessica Parker (3/24/65)

PISCES Tea Leoni (2/25/66) and LEO David Duchovny (8/7/61)

ARIES Warren Beatty (3/30/37) and GEMINI Annette Bening (5/29/58)

ARIES Al Gore (3/31/48) and LEO Tipper Gore (8/19/48)

ARIES Alec Baldwin (4/3/58) and SAGITTARIUS Kim Basinger (12/8/53)

TAURUS Barbra Streisand (4/24/42) and CANCER James Brolin (7/18/40)

TAURUS Uma Thurman (4/29/70) and SCORPIO Ethan Hawke (11/6/70)

TAURUS Carmen Electra (4/20/72) and TAURUS Dennis Rodman (5/13/61)

GEMINI Liz Hurley (6/10/65) and VIRGO Hugh Grant (9/9/60)

GEMINI Angelina Jolie (6/4/75) and LEO Billy Bob Thornton (8/4/55)

GEMINI Nicole Kidman (6/21/67) and CANCER Tom Cruise (7/3/62)

LEO Jennifer Lopez (7/24/70) and SCORPIO Sean "Puffy" Combs (11/4/69)

LEO Arnold Schwarzenegger (7/30/47) and SCORPIO Maria Shriver (11/6/55)

LEO Whitney Houston (8/9/53) and AQUARIUS Bobby Brown (2/5/69)

LEO Melanie Griffith (8/9/57) and LEO Antonio Banderas (8/10/60)

LIBRA Michael Douglas (9/25/44) and LIBRA Catherine Zeta-Jones (9/25/69)

TAURUS Jessica Lange (4/20/49) and SCORPIO Sam Shepard (11/5/43)

SCORPIO Hillary Clinton (10/26/47) and LEO Bill Clinton (8/19/46)

PISCES Kurt Russell (3/17/51) and SCORPIO Goldie Hawn (11/21/45)

SCORPIO Prince Charles (11/14/48) and CANCER Camilla Parker Bowles (7/17/47)

SAGITTARIUS Brad Pitt (12/18/63) and AQUARIUS Jennifer Aniston (2/11/69)

CAPRICORN Diane Sawyer (12/22/45) and SCORPIO Mike Nichols (11/6/46)

AQUARIUS Oprah Winfrey (1/29/54) and PISCES
Stedman Graham (3/6/51)

Now it's time to do a bit of astro-mating of your own!
Do you have what it takes to seduce these celebrity hunks?
Check your sun, moon, Mars, and Venus with theirs!

Prince William (6/21/82)

SUN: Cancer (water)
MOON: Cancer (water)
MARS: Libra (air)
VENUS: Taurus (earth)

Russell Crowe (4/7/64)

SUN: Aries (fire)
MOON: Aquarius (air)
MARS: Aries (fire)
VENUS: Gemini (earth)

Jude Law (12/29/72)

SUN: Capricorn (earth)
MOON: Scorpio (water)
MARS: Scorpio (water)
VENUS: Sagittarius (fire)

Leonardo DiCaprio (11/11/74)

SUN: Scorpio (water)
MOON: Libra (air)
MARS: Scorpio (water)
VENUS: Scorpio (water)

Matt Damon (10/8/70)

SUN: Libra (air)
MOON: Gemini (air)
MARS: Aquarius (air)
VENUS: Libra (air)

George Clooney (5/6/61)

SUN: Taurus (earth)
MOON: Capricorn (earth)
MARS: Leo (fire)
VENUS: Aries (fire)

Richard Gere (8/31/49)

SUN: Virgo (earth)
MOON: Sagittarius (fire)
MARS: Cancer (water)
VENUS: Libra (air)

Hugh Grant (9/9/60)

SUN: Virgo (earth)
MOON: Taurus (earth)
MARS: Gemini (air)
VENUS: Libra (air)

Kevin Costner (1/18/55)

SUN: Capricorn (earth)
MOON: Sagittarius (fire)
MARS: Aries (fire)
VENUS: Sagittarius (fire)

Mel Gibson (1/3/56)

SUN: Capricorn (earth)
MOON: Virgo (earth)
MARS: Scorpio (water)
VENUS: Aquarius (air)

Fabio (3/15/61)

SUN: Pisces (water)
MOON: Pisces (water)
MARS: Cancer (water)
VENUS: Aries (fire)

Brad Pitt (12/18/63)

SUN: Sagittarius (fire)
MOON: Capricorn (earth)
MARS: Capricorn (earth)
VENUS: Capricorn (earth)

Johnny Depp (6/9/63)

SUN: Gemini (air)
MOON: Capricorn (earth)
MARS: Virgo (earth)
VENUS: Taurus (earth)

Keanu Reeves (9/2/64)

SUN: Virgo (earth)
MOON: Leo (fire)
MARS: Cancer (water)
VENUS: Cancer (water)

Joaquin Phoenix (10/28/74)

SUN: Scorpio (water)
MOON: Aries (fire)
MARS: Scorpio (water)
VENUS: Scorpio (water)

CHAPTER 8

Ask the Expert—Should You Have a Personal Reading?

Though you can learn much about yourself and others from studying astrology yourself, there comes a time when you might want the objective opinion of a professional astrologer. Done by a qualified astrologer, the personal reading can be an empowering experience if you want to reach your full potential, size up a lover or business situation, or find out what the future has in store. There are so many options for readings today, however, that sorting through them can be a daunting task. Besides face-to-face consultations, there are readings by mail, phone, tape, and Internet. There are astrologers who are specialists in certain areas, such as finance or medical astrology. And unfortunately, there are many questionable practitioners who range from streetwise gypsy fortunetellers to unscrupulous scam artists. The following basic guidelines can help you sort out your options to find the reading that's right for you.

The One-on-One Reading

Nothing compares to a one-on-one consultation with a professional astrologer who has analyzed thousands of charts and can pinpoint the potential in yours. During your reading, you can get your specific questions answered. For instance, how to get along better with your mate or coworker. There are many astrologers who now combine their skills with training in psychology and are well suited to help you examine your alternatives.

To give you an accurate reading, an astrologer needs certain information from you, such as the date, time, and place where you were born. (A horoscope can be cast about anyone or anything that has a specific time and place.) Most astrologers will then enter this information into a computer, which will calculate a chart in seconds. From the resulting chart, the astrologer will do an interpretation.

If you don't know your exact birth time, you can usually locate it at the Bureau of Vital Statistics at the city hall or county seat of the state where you were born. If you still have no success in getting your time of birth, some astrologers can estimate an approximate birth time by using past events in your life to determine the chart. This technique is called *rectification.*

How to Find a Good Astrologer

Your first priority should be to choose a qualified astrologer. Rather than relying on word of mouth or grandiose advertising claims, choose your astrologer with the same care as any trusted adviser such as a doctor, lawyer, or banker. Unfortunately, anyone can claim to be an astrologer—to date, there is no licensing of astrologers or established professional criteria. However, there are nationwide organizations of serious, committed astrologers that can help you in your search.

Good places to start your investigation are organizations such as the American Federation of Astrologers or the National Council for Geocosmic Research (NCGR), which offer a program of study and certification. If you live near a major city, there is sure to be an active NCGR chapter or astrology club in your area—many are listed in astrology magazines available at your local newsstand. In response to many requests for referrals, the NCGR has compiled a directory of professional astrologers, which includes a glossary of terms and an explanation of specialties within the astrological field. Contact the NCGR headquarters (see Chapter 10, "The Sydney Omarr Yellow Pages") for information.

Be Aware of When to Beware

As a potentially lucrative freelance business, astrology has always attracted self-styled experts who may not have the knowledge or the counseling experience to give a helpful reading. These astrologers can range from the well-meaning amateur to the charlatan or street-corner gypsy who has for many years given astrology a bad name. Be very wary of astrologers who claim to have occult powers or who make pretentious claims of celebrated clients or miraculous achievements. You can often tell from the initial phone conversation if the astrologer is legitimate. He or she should ask for your birthday time and place and conduct the conversation in a professional manner. Any astrologer who gives a reading based only on your sun sign is highly suspect.

When you arrive at the reading, the astrologer should be prepared. The consultation should be conducted in a private, quiet place. The astrologer should be interested in your problems of the moment. A good reading involves feedback on your part, so if the reading is not relating to your concerns, you should let the astrologer know. You should feel free to ask questions and get clarifications of technical terms. The more you actively participate, rather than expecting the astrologer to carry the reading or come forth with oracular predictions, the more meaningful your experience will be. An astrologer should help you validate your current experience and be frank about possible negative happenings, but suggest a positive course of action.

In their approach to a reading, some astrologers may be more literal, others more intuitive. Those who have had counseling training may take a more psychological approach. Though some astrologers may seem to have an almost psychic ability, extrasensory perception or any other parapsychological talent is not essential. A very accurate picture can be drawn from the data in your horoscope chart.

An astrologer may do several charts for each client, including one for the time of birth and a "progressed chart," showing the evolution from birth to the present time. According to your individual needs, there are many other possibilities, such as a chart for a different location, if you are contemplating a change of place. Relationships between any two people, things, or events can be interpreted with a chart which compares one partner's horoscope with the other's. A composite chart, which uses the midpoint between planets in two individual charts to describe the relationship, is another commonly used device.

An astrologer will be particularly interested in transits—times when planets will pass over the planets or sensitive points in your birth chart, which signal important events in your life.

Many astrologers offer tape-recorded readings, another option to consider. In this case, you'll be mailed a taped reading based on your birth chart. This type of reading is more personal than a computer printout and can give you valuable insights, though it is not equivalent to a live dialogue with the astrologer, when you can discuss your specific interests and issues of the moment.

Phone Readings—Real or Phony?

Telephone readings come in two varieties, a dial-in taped reading, usually recorded in advance by an astrologer or a live consultation with an "astrologer" on the other end of the line. The taped readings are general daily or weekly forecasts, applied to all members of your sign and charged by the minute. The quality depends on the astrologer. *One caution*: Be aware that these readings can run up quite a telephone bill, especially if you get into the habit of calling every day. Be sure that you are aware of the per-minute cost of each call beforehand.

Live telephone readings also vary with the expertise of the astrologer. Ideally, the astrologer at the other end of the line enters your birth data into a computer, which calculates your chart. This chart will then be referred to during the consultation. The advantage of a live telephone reading is that your individual chart is used and you can ask about a specific problem. However, before you invest in any reading, be sure that your astrologer is qualified and that you fully understand in advance how much you will be charged. There should be no unpleasant financial surprises later.

About Computer Readings

Companies which offer computer programs (such as ACS, Matrix, Astrolabe) also offer a variety of computer-generated horoscope readings. These can be quite comprehensive, offering a beautiful printout of the chart plus many pages of detailed information about each planet and aspect of the chart. You can then study it at your convenience. Of course, the interpretations will be general, since there is no personal input from you, and may not cover your immediate concerns. Since computer-generated horoscopes are much lower in cost than live consultations, you might consider them as either a supplement or preparation for an eventual live reading. You'll then be more familiar with your chart and able to plan specific questions in advance. They also make a terrific gift for astrology fans. There are several companies in our "Yellow Pages" chapter which offer computerized readings prepared by reputable astrologers.

Whichever option you decide to pursue, may your reading be an empowering one!

CHAPTER 9

The "In" Sites Online

If you're curious to see a copy of your chart (or someone else's), want to study astrology in depth, or chat
with another astrology fan, log on to the Internet!
There you'll find a whole new world of astrology waiting for a click of your mouse. Thousands of astrological sites offer you everything from chart services to
chat rooms to individual readings. Even better, you'll
find *free* software, *free* charts, and *free* articles to download. You can virtually get an education in astrology
from your computer screen, share your insights with
new astrology-minded pals in a chat room or on a
mailing list, then later meet them in person at one of
the hundreds of conferences around the world.

The following sites were chosen for general interest
from vast numbers of astrology-oriented places on the
Net. Many have their own selection of links to other
sites for further exploration. *One caveat*: Though these
sites were selected with longevity in mind, the Internet
is a volatile place where sites can disappear or change
without notice. Therefore, some of our sites may have
changed addresses, names, or content by the time this
book is published.

Free Charts

Astrolabe Software at *http://www.alabe.com* distributes
some of the most creative and user-friendly programs
now available, like "Solar Fire," a favorite of top as-

trologers. Visitors to their site are greeted with a chart of the time you log on. You can get your chart calculated, with a mini-interpretation, e-mailed to you.

For an instant chart, surf to this address: *http://www.astro.ch* and check into ASTRODIENST, one of the first and best astrology sites on the Internet. Its world atlas will give you the accurate longitude and latitude of your birthplace for setting up your horoscope. You can print out your chart in a range of easy-to-read formats. One handy feature for beginners: The planetary placement is listed in words, rather than glyphs, alongside the chart (a real help for those who haven't yet learned to read the astrology glyph).

There are many other attractions at this site, such as a list of your astro-twins (famous people born on your birthdate). The site even sorts the "twins" to feature those who also have your identical rising sign. You can then click on their names and get instant charts of your famous sign-mates.

Free Software

Software manufacturers on the Web are generous with free downloads of demo versions of their software. You may then calculate charts using their data. This makes sense if you're considering investing serious money in astrology software, and want to see how the program works in advance. You can preview ASTROLABE Software programs favored by many professional astrologers at *http://www.alabe.com.* Check out the latest demo of "Solar Fire," one of the most user-friendly astrology programs available—you'll be impressed.

For a Fully Functional Astrology Program:

Walter Pullen's amazingly complete ASTROLOG program is offered absolutely free at this site: *http://www.magitech.com/~cruiser1/astrolog.htm.*

ASTROLOG is an ultrasophisticated program with all the features of much more expensive programs. It comes in versions for all formats—DOS, Windows, MAC, UNIX—and has some cool features such as a revolving globe and a constellation map. A "must" for those who want to get involved with astrology without paying big bucks for a professional-caliber program. Or for those who want to add ASTROLOG's unique features to their astrology software library. This program has it all!

Another good resource for software is Astro Computing Services. Their Web site has free demos of several excellent programs. Note especially their "Electronic Astrologer," one of the most effective and reasonably priced programs on the market. It's very easy to use, a bonus for nontechies. Go to *http://www.astrocom.com* for ACS software, books, readings, chart services, and software demos. At this writing, there are free new moon and full moon reports.

Surf to *http://www.astroscan.ca* for a free program called ASTROSCAN. Stunning graphics and ease of use make this a winner.

At Halloran Software's site, *http://www.halloran. com*, there are four levels of Windows astrology software from which to choose. The "Astrology for Windows" shareware program is available in unregistered demo form as a free download and in registered form for $26.50, at this writing. The calculations in this program may be all that an astrology hobbyist needs. The price for the full-service program is certainly reasonable.

Free Screen Saver and More

The Astrology Matrix offers a way to put your sign in view with a downloadable graphic screensaver. There are also many other diversions at this site, where you may consult the stars, the I Ching, the runes, and the tarot. Here's where to connect with news groups and online discussions. Their almanac helps you schedule the best day to sign on the dotted line, ask for a raise, or plant your rosebush. Address: *http://thenewage.com.*

Free Astrology Course

Schedule a long visit to *http://www.panplanet.com,* where you will find the Canopus Academy of Astrology, a site loaded with goodies. For the experienced astrologer, there is a collection of articles from top astrologers. They've done the work for you when it comes to picking the best astrology links on the Web, so be sure to check out those bestowed with the Canopus Award of Excellence.

Astrologer Linda Reid, an accomplished astrology teacher and author, offers a complete online curriculum for all levels of astrology study plus individual tutoring. To get your feet wet, Linda is offering an excellent beginners' course at this site, a terrific way to get off and running in astrology.

Visit an Astro-Mall

Surf to *http://www.astronet.com* for the Internet's equivalent of an Astrology Mall. ASTRONET offers interactive fun for everyone. At this writing, there's a special area for teenage astrology fans, access to popular astrology magazines like *American Astrology,* advice to the lovelorn, as well as a grab bag of horoscopes, featured guests, and a shopping area for books, reports, software, and even jewelry.

Swoon.com is another mall-like site aimed at dating, mating, and relating. It has fun features to spark up your love life, plenty of advice for the lovelorn, as well as links to all the popular fashion magazine astrology columns. Address: *http://www.swoon.com.*

Find An Astrologer Here

Metalog Directory of Astrology
http://www.astrologer.com

Looking for an astrologer in your local area? Perhaps you're planning a vacation in Australia or France and would like to meet astrologers or combine your activities with an astrology conference there? Go no further than this well-maintained resource. Here is an extensive worldwide list of astrologers and astrology sites. There is also an agenda of astrology conferences and seminars all over the world.

The A.F.A. Web Site
http://www.astrologers.com

This is the interesting Web site of the prestigious American Federation of Astrologers. The A.F.A. has a very similar address to the *Metalog Directory* and also has a directory of astrologers, restricted to those who meet their stringent requirements. Check out their correspondence course if you would like to study astrology in depth.

Tools Every Astrologer Needs Are Online

Internet Atlas
http://www.astro.ch/atlas

Find the geographic longitude and latitude and the correct time zone for any city worldwide. You'll need this information to calculate a chart.

The Exact Time, Anywhere in the World
http://www.timeticker.com

A fun site with fascinating graphics which give you the exact time anywhere in the world. Click on the world map and the correct time and zone for that place lights up.

Check the Weather Forecast
http://www.weathersage.com

More accurate than your local TV forecast is the Weathersage, which uses astrology to predict snow-storms and hurricanes. Get your long-range local forecast at this super site.

Celebrate the Queen's Birthday
http://www.zodiacal.com

A great jumping-off place for an astrology tour of the Internet, this site has a veritable Burke's Peerage of royal birthdays. There's a good selection of articles, plus tools such as a U.S. and world atlas and information on conferences, software, and tapes. The links at this site will send you off in the right direction.

Astrology World
http://astrology-world.com

Astrologer Deborah Houlding has gathered some of the finest European astrologers on this super Web site, as well as a comprehensive list of links and conferences.

Astrology Alive
http://www.astrologyalive.com

Barbara Schermer has one of the most innovative approaches to astrology. She was one of the first astrologers to go online, so there's always a "cutting edge" to this site. Great list of links.

National Council for Geocosmic Research (NCGR)
http://www.geocosmic.org

A key stop on any astrological tour of the Net. Here's where you can find local chapters in your area, get information on the NCGR testing and certification programs, and get a conference schedule. You can also order lecture tapes from their nationwide conferences, or get complete lists of conference topics to study at home. Good links to resources.

Where to Find Charts of the Famous

When the news is breaking, you can bet Lois Rodden will be the first to get accurate birthdays of the headline makers, and put up their charts on her Web site: *www.astrodatabank.com*. Rodden's research is astrology's most reliable source for data of the famous and infamous. Her Web site specializes in birthdays and charts of current newsmakers, political figures, and international celebrities. You can purchase her database program, a wonderful research tool, which gives you thousands of birthdays sorted into categories.

Another site with birthdays and charts of famous people to download is *http://www.astropro.com*.

You can get the sun and moon sign, plus a biography of the hottest new film stars here: *http://www.mrshowbiz. com*. Or go to *http://www.imdb.com* for a comprehensive list of film celebrities including bios, plus lists of famous couples from today and yesteryear.

Yet another good source for celebrity birthdates is *http://www.metamaze.com/bdays*. You can find some interesting offbeat newsmakers here.

For Astrology Books

National Clearinghouse for Astrology Books

A wide selection of books on all aspects of astrology, from basics to advanced. Many hard-to-find books. Surf to: *http://www.astroamerica.com.*

These addresses also have a good selection of astrology books, some which are unique to the site:
http://www.panplanet.com
http://thenewage.com
http://www.astrocom.com

Browse the huge astrology list of online bookstore Amazon.com at *http://www.amazon.com.*

Astrology Tapes at Pegasus Tapes
http://www.pegasustape.com

You can study at home with world-famous astrologers via audiocassette recordings from Pegasus Tapes. There's a great selection taped from conferences, classes, lectures, and seminars. An especially good source for astrologers who emphasize psychological and mythological themes.

For History and Mythology Buffs

Be sure to visit the astrology section of this gorgeous site, dedicated to the history and mythology of many traditions. One of the most beautifully designed sites we've seen. Address: *http://www.elore.com.*

The leading authority on the history of astrology, Robert Hand, has an excellent site which features his cutting-edge research. See what one of astrology's great teachers has to offer. Address: *http://www.robhand.com.*

The Project Hindsight group is devoted to restoring the astrology of the Hellenistic period (300 B.C. to about

600 A.D.), the primary source for all later Western astrology. Some fascinating articles for astrology fans. Address: *http://www.projecthindsight-tghp.com/index.html.*

C.U.R.A. is a European site for historical researchers. Address: *http://cura.free.fr.*

Readers interested in mythology should also check out *http://pantheon.org/mythical/* for stories of gods and goddesses.

Astrology Magazines

The Mountain Astrologer
http://www.mountainastrologer.com

A favorite magazine of astrology fans, *The Mountain Astrologer* has an interesting Web site featuring the latest news from an astrological point of view, plus feature articles from the magazine.

Financial Astrology

Find out how financial astrologers play the market. Here are hot picks, newsletters, specialized financial astrology software, and mutual funds run by astrology seers. Go to *www.afund.com* or *www.alphee.com* for tips and forecasts from two top financial astrologers.

CHAPTER 10

The Sydney Omarr Yellow Pages

Enter the world of astrology! If you want to find an astrology program for your computer, connect with other astrology fans, study advanced techniques, or buy books and tapes, consider this chapter "Astrology Central." Here you'll find the latest products and services available, as well as the top astrology organizations which hold meetings and conferences in your area.

There are organized groups of astrologers all over the country who are dedicated to promoting the image of astrology in the most positive way. The National Council for Geocosmic Research (NCGR) is one nationwide group that is dedicated to bringing astrologers together, promoting fellowship and high-quality education. Their accredited course system promotes a systematized study of all the different facets of astrology. Whether you'd like to know more about such specialties as financial astrology or techniques for timing events, or if you'd prefer the psychological or mythological approach, you'll find the leading experts at NCGR conferences.

Your computer can be a terrific tool for connecting with other astrology fans at all levels of expertise, as we explored in the Internet chapter in this book. Even if you are using a "dinosaur" from the 1980s, there are still calculation and interpretation programs available for DOS and MAC formats. They may not have all the bells and whistles or the exciting graphics, but they'll get the job done!

Newcomers to astrology should learn some of the basics, including the glyphs (astrology's special shorthand language) before you invest in a complex computer program. Use the chapter in this book to help you learn the symbols easily, so you'll be able to read the charts without consulting the "help" section of your program every time. Several programs, such as Astrolabe's "Solar Fire," have pop-up definitions to help you decipher the meanings of planets and aspects. Just click your mouse on a glyph or an icon on the screen, and a window with an instant definition appears.

You don't have to spend a fortune to get a perfectly adequate astrology program. In fact, if you are connected to the Internet, you can download one free. Astrology software is available at all price levels, from a sophisticated free application like *Astrology,* which you can download from a Web site, to inexpensive programs for under $100 such as Halloran's "Astrology for Windows," to the more expensive astrology programs such as "Winstar," "Solar Fire," or "Io" (for the Mac), which are used by serious students and professionals. Before you make an investment, it's a good idea to download a sample from the company's Web site or order a demo disk.

If you're baffled by the variety of software available, most of the companies on our list will be happy to help you find the right application for your needs.

Students of astrology who live in out-of-the-way places or are unable to fit classes into your schedule have several options. There are online courses offered at astrology Web sites, such as *www.panplanet.com,* and at the NCGR and AFA Web sites. Some astrology teachers will send you a series of audiotapes or you can order audiotaped seminars of recent conferences; other teachers offer correspondence courses that use their workbooks or computer printouts.

The Yellow Pages

Nationwide Astrology Organizations and Conferences

Contact these organizations for information on conferences, workshops, local meetings, conference tapes, and referrals:

National Council for Geocosmic Research

Educational workshops, tapes, conferences, and a directory of professional astrologers are available from this nationwide organization devoted to promoting astrological education. For a $35 annual membership fee, you get their excellent publications and newsletters, plus the opportunity to network with other astrology buffs at local chapter events (there are chapters in twenty states).

For general information about NCGR, contact:

NCGR
P.O. Box 38866
Los Angeles, CA 90038
Phone: 818-705-1678

Or visit their Web page, *http://www.geocosmic.org,* for updates and local events.

American Federation of Astrologers (A.F.A.)

One of the oldest astrological organizations in the United States, established in 1938. Conferences, conventions, and a correspondence course. Will refer you to an accredited A.F.A. astrologer.

A.F.A.
P.O. Box 22040
Tempe, AZ 85382

Phone: 602-838-1751
Fax: 602-838-8293

A.F.A.N. (Association for Astrological Networking)

(Networking, Legal Issues)
Did you know that astrologers are still being arrested for practicing in some states? AFAN provides support and legal information, and works toward improving the public image of astrology. Here are the people who will go to bat for astrology when it is attacked in the media. Everyone who cares about astrology should join!

A.F.A.N.
8306 Wilshire Blvd., Suite 537
Beverly Hills, CA 90211

ARC Directory

(Listing of astrologers worldwide)
2920 E. Monte Vista
Tucson, AZ 85716
Phone: 602-321-1114

Pegasus Tapes

(Lectures, conference tapes)
P.O. Box 419
Santa Ysabel, CA 92070

International Society for Astrological Research

(Lectures, workshops, seminars)
P.O. Box 38613
Los Angeles, CA 90038

ISIS Institute

(Newsletter, conferences, astrology tapes, catalog)
P.O. Box 21222
El Sobrante, CA 94820-1222
Phone: 888-322-4747
Fax: 510-222-2202

Astrology Software

Astrolabe

Box 1750-R
Brewster, MA 02631
Phone: 800-843-6682

Check out the latest version of their powerful "Solar Fire" software for Windows—it's a breeze to use and will grow with your increasing knowledge of astrology to the most sophisticated levels. This company also markets a variety of programs for all levels of expertise, a wide selection of computer astrology readings, and Mac programs. A good resource for innovative software as well as applications for older computers.

Matrix Software

407 N. State Street
Big Rapids, MI 49307
Phone: 800-PLANETS

A wide variety of software in all price ranges, demo disks, student and advanced levels, and lots of interesting readings. Check out "Winstar," their powerful professional software, if you're planning to study astrology seriously.

Astro Communications Services

Dept. AF693, PO Box 34487
San Diego, CA 92163-4487
Phone: 800-888-9983

Books, software for MAC and IBM compatibles, individual charts, and telephone readings. Find technical astrology materials here, such as "The American Ephemeris." They will calculate charts for you if you do not have a computer.

Air Software

115 Caya Avenue
West Hartford, CT 06110
Phone: 800-659-1247

Powerful, creative astrology software, like their millennium "Star Trax 2000." For beginners, check out "Father Time," which finds your best days. Or "Nostradamus," which answers all your questions. Financial astrology programs for stock market traders are a specialty.

Time Cycles Research—For Mac Users!!!

375 Willets Avenue
Waterford, CT 06385
Fax: 869-442-0625
E-mail: *astrology@timecycles.com*
Internet: *http://www.timecycles.com*

Where MAC users can find astrology software that's as sophisticated as it gets. If you have Mac, you'll love their beautiful graphic "IO Series" programs.

Astro-Cartography

(Charts for location changes)
Astro-Numeric Service Box 336-B
Ashland, OR 97520
Phone: 800-MAPPING

Astro-cartography is a sophisticated technique which superimposes an astrology chart on a map of the world. A fascinating study for serious students of astrology.

Astrology Magazines

In addition to articles by top astrologers, most have listings of astrology conferences, events, and local happenings.

AMERICAN ASTROLOGY
Dept. 4
P.O. Box 2021
Marion, OH 43306-8121

DELL HOROSCOPE
P.O. Box 53352
Boulder, CO 89321-3342

THE MOUNTAIN ASTROLOGER
P.O. Box 970
Cedar Ridge, CA 95924

Astrology Schools

Though there are many correspondence courses available through private teachers and astrological organizations, up until now, there has never been an accredited college of astrology. That is why the following address is so important.

Kepler College of Astrological Arts and Sciences

Kepler College, the first institution of its kind to combine an accredited liberal arts education with extensive astrological studies, is now in operation, after many years in planning. A degree-granting college that is also a center of astrological studies has long been the dream of the astrological community and will be a giant step forward in providing credibility to the profession. The Kepler College faculty comprises some of the most creative leaders in the astrology community.

For more information, contact:

Kepler College of Astrological Arts and Sciences
Business Office
4630 200th St. SW
Suite L-1
Lynnwood, WA 98036
Phone: 435-673-4292
Fax: 425-673-4983
Internet: *www.kepler.edu*

Your Cancer Home Pages—
All About Your Life,
Friends, Family, Work,
and Style!

An emotional water sign ruled by the fast-moving moon, you're more sensitive to the constantly changing atmosphere than any other sign. To protect your natural emotional vulnerability, you operate very much like your symbol, the crab, a sidewalker who moves indirectly at a situation, never confronting it face on, but always obliquely, subtly, and cleverly. Your keen psychic antenna gives you an intuitive understanding of the hidden motives and agendas of others, which you often use to your advantage, tuning in to this powerful sixth sense before you listen to objective reason. Read on to discover all about your Cancer sun sign's personality and preferences. Bear in mind that there are ten other planets that also color your horoscope. For example, if only the sun was in Cancer and the moon was passing through businesslike Capricorn at the time you were born, you're likely to have a cooler, less emotional personality than the typical Cancer. So, the more Cancer planets you have, the more likely the following descriptions will resemble your personality.

CHAPTER 11

Are You True to Type?

The Cancer Man—
Strong and Sensitive

You sometimes wear a hard outer shell to protect yourself from the harsh realities of life. But inside you're vulnerable and tender, afraid of being exploited if you show this nurturing side to the world. Usually, it comes forth in a professional way, through your choice of a career where you can express your feelings safely in a creative context. Many Cancer men choose nurturing fields in medicine, child care, psychology, hotel work, family businesses, or restaurants for this reason. Or they'll extend their nurturing to an extended family tribe, like the Cancer writer Ernest Hemingway, who was called "Papa" by all who knew him personally. In fact, anyone who truly wishes to understand the Cancer male would do well to read the life and works of Hemingway, who exemplified both the tough and the vulnerable sides of the Cancer man.

You have an uncanny ability to read the feelings of others, which gives you great emotional power and understanding. You know exactly how to nurture people by giving them what they need when they need it. On the other hand, you know where to inflict the most hurt (often by withholding what is needed). Your negative side, which can be cool and cruel, is actually a form of resentment in Cancers who have not been nurtured enough themselves. If you can learn how to release the past and any hurts rendered to you, and how to nurture yourself, you'll have a much better chance to reach your full potential. Many Cancers have found psychotherapy extremely helpful in doing this.

Needless to say, a Cancer man's mother is especially important to him—even more so than to other men. If this relationship is either overpowering or lacking, you may try to replace it by mothering (or smothering) others or by looking for someone else to mother you.

Though you can be extremely masculine and sensual, the Cancer man rarely embodies the stereotypical masculine attitude. There is always a special communication of tenderness in your treatment of women, which makes you one of the zodiac's great lovers. You can tap into a woman's emotional needs and treat her with great sensitivity. This subtle vulnerability is evident in Cancer celebrities such as Robin Williams, Tom Cruise, Harrison Ford, and Geraldo Rivera. Their special sensitivity is far more attractive to women than the muscle-flexing of macho types.

In a Relationship

Like the crab, the Cancer man hangs on—you're extremely possessive of whatever and whoever belongs to you. You'll hang on to old memories, old sweaters, and often your first dollar.

In a committed relationship or marriage, you're at last free to show your tender, caring, protective side. Your home is supremely important to you. It's the place where you feel most secure and can thrive in the supportive atmosphere of a long-term love. You treasure the mother of your children, who probably resembles your own mother strongly in some way.

You are usually not attracted to independent women (unless your mother was independent), preferring the more maternal, nurturing type or a romantic, creative partner. You'd like her to be interested in domestic life and be an excellent cook. (If your partner is on the go all the time, she'll come home to a crabby mate.) Since you are usually materially successful, your home can be a private paradise for enjoying the good life together.

The Cancer Woman—Moon Maiden

As an active cardinal sign, you know how to capitalize creatively on your sensitive moon-ruled feelings by finding ways to satisfy or feed others' needs. Many Cancer women have become successful in business by providing the right product at the right time, like cosmetics tycoon Estée Lauder. However, you can be quite acquisitive, and the Cancer woman will hoard money or objects as if to store up for hard times. It has been said that nothing upsets a Cancer woman more than an empty refrigerator or an empty closet.

Because of your uncanny intuition, you easily grasp the inner motivations of others, and this knowledge becomes your shell of protection. Cancer women in high places often extend their shell to become legendary mother figures for their country, such as Princess Diana, Imelda Marcos, or Nancy Reagan. The wisest and wealthiest members of your sign use their intuition for personal and professional benefit.

You are especially affected by the moon's phases, especially during the full moon, when you could become supersensitive and overreact to imagined slights. Let creative projects come to the rescue, turning your negative energies back to positive again. You can find emotional fulfillment by providing food and shelter to others; cooking a delicious family dinner is excellent therapy for the Cancer moody blues.

Family influences are more potent with Cancer than with many other signs, so it is especially important that you try to conquer or reprogram negative relationships, so you can express your creative talents fully. You keep strong family ties throughout life and you are often able to combine your career with your home life, by working either at home or in a family business.

In a Relationship

Your choice of a mate is especially important, for a good relationship can draw you out of your shell and provide the emotional security you crave. You need a partner who is devoted and demonstrative, who will give you tangible proof of his love, and who will provide you with a stable home life.

Cancer wives are famous for creating beautiful homes and family ties. Many of you marry someone who is wealthy, powerful, and protective and then provide an indispensable support system for him. Usually, you are quite possessive of your husband and anxious to fulfill his needs. Sometimes a shy Cancer will transform herself into a public person and perfect hostess if her husband's role demands it, as Nancy Reagan and Camilla Parker Bowles did. You make good partners for chief executives, since you are able to embody the feminine power role, and can be seen as a maternal figure who is the ideal complement to your mate.

Cancer in the Family

The Cancer Parent

As the "mother" of the zodiac (even if you're the dad), you're in your element as a parent. You're at your best cuddling a tiny vulnerable child. This nurturing quality extends to all children, who arouse your deepest caring, nurturing instincts. You can be fiercely protective of your brood and also possessive, hanging on to the mother role long after your children have left the nest. Often the Cancer parent will have a dynasty and sustain their parental role by bringing the children into a family business. One of your greatest lessons will be to let go when the time comes, and to find constructive outlets for your nurturing energies as you evolve out of the parental role.

The Cancer Stepparent

Since a broken home is probably one of the most traumatic events that can happen to a Cancer, you will be full of compassion for your stepchildren. You will intuitively understand their unspoken feelings and their need for emotional support. Much depends, however, on how secure you yourself feel in the new family situation, and if you are getting the emotional support you require from your mate. If not, you may have difficulty sharing your mate with a previous family. If you can be open with your feelings, this situation can be remedied. Establishing good communications can sidestep power struggles and emotional manipulation. When your caring, protective nature is channeled in the right direction, you'll easily win over the children and provide a warm, welcoming, extended family.

The Cancer Grandparent

Grandparenthood is a liberating experience for Cancers. Now you're free to enjoy young children without chores or responsibilities. You can fuss over the babies to your heart's content. You'll actually love babysitting the toddlers, pampering them with presents. Family get-togethers, when your brood gathers over a huge, delicious meal, will be important seasonal events. You'll keep close ties with everyone in the family, so your grandchildren will always feel at home with you, and there will probably always be some young visitor toddling about. Grandpa will be especially concerned that his dynasty's future will be secure and has probably provided a substantial nest egg. As you grow older, you'll pass on your sense of tradition, giving each generation the lasting pleasures of close and warm family ties.

CHAPTER 12

"In Style" the Cancer Way

The key to looking and feeling your best is to go with the style that best suits your Cancer personality, which favors specific colors, surroundings, and attitudes. Follow these tips to maximize your own Cancer star quality.

The Cancer Atmosphere

You're the master of creating an atmosphere where everyone feels at home. Some of you have become internationally famous for this talent, such as the late interior designer, Sister Parish, who was the First Lady of decorating for the rich and famous. "Sister" created a mood that was comforting, secure, and relaxing, using crystal, candlelight, silver, and mirrors, so that the home looked especially good at night, when Cancer shines brightest. You tend to accumulate sentimental treasures, so be sure there is storage space for belongings you've saved over the years. Since you love to cook, your kitchen and dining room should be equipped to prepare frequent family feasts. It will probably be the favorite gathering place in your home. A large dining table will be needed to accommodate your extended family and friends.

One room should be done in tranquil, restful colors, a place for solitary meditation. Incorporate your water element in some way in your home, perhaps with a tiny waterfall or a painting of a favorite beach. A swimming pool or a Jacuzzi tub are water-loving Cancer luxuries. Why not turn a bathroom into a home spa, a private place to relax and rejuvenate.

Your Special Sounds

Your kind of music stirs deep feelings or reminds you of happy times. Some Cancer artists that touch you are Carly Simon, Lena Horne, Courtney Love, and Diahann Carroll. Though you gravitate to blues and love songs, you should collect upbeat music that lifts your spirits and cool jazz that soothes your nerves. Why not make special tapes of your favorite songs, themed to evoke moods such as romance, relaxation, and high energy, for the perfect background music to complement meals and parties.

Cancer Travel and Leisure

Water-loving Cancers are in their element on cruises, at seaside resorts, or in tropical-island paradises. Rather than an impersonal resort, you might prefer a home-away-from-home with a family feeling, or you may bring a relative or intimate friend for company. Investigate renting your own villa or condominium at a resort rather than staying in a big hotel. This would give you both privacy and a place to entertain new friends. Cancer will actually enjoy shopping at the local food markets and serving regional specialties.

One of the zodiac's great shoppers, you'll probably bring home souvenirs for everyone in the family. Stash an extra collapsible suitcase or ballistic-nylon tote bag in your baggage to hold all your finds. Most Cancers love to take photos, so be sure you have a small camera with you at all times. The new disposable cameras are perfect for casual snapshots and eliminate any worry about theft. Some disposable cameras can take photos underwater and can be attached to your swimsuit while snorkeling.

Stomach upsets are your travel foe, so take along a portable water purifier and all the proper medication. Include a high-SPF sunscreen in all your travel kits to protect your sensitive skin. Cancer likes to be upon or under the waves, so ocean liners are the perfect floating vacation homes. Or you may rent a sailboat to cruise the Caribbean or the Greek Islands. Scuba vacations also appeal. Exotic places like Nairobi, Singapore, Istanbul, Venice, and the highlands of Scotland suit Cancer's many travel moods.

Your Special Cancer Colors

Soft, subtle shades, nothing garish or shouting, are especially soothing to Cancer. All the moonbeam shades of pearly white, silver, taupe, moss green, midnight blue, and coral are yours. Cancer decorators are specialists in using color to evoke moods, to stimulate appetites, or to soothe and comfort.

Cancer Style-Setters

Your sun sign has an intuitive fashion sense that cues you to the right dress for every occasion. You are a specialist in using clothing to evoke a mood. Like the late Princess Diana, you look best in fluid, romantic lines that play up your intense femininity. Your luminous quality is especially evident at night, when you look your best. Soft, shimmering evening wear brings out the moon maiden in you. Wear silver and pearls, iridescent fabrics, and wavy hair to play up this quality. Accent your expressive eyes with subtle makeup and take care of your sensitive skin, which can react to emotional upsets or overexposure to the sun.

Cancer Fashion Leaders

Look no further than your own sun sign for many chic fashion leaders and designers to inspire you. These designers understand the many moods and the perfect styles for your sign: Giorgio Armani, Oscar de la Renta, Pierre Cardin, Norma Kamali, and Claude Montana. Many "best-dressed" fashion icons of the past were born under Cancer such as Babe Paley, Slim Keith, Nancy Reagan, and Jacqueline de Ribes. Trendy Cancers like Liv Tyler and Courtney Love always look best when they are accenting their beautiful eyes and projecting an ethereal moonbeam quality.

Cancer fashion models have always ruled the runway. At this writing, the Brazilian sensation Gisele Bundchen's curvaceous body and undulating walk captures every mood of the moment. Jerry Hall and Karen Mulder are also fashion favorites born under your sign.

Cancer Food Fans

Your sign is unrivaled in the kitchen, especially when it comes to preparing traditional dishes and family favorites. However, many Cancers have delicate digestive systems and fare best on cooking with a light touch. Vegetarian and seafood specialties are excellent choices for your menus.

Any restaurant with a romantic view of an ocean, stream, or lake is sure to please. If you live in a city near the ocean or a well-traveled river, look for a floating restaurant, either on a barge, riverboat, or yacht, for a romantic dinner.

As one of the zodiac's natural gourmets, you'll appreciate the more creative chefs in town. Another possible night-out favorite is a family-style restaurant, with ethnic food and Mama at the stove cooking her specialties.

CHAPTER 13

The Healthy Cancer

The breast area is ruled by Cancer, a reminder to have regular checkups, according to your age and family health history of breast-related illness.

For this sign that loves good food, dieting can be especially difficult and can be laden with conflicts: you may want to be fashionably thin to appeal to a loved one, but yours is also a sign that loves to eat and becomes the family cook. So it is important not to have a feeling of deprivation. Remember to nurture yourself emotionally by airing problems and finding support to sustain healthier new eating habits, perhaps through a therapy group that is food-oriented.

Cancer rules digestive difficulties, especially gastric ulcers and eating disorders. When emotionally caused digestive problems from those stomach-knotting insecurities crop up, baby yourself with some extra pampering. If you're feeling blue, a visit with loved ones, old friends, and family could provide the support you need. Plan some special family activities that bring everyone close together.

Your natural element of water provides many solutions to emotionally related health problems: sometimes just a walk by your local pond or sitting for a few moments by a fountain can do wonders to relieve the emotional stress and tension that can lead to overeating. You'll be more likely to stick to an exercise routine if it's in your natural water element or shared with people you love. Boating and water sports provide ideal ways for you to stay fit. Make exercise a family activity by creating a family gym, playing sports together, or going to exercise classes with loved ones.

CHAPTER 14

Cancer at Work!

From behind your thick protective shell, you can figure out just what a job requires, or intuit what the public wants and needs, then put your creativity to work finding ways to fulfill those needs. It's no wonder so many millionaires were born under your sign! Your natural acquisitiveness makes you a shrewd judge of quality, and you'll build your own nest egg at the same time as you're increasing company profits.

Because you're emotionally supersensitive, look for a job that gives you a feeling of security, perhaps a family business. Your stomach rebels at constant nervous tension or stealthy political maneuvers (though you can maneuver with the best of them). Creative fields give the needed self-expression: photography, theater, music, and fashion, especially. The food, shelter, home maintenance, and child-related businesses are other natural Cancer meccas, as well as interior design and architecture. Many successful Cancers have made their fortunes in hotels, restaurants, and real estate. Marine business such as shipping, yacht sales, or marine biology are water sign havens that would put you in the seaside environment you love.

Cancer in Charge

There is no such thing as an uninvolved Cancer, especially one at the helm. You are extremely possessive of your means of security and hang on to your position despite all odds. As a boss, you operate intuitively rather than openly, which could lead others to suspect a hidden agenda. Your secretiveness can project paranoia, but you usually make up for this with a very protective attitude toward your underlings. Your emotional sensitivity is a plus when negotiating a deal, helping you intuit when to sign on the dotted line and when the competition is about to act. Though your moods may be baffling to associates, chances are they have learned never to underestimate you and to wait out your "down" times for a few days until your mood changes.

Cancer Teamwork

You are the one who has everyone fooled. While you may appear quiet and shy, you are really taking everyone's measure. This is your way of protecting yourself before you reveal your tender, caring side. You work best in a rather traditional, nurturing atmosphere, where you can express your creativity and surprise everyone with your organizational talent and perseverance. Once you feel secure, you really produce. However, it is very important to work with supportive, congenial people, since you are easily upset by criticism and office politics.

You like your office to be a home away from home, where you are taking care of people and fulfilling their needs. Though you may have up and down days, you should guard against bringing your personal problems into the workplace. Emphasize your excellent sense of marketing and a shrewd eye for quality, plus innate good taste.

To Get Ahead Fast

Pick a job with a supportive atmosphere and creative opportunities. Play up your finest attributes:

- Creativity
- Intuitive insight into the market
- Perseverance
- Shrewd judgment
- Caring, nurturing qualities
- Organizational talent

Famous Cancer Millionaires

Cancer is known as the "sign of millionaires" because so many wealthy people were born under this sign, with names like Perot, Niarchos, and Rockefeller. Study the techniques of these Cancer tycoons for tips on how to make the most of your Cancer potential:

H. Ross Perot
Leona Helmsley
Stavros Niarchos
L. B. Mayer
Merv Griffin
Richard Branson (Virgin Airlines)
Estée Lauder
Nelson Rockefeller
Daniel Ludwig
Orville Redenbacher
Roone Arledge
P. T. Barnum
Imelda Marcos
Michael Milken

CHAPTER 15

Cancer Rich and Famous!

We're fascinated by reading tabloids and gossip items about the rich, famous, and infamous in the post-Millennium, but astrology can tell you more about your heroes than most magazine articles. Like what really turns them on (check their Venus). Or what makes them rattled (scope their Saturn). Compare similarities and differences between the celebrities who embody the typical Cancer sun sign traits and those who seem atypical. Then look up other planets in the horoscope of your favorites, using the charts in this book, to see how other planets influence the horoscope. It's a fun way to get your education in astrology.

Lindsay Wagner (6/22/49)
Meryl Streep (6/22/49)
Tracy Pollan (6/22/62)
Bill Blass (6/22/22)
Klaus-Maria Brandauer (6/22/44)
Kris Kristofferson (6/22/36)
Alfred Kinsey (6/23/1894)
Bryan Brown (6/23/47)
Nancy Allen (6/24/50)
Michelle Lee (6/24/42)
Peter Weller (6/24/47)
George Michael (6/25/63)

Carly Simon (6/25/45)
Pearl S. Buck (6/26/1892)
Peter Lorre (6/26/04)
Chris Isaak (6/26/56)
Isabelle Adjani (6/27/55)
Ross Perot (6/27/30)
John Cusack (6/28/66)
Mel Brooks (6/28/26)
Kathy Bates (6/28/48)
Mary Stuart Masterson (6/28/66)
Pat Morita (6/28/32)
Ruth Warrick (6/29/15)
Gilda Radner (6/29/46)
Lena Horne (6/30/17)
Mike Tyson (6/30/66)
Liv Tyler (7/1/77)
Pamela Anderson Lee (7/1/67)
Princess Diana (7/1/61)
Olivia de Havilland (7/1/16)
Farley Granger (7/1/25)
Estée Lauder (7/1/08)
Deborah Harry (7/1/45)
Leslie Caron (7/1/31)
Dan Aykroyd (7/1/52)
Karen Black (7/1/42)
Charles Laughton (7/1/1899)
Genevieve Bujold (7/1/42)
Richard Perry (7/2/37)
Imelda Marcos (7/2/31)
Jerry Hall (7/2/56)
Ron Silver (7/2/46)
Betty Buckley (7/3/47)
Tom Cruise (7/3/62)
Aaron Tippin (7/3/58)
Geraldo Rivera (7/3/43)
Montel Williams (7/3/56)
Louis Armstrong (7/4/1900)
P. T. Barnum (7/5/1810)

Ned Beatty (7/6/37)
Sylvester Stallone (7/6/46)
Merv Griffin (7/6/25)
Nancy Reagan (7/6/21)
Ringo Starr (7/7/40)
Michelle Kwan (7/7/80)
Pierre Cardin (7/7/22)
Angelica Huston (7/8/51)
Kevin Bacon (7/8/58)
Tom Hanks (7/9/56)
Kelly McGillis (7/9/57)
Brian Dennehy (7/9/39)
Jimmy Smits (7/9/55)
O. J. Simpson (7/9/49)
John Tesh (7/9/52)
Courtney Love (7/9/65)
David Brinkley (7/10/20)
Max Von Sydow (7/10/29)
Giorgio Armani (7/11/34)
Tab Hunter (7/11/31)
Sela Ward (7/11/56)
Richie Sambora (7/11/59)
Bill Cosby (7/12/37)
Harrison Ford (7/12/42)
Richard Simmons (7/12/48)
Rolonda Watts (7/12/59)
Milton Berle (7/12/08)
Kristi Yamaguchi (7/12/71)
Cheryl Ladd (7/12/51)
Patrick Stewart (7/13/40)
Harry Dean Stanton (7/14/26)
Polly Bergen (7/14/30)
Ingmar Bergman (7/14/18)
Linda Ronstadt (7/15/46)
Brigitte Neilsen (7/15/63)
Jan-Michel Vincent (7/15/44)
Phoebe Cates (7/16/63)
Ruben Blades (7/16/48)

Ginger Rogers (7/16/11)
Corey Feldman (7/16/71)
Camilla Parker Bowles (7/17/47)
David Hasselhoff (7/17/52)
Lucie Arnaz (7/17/51)
Art Linkletter (7/17/12)
Donald Sutherland (7/17/35)
Diahann Carroll (7/17/35)
Hume Cronyn (7/18/11)
John Glenn (7/18/21)
Red Skelton (7/18/13)
James Brolin (7/18/40)
Audrey Landers (7/18/59)
Nelson Mandela (7/18/18)
Pat Hingle (7/19/24)
Diana Rigg (7/20/38)
Donna Dixon (7/20/57)
Robin Williams (7/21/52)
Alex Trebek (7/22/40)
Don Henley (7/22/47)
Danny Glover (7/22/47)

CHAPTER 16

Cancer Pairs—How You Get Along with Every Other Sign

Before you commit or sign on the dotted line, check this tip list of pluses and minuses of every combination, so you'll know what to expect before you leap into love (or any other relationship).

Cancer/Aries

PLUSES:
Cancer will give Aries hero worship and nurturing, plus shrewd business sense and a solid home base to operate from. Aries gives Cancer romance and enthusiasm—positive energy and courage to coax out the cautious crab.

MINUSES:
Aries detests complaining or whining, so you'll have to suffer in silence. Sulking and possessive behavior are other Aries turnoffs. You may balk when Aries pushes, finding their behavior too insensitive and self-centered for delicate Cancerian feelings or stomach to bear.

Cancer/Taurus

PLUSES:
In theory, this should be one of the best combinations. Taurus can't get too much affection and TLC, which Cancer provides. And Taurus protects Cancer from the cold world, with solid secure assets. Both are home-loving, emotional, and sensual.

MINUSES:
Cancer's dark moods plus Taurus's stubbornness could create some muddy moments. Both partners should look for constructive ways to let off steam, rather than brood and sulk over grievances.

Cancer/Gemini

PLUSES:
This is a very public pair with charisma to spare. Gemini charm sets off Cancer's poise with the perfect light touch. Cancer adds warmth and emotional appeal to Gemini. You can go places together.

MINUSES:
It's not easy for Gemini to deliver the emotional intimacy Cancer demands. There are too many other exciting options. Cancer's possessiveness vs. Gemini's restlessness could sink this one if you don't have strong mutual interests or projects.

Cancer/Cancer

PLUSES:
Ideally, here is someone who understands your moods, gives you the mothering care you crave, and protects

you from the cold cruel world. Your home can be a loving sanctuary for your extended family and a secure nest for each other.

MINUSES:
You both take slights so personally that disagreements can easily get blown out of proportion. And if you are both in a down mood at the same time, your relationship can self-destruct. You'll need some outside activities for balance and time away from each other to regain perspective. Creative expression can save the day by providing an outlet for your emotions.

Cancer/Leo

PLUSES:
These neighboring signs come through for each other like good buddies. Cancer gives Leo total attention, backup support, and the VIP treatment the Lion craves. Here is someone who won't fight for the spotlight. Leo gives you confidence, and this sign's positive mental outlook is good medicine for your moods.

MINUSES:
Cancer's blue moods and tendency to cling tenaciously can weigh Leo down, while Leo can steamroll sensitive Cancer feelings with high-handed behavior.

Cancer/Virgo

PLUSES:
You two vulnerable signs protect and nurture each other. Moody Cancer needs Virgo to refine and focus emotions creatively. Virgo gives Cancer protective care and valuable insight. Cancer's charming romantic

tenderness nurtures the shy side of Virgo. You'll have good communication on a practical level, respecting each other's shrewd financial acumen.

MINUSES:
Cancer's extreme self-protection could arouse Virgo's suspicion. Why must you be so secretive? Virgo's protectiveness could become smothering, making Cancer overly dependent. Virgo must learn to offer suggestions instead of criticism, to coddle your feelings at all times.

Cancer/Libra

PLUSES:
You'll bring out each other's creativity, as Cancer sensitivity merges with Libra's balanced aesthetic sense. Libra's innate sense of harmony could create a serene, elegant atmosphere where Cancer flourishes. You'll create an especially beautiful and welcoming home together.

MINUSES:
Libra's detachment could be mistaken for rejection by Cancer, while Cancer's hypersensitivity could throw Libra's scales off-balance. Emotions—and emotional confrontations—are territories Libra avoids, so Cancer may look elsewhere for sympathy and nurturing.

Cancer/Scorpio

PLUSES:
Cancer actually enjoys Scorpio's intensity and possessiveness—it shows how much they care! And like Prince Charles and Diana (or Camilla Parker

Bowles), this pair cares deeply about those they love. Strong emotions are a great bond which can survive heavy storms.

MINUSES:
Scorpio's mysterious melancholy moods can leave Cancer feeling isolated and insecure. And the more Cancer clings, the more Scorpio withdraws. Outside interests can lighten the mood—or provide a means of escape.

Cancer/Sagittarius

PLUSES:
Sagittarius gets a sensual partner who will keep the home fires burning and the coffers full, while Cancer gets a strong dose of optimism that could banish the blues. Sagittarius's carefree, outgoing, outdoor lifestyle expands Cancer's sometimes narrow point of view and gets you physically active.

MINUSES:
This joyride could reach a dead end when Sagittarius shows little sympathy for Cancer's need for mothering or runs roughshod over sensitive feelings. Cancer could withdraw into a protective shell or use claws when Sagittarius exercises a free hand with the budget.

Cancer/Capricorn

PLUSES:
A serious sense of duty, family pride, and a basically traditional outlook bring you together. The zodiac mother (Cancer) and father (Capricorn) establish a strong home base. Cancer's tender devotion could

bring out Capricorn's earthy sensual side. This couple gets closer over the years.

MINUSES:
Melancholy moods could muddy this picture. Develop a strategy for coping if depression hits. Capricorn is a lone wolf who may isolate himself emotionally, or withdraw into work, or take on an overload of duties. Cancer could look elsewhere for comfort and consolation.

Cancer/Aquarius

PLUSES:
The clue to success for this one-of-a-kind couple is basic ideals. If you two share goals and values, there is no limit to how far you can go. Cancer is turned on by the security of a high position and offers Aquarius strong support and caring qualities that touch everyone's heart, the perfect counterpoint to Aquarius charisma. Former President Ronald Reagan and his wife, Nancy, are a case in point.

MINUSES:
Cancers are at their best one-on-one, while Aquarians love a crowd. Cancers have to learn to share their love with many—Aquarians have to learn to show warmth and emotion, rather than turn off Cancer moods.

Cancer/Pisces

PLUSES:
You both love to swim in emotional waters, where your communication flows easily. Cancer's protective attention and support help Pisces gain confidence and direction. Pisces gives Cancer dreamy romance and

creative inspiration. A very meaningful relationship develops over time.

MINUSES:
You two emotionally vulnerable signs know where the soft spots are and, therefore, can really hurt each other. Pisces has a way of slipping through clingy Cancer's clutches, possibly to "dry out" after too much emotion. Learn to give each other space and find creative projects to diffuse negative moods and give you a sense of direction.

CHAPTER 17

Astrological Outlook for Cancer in 2002

If single, you are likely to marry this year. If married, you get more of the facts of life; the glow might be off your relationship. However, it is also likely that you rediscover your mate in a mental, emotional, and sexual way.

You could go into business for yourself. You will have more responsibility and pressure, but you will be up to it. With Saturn in your twelfth house, you can't seem to put your finger on where the trouble is. More and more people rely upon you, however, and you become sort of a paragon.

During September, it will be an all-out fight between those who want to dethrone you and you holding on to gains and to your own creations. During January, the burden is lifted, and you'll be glad to give up at least part of your responsibilities. During February, you make a fresh start and you make room for a new love.

Throughout the year, Capricorn and other Cancer-born natives will play dominant roles.

In matters of speculation, stick with these numbers—8, 2, 5.

During April, social activities accelerate.

With Capricorn, it is a matter of no more playing,

let's get down to business, if you don't know what to do, get off the pot. With Capricorn, a marriage figures prominently.

With another Cancer, you figure out ways to enjoy yourself, without carelessly losing what you have earned.

A Taurus will be part of your scenario, relating to your eleventh house. When things are blackest, when you feel low down, Taurus lifts your spirits.

Throughout this year, you let people know you mean business and you have a business of your own. Passionate lovemaking will be part of this scenario.

Turn the pages for your daily indications, sort of your "diary in advance." It will amaze you, how much you learn, how far ahead of your competitors you will be as a result.

CHAPTER 18

Eighteen Months of Day-by-Day Predictions—July 2001 to December 2002

JULY 2001

Sunday, July 1 (Moon in Scorpio to Sagittarius 11:13 p.m.)   Plan ahead for the holiday. Complete your invitation list or, at the very least, find out where you will be for the celebration. Attention revolves around familiar ground, your own home, making peace with a relative who misunderstood statements. Libra is involved.

Monday, July 2 (Moon in Sagittarius)   Define terms, outline boundaries, arrange with one or two young persons to coordinate the reading of the Declaration of Independence. Make the holiday more meaningful by putting forth what it means and ultimately meant to the entire world.

Tuesday, July 3 (Moon in Sagittarius)   Your earning power increases, but so do your responsibilities. Along with greater financial rewards, there is an intensified romantic relationship. If single, it might not last too long, so be discriminating, willing to love and be loved. Choose quality in products and people. Capricorn is in this picture.

Wednesday, July 4 (Moon in Sagittarius to Capricorn 8:21 a.m.) The Sagittarian moon relates to preparations, putting things in working order, including clocks, watches, and keys. Take proper precautions against injuries from firecrackers. A close friend or relative makes a long-distance call to wish you a "Happy Fourth!"

Thursday, July 5—Lunar Eclipse (Moon in Capricorn) There's a full moon, lunar eclipse in Capricorn today. Survey the situation, which is not too messy considering the holiday celebration. Make a fresh start, participate in a new project. Avoid an arrogant person who seems to think you are his or her possession. Leo and Aquarius are involved.

Friday, July 6 (Moon in Capricorn to Aquarius 7:32 p.m.) Steer clear of a get-rich-quick scheme. You receive proposals—business, career, marriage. You'll breathe deeply, saying to yourself, "I did not expect to enjoy such a meaningful Fourth!" A close friend asserts, "I wouldn't think of spending the Fourth without you!"

Saturday, July 7 (Moon in Aquarius) There could be a hot time in the old town tonight—Saturday night live! Forces tend to be scattered, so get your thoughts in order, focus on entertainment, fulfilling your creative urge. Gemini and Sagittarius figure in this scenario. Lucky lottery: 1, 6, 12, 14, 30, 35.

Sunday, July 8 (Moon in Aquarius) You'll be fascinated by touches of the occult in well-known operas, presidential declarations, implications of the occult in the signing of the Declaration of Independence. For you personally, doors previously shut tight will finally respond to locks recently repaired.

Monday, July 9 (Moon in Aquarius to Pisces 8:04 a.m.) Within 24 hours, the moon will be in your ninth house. Translated from astrological lingo, this means you will get serious about romance, travel, philosophy, the history of religions. Get your thoughts on paper, communicate with a relative in a distant city who always encouraged you to write.

Tuesday, July 10 (Moon in Pisces) Creativity abounds in your home. People become critics in connection with literature and motion pictures. Enjoy and encourage this atmosphere. The Venus keynote promotes activities in connection with the fine arts, motion pictures, materials featuring silks.

Wednesday, July 11 (Moon in Pisces to Aries 8:34 p.m.) Check with your travel agent about a proposed journey. Avoid self-deception. See people, places, and relationships in a realistic light. You'll be encouraged to read your story aloud—don't be overly shy. Step right up and say, "Get ready, fasten your seat belts, here I come!"

Thursday, July 12 (Moon in Aries) You'll be musing, "I had such a good time under this cycle that I am sorry to leave it!" Leave it you will, within 24 hours. Focus on a power play, promotion, production, the realization that another Cancer is on your side and will help your cause. Your lucky number is 8.

Friday, July 13 (Moon in Aries) You'll muse, "I don't care what the date is. I am not going to be unlucky!" The Aries moon relates to your career, fulfillment of ambitions, extra responsibility, being attractive to persons in high places. Long repressed feelings are released. Instead of making others angry, they express admiration for your frankness.

Saturday, July 14 (Moon in Aries to Taurus 7:12 a.m.) Stress independence, original thinking, the willingness to concede that some work requires revision. A dynamic Aries declares, "Let's go out and see what the world looks like tonight." An Aquarian also plays a role. Lucky lottery: 1, 3, 9, 30, 47, 50.

Sunday, July 15 (Moon in Taurus) Many of your desires, including good fortune for your family, will be fulfilled. The moon in your eleventh house in Taurus adds up to luck in finance and romance. You won't break any speed records, but you will gain objectives, much to the delight of friends and family.

Monday, July 16 (Moon in Taurus to Gemini 2:23 p.m.) A lively Monday! The Jupiter keynote equates to luck, entertainment, ability to stretch your horizons to include literature, publishing, and romance. You'll be happier as a result. Gemini and Sagittarius are in the picture, and have these letters or initials in their names—C, L, U.

Tuesday, July 17 (Moon in Gemini)) Be careful that you don't lock yourself out. Put valuables in a safe place. The spotlight is on shopping, gaining freedom in thought and action. You finally are regarded as the "main event." Don't be shy about raising your price.

Wednesday, July 18 (Moon in Gemini to Cancer 5:55 p.m.) A secret meeting concludes that you are most valuable and that you deserve a raise in pay. Focus on hospitals, institutions, theater, participation in political-charitable campaigns. Gemini, Virgo, and Sagittarius are in this picture, and have these letters in their names: E, N, W. Your lucky number is 5.

Thursday, July 19 (Moon in Cancer) Go slow and stay even-tempered if possible. The spotlight is on your home environment, beautifying your surroundings, a better understanding of music, literature, modern and classical compositions. Taurus and Libra will play fascinating roles.

Friday, July 20 (Moon in Cancer to Leo 6:42 p.m.) The new moon in your sign equates to judgment, intuition, success in taking the initiative. During this cycle, you exude personal magnetism, an aura of sensuality and sex appeal. Your credo could be, "All's fair in love and war!" Pisces is represented.

Saturday, July 21 (Moon in Leo) What failed once will now succeed. Capricorn and Leo are very much involved. Funding will be made available, so use your remarkable imagination to create a process that brings forth quality goods. On this Saturday, play these lucky numbers: 7, 8, 12, 14, 18, 23.

Sunday, July 22 (Moon in Leo to Virgo 6:28 p.m.) Luck with money is featured. The Leo moon relates to locating lost articles, successful investments, good fortune in finance and romance. Investing in entertainment stock could be profitable. Strive for universal appeal; develop a market for your products overseas.

Monday, July 23 (Moon in Virgo) On this Monday, you are presented with a shiny product that could lack solidity. Leo and Aquarius will figure prominently, and have these letters or initials in their names: A, S, J. Stress showmanship and color coordination; prepare a list of questions to ask authorities.

Tuesday, July 24 (Moon in Virgo to Libra 7:07 p.m.) The Virgo moon relates to traffic on the highways, fun and games, a night of love and laughter. Someone who previously was indifferent could now be at your feet. Another Cancer plays an interesting role. Your marital status will figure prominently.

Wednesday, July 25 (Moon in Libra)　　The moon position emphasizes design, color coordination, music, an appreciation for the arts. It might be as if you're awakening from a long sleep. Suddenly, the tones are sharp and clear. Social activities are part of this scenario; you'll be taking note of appearance and weight. Your lucky number is 3.

Thursday, July 26 (Moon in Libra to Scorpio 10:17 p.m.)　　On this Thursday, you will be asked to criticize art objects or luxury items. You might protest, "I am no expert!" Taurus, Leo, and Scorpio play outstanding roles, and could have these letters or initials in their names: D, M, V.

Friday, July 27 (Moon in Scorpio)　　Within 24 hours, the transitting moon will be in Scorpio, your fifth house of creativity, style, and challenge. For today, take note of last night's dream. With proper interpretation, the dream will prove prophetic. Gemini plays a fascinating role.

Saturday, July 28 (Moon in Scorpio to Sagittarius 4:44 a.m.)　　Attention revolves around your home, family, plans for a lively Saturday night. "I know astrology says I am a homebody. Most of the time I am, but tonight, I would like to kick up my heels!" Focus on music, drama, a gift that adds to your wardrobe. Your lucky number is 6.

Sunday, July 29 (Moon in Sagittarius)　　On this Sunday, there will be much study, talk about theology—the religions of the world. Perfect techniques, streamline procedures, find out where you stand in a special relationship—and what to do about it. Pisces and Virgo are in the picture.

Monday, July 30 (Moon in Sagittarius)   On this Monday, you find you have more responsibility than you originally anticipated. Let go of preconceived notions, accept challenges, and be willing to admit you very well might be in love. Capricorn and another Cancer figure in today's dynamic scenario.

Tuesday, July 31 (Moon in Sagittarius to Capricorn 2:16 p.m.)   A break from the past is imminent. A brief mental review of what has taken place will help you face the music of the future. You can complete an onerous task. Get unpleasantness over with, and you will then be happy. Aries and Libra will play roles, and have these letters or initials in their names: I and R.

AUGUST 2001

Wednesday, August 1 (Moon in Capricorn)   There's inferior work by a computer operator, so insist on verification of your bank account. Let it be known that you intend to check the facts and figures! The spotlight is on entertainment, diversity, humor, the ability to retrace your steps and catch an original error. Pisces is involved.

Thursday, August 2 (Moon in Capricorn)   A family member helps track down a culprit who deliberately jammed your computer. Focus on security, home, fire protection, assurance aimed at letting people know that you have their best interests at heart. An insurance policy requires review—you are acting in a responsible way.

Friday, August 3 (Moon in Capricorn to Aquarius 1:52 a.m.) What had been a burden will be removed. You'll be asking yourself, "What took me so long to get rid of this situation?" Highlight humor, versatility, a willingness to provide an incentive for people to perform their duties. An Aries figures prominently.

Saturday, August 4 (Moon in Aquarius) What a Saturday! The full moon in Aquarius relates to partnership, cooperative efforts, public appearances, your marital status. Make a fresh start, highlight independence, courage, your pioneering spirit. A new love is on the horizon. Celebrate tonight with a gourmet dinner.

Sunday, August 5 (Moon in Aquarius to Pisces 2:29 p.m.) The lunar position accents trips, visits, a relative who wants to make peace by admitting, "It was my error, and now I confess it!" It's catch-up time! Recently, you fell behind. Now catch up, plug the loopholes. A Capricorn is in a preaching mood.

Monday, August 6 (Moon in Pisces) Listen to statements but don't believe everything you hear. People consult you about fashion and international affairs. Be open to creative questions about a theatrical performance you could witness tonight. A Sagittarian will play a significant role.

Tuesday, August 7 (Moon in Pisces) A mystery is solved. What was missing will once again appear, and this in itself will provide the answers to questions. A clock that had been repaired is again in working order. Place valuables under lock and key. Taurus and Scorpio play exciting roles.

Wednesday, August 8 (Moon in Pisces to Aries 3:03 a.m.) You are given the green light for original work. Breathe an air of creative freedom. The spotlight is on a change of scene, variety, plans for a trip involving relatives. Gemini, Virgo, and Sagittarius play outstanding roles. Lucky lottery: 4, 5, 7, 8, 12, 30.

Thursday, August 9 (Moon in Aries)   Highlight diplomacy; check the budget for a needed domestic adjustment that could include furniture, art, luxury items. The focus is also on music, your ability to get into your own rhythm and to dance to your own tune. Aries and Libra will play sensational roles.

Friday, August 10 (Moon in Aries to Taurus 2:21 p.m.)   Define terms; engage in a clash of ideas with Aries. Check legal rights and permissions. Yet another fire sign, Sagittarius, will join in a dispute and the three of you—Cancer versus two fire signs—will make a big splash. Have luck with number 7.

Saturday, August 11 (Moon in Taurus)   A power play day! The Taurus moon equates to your ability to win friends and influence people. The Saturn numerical cycle emphasizes promotion, production, discipline, being on time. A Capricorn declares, "This is my cup of tea—I will not let myself or anyone else down."

Sunday, August 12 (Moon in Taurus to Gemini 10:56 p.m.)   Let go of preconceived notions, extricate yourself from an unsavory situation. A love relationship might have run its course. You are being taken for granted. A journey overseas is a distinct possibility for the purpose of promoting your product or talent.

Monday, August 13 (Moon in Gemini)   Within 24 hours, the moon will be in Gemini; that twelfth house influence equates to secret meetings, institutions, and possibly an illicit love affair. Discretion is the order

196

of the day, so overcome a temptation to blurt out the facts. Leo will play a dramatic role.

Tuesday, August 14 (Moon in Gemini)   Focus on love, food, and serious consideration of marriage. The moon is moving toward your higher cycle. Hang on. Your hand is just about to be raised in victory. The moon will be in your sign shortly. In the meantime, your vitality returns. You could be in the midst of a courtship.

Wednesday, August 15 (Moon in Gemini to Cancer 3:53 a.m.)   For racing luck at all tracks: post position special—number 5 p.p. in the seventh race. Pick six: 5, 5, 1, 8, 3, 4. Watch for these letters or initials in the names of potential winning horses or jockeys: C, L, U. Hot daily doubles: 5 and 5, 3 and 3, 1 and 4. A lucky Sagittarian jockey wins in a photo finish.

Thursday, August 16 (Moon in Cancer)   The moon finally has reached your sign. Your judgment and intuitive intellect will prove accurate. During this cycle, you exude personal magnetism, an aura of sensuality and sex appeal. A young person in a kind of whine asks for more money, declaring, "You give everybody else things and, when I ask for more money, you balk!"

Friday, August 17 (Moon in Cancer to Leo 5:24 a.m.)   Get ready for change, travel, a variety of experiences and sensations. Today is a precursor to what will be a lively weekend. Emerge from your emotional shell, let others know exactly where you stand, politically and otherwise. Written material is accepted!

Saturday, August 18 (Moon in Leo)   The financial picture is bright. A gift is received that adds to the beauty of your abode. Silverware is featured. This could be a hint for an invitation to dinner. A domestic adjustment is featured. Family members will dispute the division of profits or property. Lucky lottery: 6, 12, 18, 24, 31, 42.

Sunday, August 19 (Moon in Leo to Virgo 4:52 a.m.) The new moon in your money house indicates, like a bolt out of the blue, that the necessary funding will be available. Beware of self-deception. See people, situations, and relationships as they are, and not merely as you wish they might be. Get promises relating to money in writing.

Monday, August 20 (Moon in Virgo) Be open to criticism. Show that you are not ultrasensitive. Define meanings, check real estate holdings, perfect techniques, and streamline procedures. People expect you to organize, to get your files in order, to work overtime so that a project can be completed and show a profit.

Tuesday, August 21 (Moon in Virgo to Libra 4:18 a.m.) You exude aura of universal appeal. Learn more about language. Communicate with someone representing your interests overseas. The Virgo moon, plus the Mars keynote, means you are now capable of making a fiery speech. Aries, Libra, and Taurus are heavily involved.

Wednesday, August 22 (Moon in Libra) A family member hints, "I want very much to be on my own. I must see if I can make it, if I depend solely on myself." Stress innovative procedures; make a fresh start; wipe your slate clean of preconceived notions. Lucky lottery: 1, 4, 11, 19, 22, 33.

Thursday, August 23 (Moon in Libra to Scorpio 5:49 a.m.) What a Thursday! Attention revolves around basic values, property, participation in an enterprising project that requires imagination, derring-do. Today's emphasis stresses the need to make up your mind about a partnership or your marital status.

Friday, August 24 (Moon in Scorpio) Highlight diversity, versatility, and intellectual curiosity. You'll be involved in a publishing project, even if on the edge of it. Maintain your emotional equilibrium—and sense of humor. Luck rides with you. Pay close attention to racing selections; you're due for a big score.

Saturday, August 25 (Moon in Scorpio to Sagittarius 10:59 a.m.) Expect postponement. Do not equate delay with defeat. A missing piece of machinery you sent for two months ago is finally being dispatched. It is time to rebuild on a more solid structure. Leo and Scorpio figure in today's dynamic scenario.

Sunday, August 26 (Moon in Sagittarius) Regard these numbers as lucky for you: 5, 9, 12. The Sagittarian moon tells of a need for a health checkup. A bruise on the right side of your right eye needs attention. Settle a dispute with a family member, which relates to money and music. Gemini is represented.

Monday, August 27 (Moon in Sagittarius to Capricorn 8:01 p.m.) Trying to fix a traffic ticket would be an error. Go slow, be diplomatic, and accept a friendly reprimand in the spirit in which it is given. A domestic adjustment relates to where you live, beautifying your surroundings, your marital status. Libra urges, "Let's go!"

Tuesday, August 28 (Moon in Capricorn) Play the waiting game. Within 24 hours, you'll be offered a legal agreement. Obtain a hint about public relations—you are going places, but are not too sure of where. Meditation will help. Heed your inner voice. Pisces and Virgo play exciting roles.

Wednesday, August 29 (Moon in Capricorn)   For racing luck at all tracks: post position special—number 8 p.p. in the ninth race. Pick six: 4, 3, 8, 1, 2, 7. Watch for these letters or initials in the names of potential winning horses or jockeys: H, Q, Z. Hot daily doubles: 4 and 3, 7 and 8, 6 and 2. Favorites win, long shots are out of the money.

Thursday, August 30 (Moon in Capricorn to Aquarius 7:47 a.m.)   Complete a project; take charge: let others know: "There are two ways to do things: the right way and my way!" Some will complain, others might have a good laugh, but most will follow your orders to the T. Aries will play a stunning role.

Friday, August 31 (Moon in Aquarius)   Make a fresh start in a new direction. Your energy level is up again. Display derring-do. Wear bright colors and make personal appearances. A different kind of love is on the horizon. Leo and Aquarius will play unusual roles, and have these letters or initials in their names: A, S, J.

SEPTEMBER 2001

Saturday, September 1 (Moon in Aquarius to Pisces 8:31 p.m.)   A complete change of routine is due today. You'll be delving into waters generally identified as occult. The Aquarian moon represents your eighth house and blends with your Saturn keynote and tonight finds you defending subjects mostly vilified. Stick with number 8!

Sunday, September 2 (Moon in Pisces)   On this Sunday, there is a full moon in Pisces, in your ninth house, which represents theology, travel, striving to understand the viewpoints of people who might be hungry and homeless. Stress universality; look beyond the immediate; break free from an unsavory situation.

Monday, September 3 (Moon in Pisces)   On this Monday, get ready for a new assignment, a fresh start in a different direction, the possibility of a different kind of love. The light shines in areas previously dark. Leo and Aquarius play long-delayed roles. The message will be clear by tonight.

Tuesday, September 4 (Moon in Pisces to Aries 8:57 a.m.)   On this Tuesday, it will be necessary to keep your valuables under lock and key. Changing the lock might not be a bad idea! A family member confides a desperate situation. Capricorn and another Cancer play leading roles, and could have these initials in their names: B, K, T.

Wednesday, September 5 (Moon in Aries)   Focus on direction, motivation, the need to play a leading role. Steer clear of someone who refuses to advocate versatility, diversity, exploration, and the excitement of discovery. Gemini and Sagittarius are in this picture, and have these letters in their names: C, L, U. Your lucky number is 3.

Thursday, September 6 (Moon in Aries to Taurus 8:16 p.m.)   The emphasis is on whether or not you will be made privy to secrets relating to high finance. Break free from foolish restrictions; maintain creative control. The Aries moon continues to equate to success, freedom, motivation, and direction. Scorpio is involved.

Friday, September 7 (Moon in Taurus)   Within 24 hours, many of your fondest hopes and wishes could be fulfilled. Additional written material is required. Write in your own style, avoid instructions or orders from someone who is hopelessly old fashioned. Virgo plays a top role.

Saturday, September 8 (Moon in Taurus)   On this Saturday, wishes involve the appearance of your home, furniture, luxury items, and art objects. Many of your wishes will be fulfilled. You will experience good fortune in matters of finance and romance. The financial picture shows marked improvement. Lucky lottery: 5, 11, 12, 13, 22, 50.

Sunday, September 9 (Moon in Taurus to Gemini 5:40 a.m.)   You will benefit from meditation. You will locate missing money; you could reunite with former lover or spouse. Because of an amazing series of coincidences, what was taken from you will be returned. When you relate this, people will be amazed. Pisces is represented.

Monday, September 10 (Moon in Gemini)   The emphasis is on responsibility, the pressure of meeting and beating a deadline. An older person decides, "I am the first to admit that we need new blood around here!" A love relationship is exciting, energizing, relates to a past investment that is finally showing life.

Tuesday, September 11 (Moon in Gemini to Cancer 12:07 p.m.)   Don't be caught napping in connection with new issues. Be familiar with foreign exchange rates. Doors open to adventure, investment, a love relationship that could be getting too hot not to cool down. Wear shades of red; make personal appearances.

Wednesday, September 12 (Moon in Cancer)   For racing luck at all tracks: post position special—number 7 p.p. in the first race. Pick six: 7, 3, 4, 8, 2, 1. Look for these letters or initials in the names of potential winning horses or jockeys: A, S, J. Hot daily doubles: 7 and 3, 1 and 1, 6 and 4. Leo jockeys win with speed horses, pay long-shot prices.

Thursday, September 13 (Moon in Cancer to Leo 3:14 p.m.) Your cycle is high, so take the initiative and designate where the action will be. The moon in your sign represents a time when ideas click, when you exude an aura of personal magnetism, sensuality, and sex appeal. Capricorn and another Cancer play exciting roles, and have these letters or initials in their names: B, K, T.

Friday, September 14 (Moon in Leo) An opportunity exists to show you are human enough to laugh at your own mistakes and foibles. People find you a marvelous companion, actually compete to see who will have the privilege of wining and dining you. Show appreciation, without being obsequious.

Saturday, September 15 (Moon in Leo to Virgo 3:38 p.m.) The Leo moon relates to money, payments, collections, an opportunity to transform what was worthless into "pure gold." Review articles; do research about early alchemy. You might be surprised to learn that scientists such as Sir Isaac Newton devoted much time to the study, not only of astrology, but also of alchemy.

Sunday, September 16 (Moon in Virgo) A relative provides a tip on a game of chance; it's worth looking into and taking a chance. That relative, a Virgo often grumpy, will turn out to be a delight this time. The spotlight is on the written word, personal magnetism, sex appeal. Have luck with number 5.

Monday, September 17 (Moon in Virgo to Libra 2:59 p.m.)   Once again, a Virgo will play an important role, and will have these letters or initials in their name: E, N, W. The emphasis is on music, entertainment, investment in a high-brow product. A former teacher arrives who wasn't invited; you apparently forgot.

Tuesday, September 18 (Moon in Libra)   Everything seems to be emphasized today. This applies to the good and the bad. Spotlight is on where you live, general appearances, a willingness to delve deep in order to investigate the truth or falsity of sensational claims. A Pisces figures prominently.

Wednesday, September 19 (Moon in Libra to Scorpio 3:27 p.m.)   On this Wednesday, you can win money by sticking with number 8. Capricorn and another Cancer play memorable roles, and will have these letters or initials in their names: H, Q, Z. Property value varies. A Libra makes a serious offer that should be considered.

Thursday, September 20 (Moon in Scorpio)   Finish what you start; show enthusiasm in the promotion of your product, talent. Communicate with your overseas representative. The world will look different. You are in love, so emotions dominate. All of this applies, no matter what your chronological age.

Friday, September 21 (Moon in Scorpio to Sagittarius 7:02 p.m.)   Imprint your style, refuse to be haunted by the past, display initiative and originality. Avoid heavy lifting. If someone breaks your heart, let it be—you cannot force love. Participate in a pioneering project. Before you know it, the opportunity for new love will happen.

Saturday, September 22 (Moon in Sagittarius)   Today the emphasis is on a spousal relationship. A mate decides, "I am not getting all the attention I am entitled to, so I might be leaving soon!" Tonight, you'll experience a "Saturday night live!" A reunion with a former lover could result in an awkward situation.

Sunday, September 23 (Moon in Sagittarius)   A pleasant Sunday, especially if travel is involved. You receive an excellent health report, along with dietary suggestions, not necessarily restrictive. Gemini and Sagittarius play outstanding roles, and could have these letters or initials in their names: C, L, U.

Monday, September 24 (Moon in Sagittarius to Capricorn 2:48 a.m.)   An escape route is sought. When you ask yourself, "What am I escaping from?" there is no real answer. Keep a steady pace and emotional equilibrium. If people comment on the vacant look in your eyes, respond, "I am just waking up to who I am and what to do about it."

Tuesday, September 25 (Moon in Capricorn)   You realize tonight that you have successfully met a challenge. Legal clearance will be obtained for initiating a project. Gemini, Virgo, and Sagittarius will play roles, and will engage in a clash of ideas. Ultimately, your word will be the final word. Have luck with number 5.

Wednesday, September 26 (Moon in Capricorn to Aquarius 2:04 p.m.)   Focus on peace and harmony. This applies especially to your domestic life. Taurus, Libra, and Scorpio figure in today's dramatic scenario, and could have these letters or initials in their names: F, O, X. Push that third helping away from the table. Save your appetite for another, more appropriate time.

Thursday, September 27 (Moon in Aquarius) You'll find many things funny. Some discoveries might reveal that the laugh is bitter, however. Romance creates rivalry. Remember the saying, "All's fair in love and war!" Pisces and Virgo figure in today's dynamic scenario, and have these initials in their names: G, P, Y.

Friday, September 28 (Moon in Aquarius) On this Friday, you could be attending a secret initiation for people seeking to become members of a unique organization. Remember the adage, "Don't judge lest you be judged!" Capricorn and another Cancer will play memorable roles.

Saturday, September 29 (Moon in Aquarius to Pisces 2:49 a.m.) Today, you will be concerned with food, entertainment, visiting firemen. You might be amused, but also confused. This is a most unusual day. You may be tired, but you won't want to miss a thing! Lucky lottery: 1, 4, 29, 30, 37, 38.

Sunday, September 30 (Moon in Pisces) Break free from inhibitions; make a fresh start in a different direction. Wear attractive colors, including sea green. You will meet a dynamic Leo who states, "You are big time; you belong in the big leagues. I could fall in love with you in a minute!"

OCTOBER 2001

Monday, October 1 (Moon in Pisces to Aries 3:06 p.m.) Accept the opportunity to travel. A change of scene would be most beneficial. Release yourself from an obligation that was foolish for you to accept in the first place. Aries and Libra play meaningful roles, have these letters or initials in their names: I and R.

Tuesday, October 2 (Moon in Aries)   The full moon in Aries relates to your career. Handle with care a relationship that starts at work and gets out of hand. Wear bright colors and explain to one and all, "I feel I might be in love and don't know what to do about it!" Leo is in this picture.

Wednesday, October 3 (Moon in Aries)   An Aries would like to be your friend. Seize the moment! The Aries in your life is climbing up the ladder—swiftly. Today's scenario features food, style, rhythm, affection, settling a dispute with a loved one. Have luck with number 2.

Thursday, October 4 (Moon in Aries to Taurus 1:59 a.m.)   Avoid scattering your forces. Don't attempt to please everyone—that is the sure road to madness. The element of luck rides with you. Blend humor with an ability to pick winners. At the racetrack, you'll have good luck with number 3 post position.

Friday, October 5 (Moon in Taurus)   The Taurus moon equates to the fulfillment of hopes, desires, and sexual attraction. Practice a degree of restraint. Know when to say, "Enough is enough!" Dinner tonight consists of steamed lobster. Taurus, Leo, and Scorpio will play magnificent roles.

Saturday, October 6 (Moon in Taurus to Gemini 11:10 a.m.)   Lucky lottery: 2, 5, 12, 20, 37, 50. You win friends and influence people. You receive carloads of affection and compliments. You'll be musing, "I don't know where all of this came from, but I sure do like it!" Virgo plays a role.

Sunday, October 7 (Moon in Gemini)   Regard these numbers as being lucky for you tonight: 5, 30, 47. The spotlight is on art, music, literature, the need to be discreet. A Libra declares, "I have the distinct feeling that you are going to the top and will remain there for some time!"

Monday, October 8 (Moon in Gemini to Cancer 6:18 p.m.)   The Gemini moon relates to secrets, theater, someone who attempts an underhanded play. Your cycle moves up, so be sure you can handle success. You might secretly prefer to be among the losers. Pisces and Virgo play dynamic roles, and have these initials in their names: G, P, Y.

Tuesday, October 9 (Moon in Cancer)   Those who claimed you missed the boat will be embarrassed—tonight you make a vigorous comeback. The moon is in your sign, with a Saturn keynote, so you'll be asked to control the crowd, to explain why entertainment might be cut short. Your lucky number is 8.

Wednesday, October 10 (Moon in Cancer to Leo 10:52 p.m.)   For racing luck at all tracks: post position special—number 8 p.p. in the first race. Pick six: 8, 2, 7, 4, 7, 3. Be alert for these letters or initials in the names of potential winning horses or jockeys: I and R. Hot daily doubles: 8 and 2, 7 and 1, 3 and 6. Aries and Libra jockeys will be in the money, aboard favorites.

Thursday, October 11 (Moon in Leo)   Make a fresh start. You'll be rid of a losing proposition. A love relationship that grew tired will be revitalized. Make personal appearances, wear yellow and gold, and put aside preconceived notions. Leo and Aquarius play outstanding roles. Your lucky number is 1.

Friday, October 12 (Moon in Leo)   You have the best of both worlds today! Highlight showmanship, color coordination, the ability to blend entertainment with education. Caution: Don't ask for more than you can handle! Capricorn and another Cancer play exciting roles, and have these letters in their names: B, K, T.

Saturday, October 13 (Moon in Leo to Virgo 12:56 a.m.) A crisis passed—you had a close call. This Saturday night, express thanks to those who helped you get by a ticklish situation. Gemini and Sagittarius will play intriguing roles, and have these letters or initials in their names: C, L, U. Your lucky number is 3.

Sunday, October 14 (Moon in Virgo) What had been disorderly conduct will finally settle down. This applies to inanimate objects as well as people; you are charged for getting everything in place. Relatives are involved. Don't be inveigled into taking an automobile trip. Say as politely as possible, "You are on your own!"

Monday, October 15 (Moon in Virgo to Libra 1:25 a.m.) The emphasis is on Mercury, the planet of communication. You will be dealing in secret arrangements, hiding places. Do not drive with a license that has expired. Read and write, listen and follow legal instructions. Gemini, Virgo, and Sagittarius will play fascinating roles.

Tuesday, October 16 (Moon in Libra) The new moon in Libra represents a different look in your home. The spotlight is on where you live. You soon will be entertaining very important people. Brush up on exotic recipes—steer away from the ordinary. Taurus, Libra, and Scorpio figure in today's dynamic, mysterious scenario.

Wednesday, October 17 (Moon in Libra to Scorpio 2:02 a.m.) For racing luck at all tracks: post position special—number 7 p.p. in the third race. Pick six:

5, 4, 7, 2, 1, 8. Watch for these letters or initials in the names of potential winning horses or jockeys: G, P, Y. Hot daily doubles: 5 and 4, 6 and 6, 1 and 5. Horses that run well on off-tracks will be in the money.

Thursday, October 18 (Moon in Scorpio) A power play! Grab the leadership position and hold on to it. Focus on romance, creativity, style, and passion. The key is to wake up and live! You'll meet an architect very much impressed with you. Be modest, not obsequious. Capricorn will play a dynamic role.

Friday, October 19 (Moon in Scorpio to Sagittarius 4:46 a.m.) This is the precursor to an exciting weekend! The Scorpio moon equates to children, challenge, change, variety, and sex appeal. People comment, "You really are making the most of this Friday night." Aries and Libra will take leadership roles—like it or lump it!

Saturday, October 20 (Moon in Sagittarius) Do something different! Coworkers or others who share your interest will be active and encouraging. Be prepared for a new love, different challenges, better understanding of colors, those in harmony or otherwise. Leo and Aquarius play dramatic roles. Your lucky number is 1.

Sunday, October 21 (Moon in Sagittarius to Capricorn 11:12 a.m.) Focus on direction, motivation, and family relationships. A health report is perhaps better than you originally anticipated. A minor digestive problem requires attention—don't let it go too far! A gourmet Sunday night dinner will feature another Cancer who likes you.

Monday, October 22 (Moon in Capricorn) Forces are scattered, so be sure you are legally in the right.

The Capricorn moon in your seventh house relates to people who excite your creative juices. You will receive proposals; this includes career, special appearances, and marriage. Your lucky number is 3.

Tuesday, October 23 (Moon in Capricorn to Aquarius 9:26 p.m.)   For racing luck at all tracks: post position special—number 4 p.p. in the fourth race. Pick six: 4, 1, 2, 4, 6, 3. Watch for these letters or initials in the names of potential winning horses or jockeys: D, M, V. Hot daily doubles: 4 and 1, 2 and 2, 3 and 8. Favorites win on slow tracks. A Scorpio apprentice jockey surprises everyone by bringing in a long shot.

Wednesday, October 24 (Moon in Aquarius)   Your interest in the occult surprises your friends and associates. A revelation concerns your income, the financial position of someone close to you, possibly your spouse. Your question: "Where have you been keeping this hidden wealth?" You will be answered with silence. Please be patient!

Thursday, October 25 (Moon in Aquarius)   Attention revolves around decorating, remodeling, making your home a more comfortable, inviting place. Color coordination is important, together with design and architecture. Music is in the picture. You will have to dance—to your own tune. Libra plays a top role.

Friday, October 26 (Moon in Aquarius to Pisces 9:54 a.m.)   Dig deep for information, play the waiting game. Answers required will be provided on the proverbial silver platter. The Neptune keynote means be careful that you don't fool yourself. See people, places, and relationships as they exist, not merely as you wish they might be.

Saturday, October 27 (Moon in Pisces) A power-ful Saturday night! Travel plans are discussed. Also featured will be publishing, photography, history, and a love relationship. The Pisces moon guarantees ro-mance, style, and creative excitement. Capricorn and another Cancer will be featured. Lucky lottery: 1, 15, 25, 26, 30, 48.

Sunday, October 28—Daylight Saving Time Ends (Moon in Pisces to Aries 9:13 p.m.) Spiritual val-ues take precedence. It's important to let go of pre-conceived notions. *Impossible* is an adjective used by fools, so insisted Napoleon. Tonight, you could partici-pate in what has all the appearances of a miracle. An Aries figures prominently.

Monday, October 29 (Moon in Aries) Within 24 hours, your life will change abruptly. You will have more responsibility, the pressure of a deadline, and a rare opportunity to hit the emotional-financial jackpot. A romantic relationship is hot, and could get too hot not to cool down. Your lucky number is 1.

Tuesday, October 30 (Moon in Aries) On this Tuesday, the moon will be in Aries, your tenth house. All of this adds up to leadership, promotion, initiative, the courage of your convictions. A special member of the opposite sex openly declares, "I can hardly keep my hands off you!"

Wednesday, October 31 (Moon in Aries to Taurus 7:46 a.m.) Enjoy a Halloween party, but don't be-lieve everything they tell you. One falsehood could be put forth during a fake séance. Remember, just be-cause fake jewelry exists doesn't mean the real thing is not also available. Bessie Houdini insisted her hus-band did come back!

212

NOVEMBER 2001

Thursday, November 1 (Moon in Taurus)   On this first day of November, with the full moon in Taurus, you feel revitalized. Prepare for some stunning surprises. You win friends and influence people. Financial aid comes from a surprise source. Leo and Aquarius will play fantastic roles, and have these letters in their names: A, S, J.

Friday, November 2 (Moon in Taurus to Gemini 4:11 p.m.)   The Taurus moon relates to your eleventh house; that section of your horoscope tells that you will be fortunate in finance and romance. This can be your lucky day, especially if you stick with number 2. Capricorn and another Cancer play top roles.

Saturday, November 3 (Moon in Gemini)   With the Gemini moon and Jupiter keynote, this indeed will be a lively Saturday night. Emphasize humor. Laugh at your own foibles. Be up-to-date in your wardrobe. Strive for sartorial splendor! Gemini and Sagittarius play memorable roles and have these letters or initials in their names: C, L, U.

Sunday, November 4 (Moon in Gemini to Cancer 10:42 p.m.)   Light battles darkness. You gain greater insights into friends and lovers. Focus on church, theater, a deeper appreciation for those who write and act in plays. Taurus, Leo, and Scorpio will play sensational roles and have these letters or initials in their names: D, M, V.

Monday, November 5 (Moon in Cancer)   On this Monday, you awaken with this premonition—something intriguing and challenging is about to happen. Throughout the day, you send and receive messages; you read, write, e-mail, and telephone. Gemini, Virgo, and Sagittarius figure in today's active scenario, and will have these initials in their names: E, N, W.

Tuesday, November 6 (Moon in Cancer)   There's music in your life. Backstage rehearsals are part of today's intriguing scenario. The moon in your sign equates to your high cycle. You will show appreciation for those who write or act in special productions. Taurus, Libra, and Scorpio figure prominently. Your lucky number is 6.

Wednesday, November 7 (Moon in Cancer to Leo 3:32 a.m.)   Slow down! Time is on your side, so play the waiting game. Keep an aura of mystery and intrigue. Avoid self-deception; this means seeing people and places as they are, not merely as you wish they might be. Pisces and Virgo play outstanding roles, and have these letters in their names: G, P, Y.

Thursday, November 8 (Moon in Leo)   A power play! The Leo moon relates to earnings, locating lost articles, helping a restaurant owner by volunteering your unique recipes. You'll be dealing with Capricorn and another Cancer. The focus will be on the legal aspects of activities, timing, the possibility of falling madly in love.

Friday, November 9 (Moon in Leo to Virgo 6:48 a.m.)   You have universal appeal! You learn more about people in other countries, their habits, their diets, their ambitions. Accent showmanship, investigations, art, literature, and music. You'll meet Aries and Libra who promise full cooperation in completing your project.

Saturday, November 10 (Moon in Virgo)   Someone who took something without your permission will now say, "I know how you feel, because someone lifted what I took from you in the first place." Because of your sense of humor and innate wisdom, you dub the situation "a comedy of errors." Aquarius is involved.

Sunday, November 11 (Moon in Virgo to Libra 8:52 a.m.)   Espouse a conservative point of view. Highlight versatility, especially in connection with family values. The spotlight is on dining in style, giving and receiving tokens of affection, letting others know exactly how you feel. Another Cancer reveals a creative procedure. Do it!

Monday, November 12 (Moon in Libra)   A Jupiter-Venus combination—not easy to defeat. Look beyond the immediate, blend humor with wisdom, discuss lessons in astrology, numerology, and palmistry. Gemini and Sagittarius are set to surprise you, to knock you off balance. Enjoy the antics of a clown!

Tuesday, November 13 (Moon in Libra to Scorpio 10:44 a.m.)   While out walking, you pass someone in the street who looks remarkably like an old acquaintance. Both of you keep walking; you'll dub the experience, "an almost encounter!" Taurus, Leo, and Scorpio play astonishing roles, and will have these letters in their names: D, M, V.

Wednesday, November 14 (Moon in Scorpio)   For racing luck at all tracks: post position special—number 3 p.p. in the seventh race. Pick six: 1, 4, 3, 5, 2, 1. Watch for these letters or initials in the names of potential winning horses or jockeys: E, N, W. Hot daily doubles: 1 and 4, 2 and 6, 2 and 7. Speed horses get out in front and win—Virgo jockeys are in the winner's circle.

Thursday, November 15 (Moon in Scorpio to Sagittarius 1:51 p.m.)   The new moon in Scorpio relates to your fifth house. This means you emit an aura of sensuality and sex appeal. Your creative juices stir, so highlight originality. Be willing to make a fresh start in a different direction. Definite gains as a result of the written word.

Friday, November 16 (Moon in Sagittarius)   You win the friendship of a very important person who shares your interest in mechanical objects, including an automobile and boats. You may feel the urge to travel, but realize there is much to be done at home. Pisces and Virgo figure in today's action.

Saturday, November 17 (Moon in Sagittarius to Capricorn 7:39 p.m.)   This is a very lively, productive Saturday. Some will ask, "How does your energy last so long?" Respond: "I regard almost every day as a training day!" Capricorn and another Cancer figure in this exciting scenario. Lucky lottery: 7, 8, 12, 16, 25, 26.

Sunday, November 18 (Moon in Capricorn)   Within 24 hours, the spotlight turns to cooperative efforts, the study of legal rights, partnership, and marriage. Spiritual values surface. You gain new understanding of people who live in other countries. Locate a representative; find out what to do in order to win favor.

Monday, November 19 (Moon in Capricorn)   There's lovelight in your eyes today. The Capricorn moon equates to legal rights, cooperative efforts, partnership, and marital status. Imprint your own style, do not follow others! Leo and Aquarius will play colorful roles, and provide numerous hints about advertising, publicity, and showmanship.

Tuesday, November 20 (Moon in Capricorn to Aquarius 4:54 a.m.)   The emphasis continues on marriage, publicity, the ability to gain allies when most needed. The moon keynote emphasizes quality, durability, a gourmet dinner tonight—it will be seafood, possibly lobster. Capricorn and another Cancer will play dynamic, dramatic roles.

Wednesday, November 21 (Moon in Aquarius)   Give full play to your intellectual curiosity—ask questions, receive answers about the world of the occult. Keep recent resolutions about exercise, diet, and nutrition. An attractive member of the opposite sex confides, "For me, you are everything!" Your lucky number is 3.

Thursday, November 22 (Moon in Aquarius to Pisces 4:51 p.m.)   It's Thanksgiving! You could be dining with Taurus, Leo, and Scorpio. The choice of dark meat will outnumber those who request white meat. Scorpio will relate the story of Thanksgiving in a poignant way. Although most people celebrate, many of the Native American population regard it as a day of mourning.

Friday, November 23 (Moon in Pisces)   You will be active, reading and writing, discerning the mystery of the holidays, determined to learn truth from all angles. You'll be provided with a gift, a book, telling of the travails of Native Americans who yesterday mourned the death of friends and family members.

Saturday, November 24 (Moon in Pisces)   Attention revolves around home, family, music, style, and possibly the purchase of shoes. The spotlight is on discovering your own rhythm, learning more about the lives of composers. Keep this up, and you'll be asked to lecture on the lives of composers, their foibles and genius.

Sunday, November 25 (Moon in Pisces to Aries 5:20 a.m.) Spiritual values surface. An Aries talks about career, promotion, the completion of negotiations with an overseas representative. Pisces and Virgo are also in this picture, and have these letters or initials in their names: G, P, Y. You'll ask, "Why are we here?"

Monday, November 26 (Moon in Aries) You get a push up the ladder. You win the confidence of executives, people who need someone they can trust. You are carrying a heavy load. With all of this, you are urged to take a chance on romance. Capricorn and another Cancer will play major, amusing, creative roles.

Tuesday, November 27 (Moon in Aries to Taurus 4:04 p.m.) The Aries moon relates to your career, ambition, a fiery kind of physical attraction to Leo. A financial burden will be removed within three days. Like a bolt out of the blue, you learn that everything truly will turn out all right! Libra is in the picture.

Wednesday, November 28 (Moon in Taurus) Lucky lottery: 1, 4, 5, 11, 20, 22. Be yourself, don't follow others. You will discover a money-making proposition. You'll attract attention with a product that will appeal to new parents. Leo and Aquarius will stop the show.

Thursday, November 29 (Moon in Taurus) You will understand what previously escaped you. Your intuition plays a major role. You will know what to do to achieve your goal and what will happen after that. The sound of money rings clear. You are going to be amply rewarded for your efforts. Another Cancer is involved.

Friday, November 30 (Moon in Taurus to Gemini 12:02 a.m.) The moon is leaving Taurus, so within

24 hours, it will be in your twelfth house. Then you learn secrets, and spice will be added to your life. Gemini and Sagittarius play exciting, dynamic, and dramatic roles. Equate humor with intelligence. Have luck with number 3.

DECEMBER 2001

Saturday, December 1 (Moon in Gemini)   On this first day of December, secrets pop up from everywhere. The Gemini moon relates to communication with someone temporarily confined to home or hospital. The emphasis is on direction and motivation, private conferences with a close family member.

Sunday, December 2 (Moon in Gemini to Cancer 5:29 a.m.)   On this Sunday, people around you tell stories, relate anecdotes, and despite laughter and fun, there will be a serious note about theology and the Bible. Gemini and Sagittarius play leading roles, and have these letters or initials in their names: C, L, U.

Monday, December 3 (Moon in Cancer)   The Cancer moon relates to your high cycle. This means take the initiative, and heed your own counsel. The spotlight is on food, energy, the ability to whip up a meal in record time. Taurus, Leo, and Scorpio play outstanding roles, and have these letters in their names: D, M, V.

Tuesday, December 4 (Moon in Cancer to Leo 9:14 a.m.)   What blocked your way 24 hours ago will now be wide open. You will experience more freedom of thought, action. Your writing skills surge to the forefront. A variety of sensations are featured. You'll ask, "Are these everyday experiences? These feelings are new to me!"

Wednesday, December 5 (Moon in Leo)   The Leo moon equates to money, payments collection, showmanship, and entertainment—all for a good cause! What appeared to be out of reach will be made available in a dramatic way. Promote harmony at home. A major domestic adjustment relates to your income potential and marriage.

Thursday, December 6 (Moon in Leo to Virgo 12:10 p.m.)   Define terms, outline boundaries, inform yourself about real estate. Those who said you could not complete a project will be dining on crow. You become more objective and win in a sensational way. Pisces and Virgo could be playing behind-the-scene roles.

Friday, December 7 (Moon in Virgo)   "A date which will live in infamy!" People will be talking about Japan's sneak attack on Pearl Harbor. Absorb information, enter a discussion about World War II and whether or not we were wise in our handling of Tojo, Mussolini, and Hitler.

Saturday, December 8 (Moon in Virgo to Libra 2:56 p.m.)   Lucky lottery: 6, 9, 12, 16, 26, 42. Tie up loose ends. Investigate the possibility of participating in travel with a special group. Those who attempt to discourage you should be ignored. Aries and Libra play dynamic roles.

Sunday, December 9 (Moon in Libra)   On this Sunday, make a fresh start, highlight your inventiveness and pioneering spirit. People who are accustomed to being couch potatoes will not feel comfortable around you. You make them get up and go, shape up or ship out! Leo is in this picture.

Monday, December 10 (Moon in Libra to Scorpio 6:08 p.m.)   On this Monday, you get involved with a family that complains, "Please talk to our problem child!" On a personal level, you will be in touch with someone who attracts you despite your defenses. An Aquarius knows the ins-and-outs of most problems.

Tuesday, December 11 (Moon in Scorpio)   Focus on philosophy, theology, and psychology. Someone you "treated" last year makes a surprise appearance. Almost immediately, you are aware that your psychological sessions had positive results. Gemini and Sagittarius figure prominently, and have these initials in their names: C, L, U.

Wednesday, December 12 (Moon in Scorpio to Sagittarius 10:29 p.m.)   The moon in your fifth house stirs up creative juices. The spotlight is on children, change, challenge, and variety. Repair locks, keys, and watches. You'll have a good feeling, "I now know that I have really accomplished something!" Your lucky number is 4.

Thursday, December 13 (Moon in Sagittarius)   You once again discover the power of words. Your physical condition improves. You'll feel better and act better. Vitality makes a dramatic comeback. You will hear words perhaps not heard in some time: "You are a creative, sensual, sexy person!" Virgo is involved.

Friday, December 14—Solar Eclipse (Moon in Sagittarius)   The new moon, solar eclipse is in your sixth house. This means the emphasis is on health, employment, skill in handling basic issues, and challenges. The focus is also on music, style, fashion, art objects, and luxury items. Aries and Libra will play fascinating roles. Your lucky number is 6.

Saturday, December 15 (Moon in Sagittarius to Capricorn 4:47 a.m.)   For racing luck at all tracks: post position special—number 1 p.p. in the eighth race. Pick six: 4, 6, 1, 2, 5, 3. Look for these letters or initials in the names of potential winning horses or jockeys: G, P, Y. Hot daily doubles: 4 and 6, 3 and 7, 1 and 2. Speed records are broken by horses that usually lay back, appearing too lazy to run. Big payoff!

Sunday, December 16 (Moon in Capricorn) A Capricorn steers talk to your business, career. The moon in your seventh house relates to public relations, legal agreements, marriage. The emphasis is also on promotion, production, meeting and beating a deadline. Another Cancer plays the top role.

Monday, December 17 (Moon in Capricorn to Aquarius 1:43 p.m.) Stress universal appeal, widen markets. Don't stop now—you are on your way to possible fame and fortune. A love relationship coincides with a journey, perhaps overseas. Get rid of an unsavory situation. An Aries declares, "I want always to be a part of your life!"

Tuesday, December 18 (Moon in Aquarius) Be yourself. Do not follow others! Interest in hidden forces will get you started on a new trail of investigation. The moon in your eighth house equates to mystery, intrigue, an accusation that you are in the playground of the occult.

Wednesday, December 19 (Moon in Aquarius) Take time to check your gift list and make plans for the New Year. Food preparation is time consuming. Another Cancer gives you a helping hand. A Capricorn talks about legal rights, career, partnership, and marriage. Lucky lottery: 9, 12, 15, 18, 22, 40.

Thursday, December 20 (Moon in Aquarius to Pisces 1:09 a.m.) Focus on diversity and versatility.

You'll discover that humor equates with intelligence. Contemplate, study, be pleased with yourself, so that you are not lonely when alone. You can be lonely in a crowd—know it and respond accordingly. A Sagittarian is in this picture.

Friday, December 21 (Moon in Pisces) Do not underrate the opposition. Some people are planning a surprise for you, not necessarily pleasant. A door that had been shut tight will respond to a new key. No question about it, you will be surprised. Taurus, Leo, and Scorpio play exciting roles.

Saturday, December 22 (Moon in Pisces to Aries 1:44 a.m.) For racing luck at all tracks: post position special—number 3 p.p. in the second race. Pick six: 1, 3, 2, 2, 6, 2. Watch for these letters or initials in the names of potential winning horses or jockeys: E, N, W. Hot daily doubles: 1 and 3, 6 and 6, 5 and 7. Speed horses win. Gemini and Virgo jockeys will be aboard winners.

Sunday, December 23 (Moon in Aries) On this Sunday, a major domestic adjustment takes place. Your home appears different, which is all for the better. Aries and Libra play roles and will have these letters or initials in their names: F, O, X. A visitor from a distant city makes valid suggestions, and helps to put things in order.

Monday, December 24 (Moon in Aries) Christmas Eve! You decide, "The wise man controls his destiny; astrology points the way!" Put succinctly, you take charge of your own fate on this Christmas Eve. During meditation, you get major clues to understanding this special holiday. Pisces is represented.

Tuesday, December 25 (Moon in Aries to Taurus 1:10 a.m.) On this Christmas Day, your cycle moves to your money house. Following an initial shock, you will know you did it right! The gift list swelled almost as you observed. Don't worry—the money was well spent! Capricorn and another Cancer play featured roles. Gifts received dwarf other years.

Wednesday, December 26 (Moon in Taurus) You reach your objective. Toss aside preconceived notions, and recognize that you are a fighter against fear, ignorance, and prejudice. People seek to enlist your aid promoting idealistic causes. About that New Year's Eve celebration—where will it be held and who will be in charge?

Thursday, December 27 (Moon in Taurus to Gemini 9:37 a.m.) Get started; be active, creative, and confident. Your light shines and people are drawn to you, especially members of the opposite sex. A Leo confides, "To tell the truth, I can hardly keep my hands off you!" An Aquarian insists, "Please let me take care of everything!"

Friday, December 28 (Moon in Gemini) Get together with another Cancer. Plan the success you can achieve by cooperating with each other. A gourmet feast is on tonight's agenda. Be sure you have reservations at the restaurant. Whatever your chronological age, you could fall in love almost before you know it!

Saturday, December 29 (Moon in Gemini to Cancer 1:38 p.m.) What a Saturday! The Gemini moon shows that people usually shy will consult and confide in you. Step right up; get out of your emotional shell. Dance to your own tune. Let people know, "Here I am. You get what you see!" Lucky lottery: 3, 6, 9, 12, 18, 33.

Sunday, December 30—Lunar Eclipse (Moon in Cancer) The full moon, lunar eclipse falls in your sign. You will not only be in the news, you'll be making news. A scientific invention is involved, together with a different astrological technique. Take a chance on romance. Be bold, and display a different side of your character.

Monday, December 31 (Moon in Cancer to Leo 5:08 p.m.) New Year's Eve! It's a stunning night; the moon will be in your sign. You will meet people destined to play major roles in your life. Words are important, so start a diary. Gemini, Virgo, and Sagittarius help you celebrate the coming of another year.

HAPPY NEW YEAR!

JANUARY 2002

Tuesday, January 1 (Moon in Leo) A new outlook is necessary—take the broad view, put aside previous ideas. You learn there is more on heaven and earth that might fit your philosophy. You deal with this day with Leo and Aquarius. Preconceived notions will fall apart at the seams. Have luck with number 1.

Wednesday, January 2 (Moon in Leo to Virgo 6:33 p.m.) Your marital status figures prominently. The emphasis is on direction, ambition, and meditation. Another Cancer invites you to dine—don't hesitate to accept! It is likely to be seafood, specifically broiled lobster. Lucky lottery: 5, 12, 14, 18, 22, 27.

Thursday, January 3 (Moon in Virgo) Racing luck—all tracks: post position special— number 3 p.p. in third race. Foreign horses will do very well—Sagittarian jockeys win photo finishes. Literally speaking, this could be your lucky day. Keep resolutions about your health.

Friday, January 4 (Moon in Virgo to Libra 8:23 p.m.)   Be willing to tear down in order to rebuild—you might say this is your "makeover day." Some materials require more proofreading and rewriting. Before this day is finished, you will be on more solid ground, and be appreciated by a Scorpio who had been indifferent.

Saturday, January 5 (Moon in Libra)   This could be the start of a winning streak. What had blocked your intuitive qualities will be removed. An excellent time for buying or selling property. Read and write, teach and learn. Someone of the opposite sex confides, "At times I can hardly keep my hands off you!"

Sunday, January 6 (Moon in Libra to Scorpio 11:41 p.m.)   Attention revolves around where you live, your marital status, music and sound. Beautify your surroundings. You'll have an important visitor, possibly unannounced. Keep resolutions about exercise, diet, and nutrition. Libra plays a distinctive role.

Monday, January 7 (Moon in Scorpio)   Focus on balance, justice, and willingness to fight if the cause is right. Ignore someone who proposes a dubious scheme. Pay more attention to your mate or loved one. Strive for emotional equilibrium. Above all, avoid self-deception.

Tuesday, January 8 (Moon in Scorpio)   A power play day! The moon in your fifth house equates to the stirring of your creative juices. Imprint your style; take notes, especially of dreams. Jung, the Leo Swiss psychologist, said dreams are the guideposts to our future. Capricorn or another Cancer figure in this scenario.

Wednesday, January 9 (Moon in Scorpio to Sagittarius 4:57 a.m.)   Lucky lottery: 9, 14, 18, 27, 29, 36. Finish what you start today. Avoid making commitments you know cannot be fulfilled. A bright Aries challenges your veracity. Roll with the punches, ride with the tide. Libra is also in the picture.

Thursday, January 10 (Moon in Sagittarius)   On this Thursday, give yourself words of encouragement. You are about to enter a new phase of your life—do not beat yourself with sledgehammer words. Make a fresh start in a new direction. Tell yourself you are pretty good and have proven it.

Friday, January 11 (Moon in Sagittarius to Capricorn 12:18 p.m.)   Out of confusion will come positive results. Follow your hunch. Pay respect to your intuitive intellect. Another Cancer and an Aquarian will play major roles. Money comes from a surprise source, perhaps past royalties, or a debt you never thought would be paid.

Saturday, January 12 (Moon in Capricorn)   On this Saturday, the lunar emphasis is on legal affairs, your reputation, public relations, and partnership and marriage. Welcome the competition. Be willing to display abilities and don't be afraid to show sentiment. Have luck with number 3.

Sunday, January 13 (Moon in Capricorn to Aquarius 9:41 p.m.)   The new moon in your seventh house means attention continues to revolve around cooperative efforts, business acumen, proposals relating to your partnership, and marital status. Do plenty of proofreading and research. Taurus plays a top role.

Monday, January 14 (Moon in Aquarius)   Be ready for a change, travel, and a variety of sensations.

The moon continues in Capricorn, your seventh house. That section of your horoscope relates to partnership and marriage. Whatever you do, don't give up the ship. You are midway across—almost before you know it, you'll have completed your mission.

Tuesday, January 15 (Moon in Aquarius) A family member helps you overcome "shortcomings." The Aquarian moon relates to your eighth sector—that means it is necessary to review accounting methods. Don't rely too much on computers. Dig deep for information. You'll find out more than you want to know about you partner or mate's financial status.

Wednesday, January 16 (Moon in Aquarius to Pisces 9:01 a.m.) You could be stymied by a situation that is not at all familiar. People who say they want to help you could be sincere, but sincerely misinformed. Pisces and Virgo will play outstanding roles. The number 7 will figure prominently.

Thursday, January 17 (Moon in Pisces) You are down to earth; 24 hours ago, you were puzzled and frustrated. Today, you take charge of your own destiny. Focus on added responsibility and participation in major financial arrangement. Capricorn will play an amazing role.

Friday, January 18 (Moon in Pisces to Aries 9:34 p.m.) Look beyond the immediate. Plan ahead for a journey that could take you overseas. A spiritual individual wants very much to "uplift you." A Pisces figures prominently, but lacks funding. Aries and Libra are also part of this scenario.

Saturday, January 19 (Moon in Aries) As the moon catches Aries, you take charge of who you are and why you are here. Meantime, much emotional debris is brought together, so that once again you feel whole. Get ready for a fresh start, new direction, and the possibility of a new, exciting romance.

Sunday, January 20 (Moon in Aries)   A family member comments, "You seem more like yourself today, independent and creative!" It is true. You are beginning a different phase of your life. Capricorn and another Cancer will play significant roles. In speculating, stick with number 2.

Monday, January 21 (Moon in Aries to Taurus 9:45 a.m.)   Give full pay to your intellectual curiosity. The Aries moon represents your tenth house—career, promotion, responsibility and possibly fame and fortune. Your popularity rating is on the rise. You have the ability to make people laugh, even through their grief.

Tuesday, January 22 (Moon in Taurus)   Some of your fondest hopes and wishes can be fulfilled in a surprising way! Money is involved. You'll obtain funding and will succeed despite the odds. The moon in Taurus, your eleventh house, assures that you will have strength enough to complete a project.

Wednesday, January 23 (Moon in Taurus to Gemini 7:26 p.m.)   Lucky lottery: 1, 2, 3, 5, 7, 50. Read, write, teach, and learn. What begins as a mild flirtation could go further than you originally anticipated. A relationship could get too hot not to cool down. Gemini and Virgo will play dynamic, dramatic roles.

Thursday, January 24 (Moon in Gemini)   Attention revolves around your home, where you live, your marital status. Someone who was supposed to mail an insurance payment fell asleep instead. Know it, and do some double-checking. A mysterious stranger comes into your life, lending spice. Libra is in this picture.

Friday, January 25 (Moon in Gemini) You receive the answers to numerous queries. A secret meeting will be held, although it will not be regarded as a "secret." Pisces and Virgo play featured roles and will confide they have been "holding back." Do not tell all!

Saturday, January 26 (Moon in Gemini to Cancer 1:15 a.m.) Let others know once and for all that you mean business and are finished playing games. Money and investments are involved. A lost article is located. Express gratitude; make no accusations. Capricorn and another Cancer-born dominate this scenario. Lucky number is 8.

Sunday, January 27 (Moon in Cancer) A family member confides a problem concerning funding. A little more financial aid is required, if a project is to be completed. A debt will be paid, and that will help, but it still is not enough. Aries and Libra stand by and will do their best to help.

Monday, January 28 (Moon in Cancer to Leo 3:29 a.m.) The spotlight is on a short trip involving a relative. A flamboyant Leo pretends to know all the answers. Be amused, but don't take it seriously. Special care must be taken in traffic with the full moon in your second house. Sex appeal pays dividends!

Tuesday, January 29 (Moon in Leo) Focus on cooperative efforts, making necessary investments to maintain your family harmony. Accent a division of property and marital status. Capricorn and another Cancer figure in today's dynamic scenario. Research will reveal the actual value of property in question.

Wednesday, January 30 (Moon in Leo to Virgo 3:39 a.m.) Your critical sense surges forth—insist on verification of claims. Be lenient. Let the opposition have "wriggle room." Your popularity is on the rise, so avoid scattering your forces. Gemini could become your valuable ally. At the track: post position special—number 5 p.p. in the third race.

Thursday, January 31 (Moon in Virgo) On this last day of January, check the details, be thorough, and maintain your self-confidence. State the case clearly and face the music. Taurus, Leo, and Scorpio play significant roles, and are likely to have these letters or initials in their names—D, M, V.

FEBRUARY 2002

Friday, February 1 (Moon in Virgo to Libra 3:44 a.m.) Prepare this month to "change banks." Accent innovative methods. It will be to your advantage to take a chance on romance. Much talk will concern your marital status. Protect your assets; count your change! Another Cancer is involved.

Saturday, February 2 (Moon in Libra) It could be a lively Saturday night—you will meet a "world traveler." Ask questions and show interest, without appearing naive. Gemini and Sagittarius will play major roles. You will know them by these letters in their names—C, L, U. Your lucky number is 3.

Sunday, February 3 (Moon in Libra to Scorpio 5:34 a.m.) Be willing to revise, review, and rewrite—tear down in order to rebuild. Your property value commands more-than-usual attention. A Scorpio is sincere, but could be sincerely misinformed. Rely upon your own intuitive intellect—follow your instincts and your heart.

Monday, February 4 (Moon in Scorpio)   Letter writing is important and could make a difference in getting or losing money. Give full play to your intellectual curiosity—insist on answers, not evasions. Someone of the opposite sex confides, "At times I can hardly keep my hands off you!"

Tuesday, February 5 (Moon in Scorpio to Sagittarius 10:21 a.m.)   Attention revolves around your children, home, and marital status. Strive for harmony, without abandoning your principles. There will be music in your life; dance to your own tune. Taurus and Libra will play fascinating roles.

Wednesday, February 6 (Moon in Sagittarius)   Lucky lottery: 5, 7, 12, 16, 38, 50. Lie low; play the waiting game. A restless relative could involve you in a wild-goose chase—if you so permit. Avoid self-deception. See people, places, and relationships in a realistic way. A Pisces figures prominently.

Thursday, February 7 (Moon in Sagittarius to Capricorn 6:07 p.m.)   An answer is received to a request for additional material and funding. It's a favorable response, with limitations. There will be more accounting for what you receive and what you do with it. Capricorn and another Cancer play outstanding roles.

Friday, February 8 (Moon in Capricorn)   A relationship is "on edge." You are asked to make a commitment, one way or another. The lunar position highlights your partnership and marital status. Check legal rights and permissions. Aries and Libra will play dramatic roles.

Saturday, February 9 (Moon in Capricorn) New people come into your life and your marriage continues to be featured in "serious discussions." Imprint style; do not follow others. Wear bright colors, and make personal appearances. A relationship could get "too hot not to cool down." Have luck with number 1.

Sunday, February 10 (Moon in Capricorn to Aquarius 4:14 a.m.) Within 24 hours, a sale will be made, much to your relief. Prepare your travel plans, and make yourself "more interesting" to a special member of the opposite sex. On this Sunday, communicate with a family member who needs to hear from you. Another Cancer is involved.

Monday, February 11 (Moon in Aquarius) In matters of speculation, stick with number 3. The moon in Aquarius coincides with health requirements, with special attention to exercise, diet, and nutrition. Gemini and Sagittarius will play "interesting" roles. Many laughs tonight!

Tuesday, February 12 (Moon in Aquarius to Pisces 3:52 p.m.) The new moon in Aquarius, your eighth house, reveals an interest in the occult and the mantic arts and sciences. Unorthodox methods and procedures will see you "winning the game." You make discoveries about the finances of someone close to you, possibly your mate or partner.

Wednesday, February 13 (Moon in Pisces) A favorable moon position equates to philosophy, travel, publishing, and advertising. If you have something to offer, today is the day to let the world know about it! Interest in theology is emphasized. A discussion ensues about the possibility of "life after death."

Thursday, February 14 (Moon in Pisces) It will be your task to encourage family members. Tell them to wait and see—Valentine cards will appear, possibly all at once. You yourself will receive a Valentine note reassuring you of love. Taurus, Libra, and Scorpio will play outstanding roles.

Friday, February 15 (Moon in Pisces to Aries 4:24 a.m.) Within 24 hours, questions will be answered about legal rights and permissions. Avoid premature actions. Someone destined to play an important role in your life will appear in a nondramatic way. Pisces and Virgo play quiet, but dramatic, roles today.

Saturday, February 16 (Moon in Aries) A promise that appeared to be broken will be mended. The moon position coincides with possible promotion and a dialogue with a "higher-up." You could be handed a leadership role, whether or not you seek it. Have material ready; don't go hat in hand. Your lucky number is 8.

Sunday, February 17 (Moon in Aries to Taurus 4:57 p.m.) Finish what you start. Be with individuals of a "spiritual bent." Look beyond the immediate; perceive potential. Give some study to language; open lines of communication. You could locate a key person to represent your talent and product in another nation.

Monday, February 18 (Moon in Taurus) Many of your hopes and wishes will be fulfilled. With the moon in Taurus, your eleventh house, you win friends and influence people and you obtain more funding. Stress originality; display your pioneering spirit. Leo and Aquarius will play major roles.

Tuesday, February 19 (Moon in Taurus) Give
yourself time to meditate, to make decisions about
direction, location, partnership, and marriage. Another Cancer claims to be a "mind reader." Be
amused, not confused. A Capricorn wants to relieve
you of minor duties.

***Wednesday, February 20 (Moon in Taurus to Gemini
3:48 a.m.)*** During social activity, you learn that a
secret has been kept and you have been kept "in the
dark." A voluble Gemini lets the cat out of the bag.
Maintain your equilibrium; don't make a "federal
case" of it. A friend returns from the hospital, and
needs reassurance that he, or she, is still needed.

Thursday, February 21 (Moon in Gemini) Get
ready for a quick change of plans. Your original itiner-
ary is no longer valid. Someone you counted on turns
out to be "counting on you." Avoid panic; laugh at
your own foibles. Taurus, Leo, and Scorpio will play
memorable roles.

***Friday, February 22 (Moon in Gemini to Cancer
11:13 a.m.)*** Your cycle is high, so take the initiative. You will be at the right place at a special moment
almost effortlessly. People comment, "You look different and you certainly look sexy!" Someone who
previously ignored you will now confide, "I'm irresist-
ibly drawn to you!"

Saturday, February 23 (Moon in Cancer) This is
the time to change your residence or marital status.
You've said, "If only I had the money!" By tonight,
you will have the money—do something about your
current situation. First, stay away from those who take
you for granted. Libra is in this picture.

Sunday, February 24 (Moon in Cancer to Leo 2:34 p.m.)   Spiritual values surface. You are both frustrated and relieved. People seek you out and consult you. You might be asking, "Where is my precious privacy?" A Pisces seeks permission to "hypnotize you." Respond: "Meditation does the trick!"

Monday, February 25 (Moon in Leo)   This could be your power play day—follow a hunch. Decisions will be based on past experience. Exude confidence. Realize your personal magnetism makes you attractive and provides sex appeal. A Capricorn encourages, "Why don't we become partners?"

Tuesday, February 26 (Moon in Leo to Virgo 2:48 p.m.)   You locate lost articles and finally feel as if you have the right to "lead the way." People who took you for granted will no longer do so; you won't permit it! Finish what you started three months ago. There's a dramatic reunion tonight. Aries plays the top role.

Wednesday, February 27 (Moon in Virgo)   The full moon in Virgo, your third house, coincides with a hearing from a relative you thought had dropped off the Earth. Take special care in traffic. Don't drive with a heavy drinker. Make a fresh start in a new direction; be open to the possibility of a new love.

Thursday, February 28 (Moon in Virgo to Libra 1:46 p.m.)   On this last day of February, a decision will be made about an important investment. A Capricorn and another Cancer figure prominently. You'll receive proposals about your career, business, and marriage. Be discriminating—choose the best and ignore the rest.

Friday, March 1 (Moon in Libra)   On this Friday, the first day of March, you learn more about your financial holdings. Beautify your surroundings. Social activities will soon be featured. This Friday night is the precurser to a lively weekend. A Sagittarian will play a key role.

Saturday, March 2 (Moon in Libra to Scorpio 1:52 p.m.)   Entertain at home, if possible. Invite a family member who recently complained, "Nobody cares about me!" Keep resolutions about exercise, diet, and nutrition. Taurus, Leo, and Scorpio play meaningful roles, and have these initials in their names—D, M, V.

Sunday, March 3 (Moon in Scorpio)   The moon in your fifth house equates to personal magnetism, sensuality, creativity, and sex appeal. This is one Sunday you won't soon forget! The spotlight is also on children, challenge, change, and variety. Beneficial if you write, take notes, and strive to creatively interpret dreams.

Monday, March 4 (Moon in Scorpio to Sagittarius 4:54 p.m.)   On this fourth day of the month, you pay more attention to your land, family, and security. If attending an auction, a bargain is available in connection with a luxury item. Beautify your home surroundings. You'll be counted on to entertain important visitors.

Tuesday, March 5 (Moon in Sagittarius)   Idealism "rules the day." You can imagine what you want—and obtain it. Pay close attention to your "psychic impressions." In plain language, that means heed your inner feelings. Pisces and Virgo figure in this dynamic scenario.

Wednesday, March 6 (Moon in Sagittarius to Capricorn 11:48 p.m.)   Lucky lottery: 6, 8, 12, 14, 18, 22. Someone who shares your beliefs will help you out of a "tight spot." You'll have more responsibility and will be financially rewarded accordingly. Capricorn plays an important role. Deal gingerly with an older person.

Thursday, March 7 (Moon in Capricorn)   Racing luck—all tracks: post position special—number 1 p.p. in the seventh race. Focus on your personality, entertainment, and sex appeal. Aries and Libra play meaningful roles. Look beyond the immediate. Communicate with someone who is preparing for a trip to another country.

Friday, March 8 (Moon in Capricorn)   The moon in Capricorn, your seventh house, emphasizes your reputation, public relations, cooperative efforts, and marriage. A Capricorn becomes impatient, but will cool down. Maintain your own emotional equilibrium. Have luck with number 1.

Saturday, March 9 (Moon in Capricorn to Aquarius 9:56 a.m.)   On this Saturday, the emphasis continues on your legal rights and marital status. You get publicity, desirable or otherwise. If dining out, check reservations and prices. Another Cancer native is willing to cooperate if you so permit. Lucky lottery: 12, 16, 19, 21, 24, 51.

Sunday, March 10 (Moon in Aquarius)   You'll have reason to celebrate! An accounting error is corrected in your favor. Thank your lucky stars! People who disparage astrology will face considerable debate from you. Gemini and Sagittarius will play fascinating roles.

Monday, March 11 (Moon in Aquarius to Pisces 9:56 p.m.) Although confused earlier in the day, you come back in a bright, dynamic way. Be willing to revise, rewrite, review, and also tear down in order to rebuild. Taurus, Leo, and Scorpio play meaningful roles, and have these initials in their names—D, M, V.

Tuesday, March 12 (Moon in Pisces) A burden is removed. As a result, you experience more freedom of thought and action. A sexual attraction is featured. You receive compliments and flattery. Be realistic. This technique does not necessarily improve with age. Read and write, learn by sharing knowledge, by teaching.

Wednesday, March 13 (Moon in Pisces) Attention revolves around your "philosophy of life." The spotlight is on a domestic adjustment that could include a change of residence or marital status. A long-distance journey is in your stars, perhaps not today, but in the near future. Plan ahead!

Thursday, March 14 (Moon in Pisces to Aries 9:01 p.m.) The new moon in Pisces, your ninth house, reveals that interest in religion, philosophy, and arcane literature is highlighted. You will travel "with a purpose." What you observe during a journey will enhance your character and potential. Virgo figures prominently.

Friday, March 15 (Moon in Aries) A contract could be signed; your career gets a boost. Avoid meeting people with hat in hand—instead, exude confidence and personal magnetism. Your attitude during this day is of most importance. Be a winner, not a loser! Capricorn and another Cancer dominate this dramatic scenario.

Saturday, March 16 (Moon in Aries to Taurus 10:59 p.m.)   The emphasis is on "universal appeal." Avoid being narrow-minded in any sense. Participate in political-charitable activities. Perceive potential, predict your future, and make it come true! Aries and Libra insist on grabbing featured roles.

Sunday, March 17 (Moon in Taurus)   On this St. Patrick's Day, accent moderation. Focus on adult beverages and not too many of them! You'll meet new people, and this should plant the seeds for a different kind of relationship. Wear bright colors, including green, of course. Have luck with number 1.

Monday, March 18 (Moon in Taurus)   Remember that to divide is to conquer. Stand firm for your principles. Confer with your partner or mate. Your marital status figures prominently. A Capricorn and another Cancer act in this memorable scenario. Find out where you stand in connection with a real estate transaction.

Tuesday, March 19 (Moon in Taurus to Gemini 10:18 a.m.)   A surprising turn of events increases your popularity. The moon in Taurus, your eleventh house, tells of money, payments, collections, and wishes that come true. The focus is also on social activity, luck, and perhaps the start of a winning streak.

Wednesday, March 20 (Moon in Gemini)   Racing luck—all tracks: post position special—number 4 p.p. in the fourth race. Look behind the scenes for pertinent information. A Gemini has been "following you." Stop, look, listen, and ask. Details unravel in your favor.

Thursday, March 21 (Moon in Gemini to Cancer 9:05 p.m.)   This could be your "discovery day." You solve puzzles, mathematical and people. Your ability to analyze character will surface. A family member expresses appreciation for all you have done. Gemini, Virgo, and Sagittarius figure prominently and have these initials in their names—E, N, W.

Friday, March 22 (Moon in Cancer)   The emphasis is on home, a domestic situation, food, and security. There's music in your life tonight, so dance to your own tune. Taurus, Libra, and Scorpio figure in today's dynamic scenario. Some could have these letters or initials in their names—F, O, X. Your lucky number is 6.

Saturday, March 23 (Moon in Cancer)   The moon in your sign represents your high cycle. Even as you read these words, circumstances are turning in your favor. Be selective, choose quality, and let others have bargains, while you take the best that is offered. Pisces is in this picture.

Sunday, March 24 (Moon in Cancer to Leo 12:10 a.m.)   The emphasis is on showmanship, color coordination, entertainment, and advertising. Money comes your way from an unusual source. Feel good about yourself—you deserve it! Those who say otherwise are merely envious and are "little people." Capricorn is in this scenario.

Monday, March 25 (Moon in Leo)   On this Monday, there is good news and news not so good. The "good news" is that what you lost will be returned. The "bad news" is that you must wait awhile until receiving more money from various sources, including employment. Aries is in this picture.

Tuesday, March 26 (Moon in Leo to Virgo 1:42 a.m.) Make a fresh start, and emphasize independence, originality, and a willingness to take a chance on romance. Do your own thing. Do not follow others. Avoid plagiarism like the plague. Be sure your work is fresh, original, and daring in concept. Have luck with number 1.

Wednesday, March 27 (Moon in Virgo) Racing luck—all tracks: post position special—number 6 p.p. in the fifth race. Focus on family, security, property value, and real estate. A family member complains about a possible loss—make it clear you are not a "crying towel." Capricorn is involved.

Thursday, March 28 (Moon in Virgo to Libra 1:03 a.m.) The full moon in Libra represents your fourth house, which in turn highlights land, your domicile, and future prospects. Do not stop in midstream. It is not yet time to "change horses." Gemini and Sagittarius play leading roles and have these initials in their names—C, L, U.

Friday, March 29 (Moon in Libra) Insist on a "square deal." Do some research on land value and language. Let people know you did not recently fall off a turnip truck. Drive a hard bargain—if you don't, people will think you don't know any better. Scorpio plays a role.

Saturday, March 30 (Moon in Libra to Scorpio 12:21 a.m.) Within 24 hours, you'll experience more freedom of thought and action. A sale will be made, a burden lifted. Maintain your personal rhythm. Refuse to get out of step to please mediocre individuals. Lucky lottery: 4, 12, 18, 36, 49, 50.

Sunday, March 31 (Moon in Scorpio) Exude confidence—people are attracted to you, especially the opposite sex. Your creative juices stir. You give off an aura of sensuality and sex appeal. Don't exploit this; don't break too many hearts! At the very least, offer tea and sympathy.

Monday, April 1 (Moon in Scorpio to Sagittarius 1:49 a.m.)   No one can really fool you, but please avoid self-deception. Check details, proofread, and do reasonable research. Taurus, Leo, and Scorpio play fascinating roles and could have these letters or initials in their names—D, M, V.

Tuesday, April 2 (Moon in Sagittarius)   Be ready for change, a variety of sensations. Get to know co-workers. Remember that to get a smile, you must smile first. Toss aside preconceived notions. As Shakespeare said, "There are more things in heaven and earth . . . than are dreamt of in your philosophy."

Wednesday, April 3 (Moon in Sagittarius to Capricorn 6:58 a.m.)   On the domestic front, make intelligent concessions without abandoning your principles. Give the other party, family or otherwise, wiggle room. Decorate, remodel, beautify your home. An important guest from another nation will arrive, perhaps unannounced.

Thursday, April 4 (Moon in Capricorn)   Racing luck—all tracks: post position special—number 7 p.p. in the seventh race. Time is on your side. You can afford to play the waiting game. A Pisces of the opposite sex wants to take you for a proverbial ride. Don't permit it!

Friday, April 5 (Moon in Capricorn to Aquarius 4:06 p.m.)   The lunar position emphasizes publicity, legal affairs, your reputation, cooperative efforts, and marital status. Be kind, but firm. Let others know you are not to be "trifled" with—this applies especially in dealing with an attorney. Capricorn is involved.

Saturday, April 6 (Moon in Aquarius)   Dig deep for information. You might be stunned upon discovering that your partner or mate has held back vital information about finances. Settle down; don't fly off the handle. Questions will be answered. Let it be known: "Don't let it happen again!"

Sunday, April 7—Daylight Saving Time Begins (Moon in Aquarius)   Spiritual values surface; maintain an aura of mystery and intrigue. This means don't tell all; don't confide or confess. Let others play a guessing game. Protect yourself in emotional clinches. Leo and Aquarius play memorable roles, have these letters in their names—A, S, J.

Monday, April 8 (Moon in Aquarius to Pisces 4:57 a.m.)   As the day draws to an end, pay attention to travel news. You will be combining business with romance. Find out where you stand, where you might go, and why. Questions of legal agreements, partnership, and marriage figure prominently.

Tuesday, April 9 (Moon in Pisces)   Diversify, predict your own future and make it come true! A former love relationship could reignite. Pisces is very much involved. Don't pay too much attention to words. Ask, "Would you mind putting that in writing?" Have luck with number 3.

Wednesday, April 10 (Moon in Pisces to Aries 5:39 p.m.)   Lucky lottery: 7, 10, 12, 18, 22, 33. Focus on advertising, publishing, and letting the world know you intend to make a difference. Some people call you haughty but that is because they are jealous and small. Scorpio is in picture.

Thursday, April 11 (Moon in Aries)   Trust your inner feelings and your heart. People who give evasive

244

answers don't want you to know the truth. Be aware, alert, don't accept excuses. Focus on dealing with superiors, production, promotion, and understanding your role and why you are here.

Friday, April 12 (Moon in Aries to Taurus 5:54 a.m.)   The new moon position highlights your career and promotion. Many express confidence. You will do okay. Taurus, Libra, and Scorpio play important roles and are apt to have these letters or initials in their names—F, O, X. Have luck with number 6.

Saturday, April 13 (Moon in Taurus)   Don't torture yourself with sledgehammer words such as *should have, might have, could have.* Define terms, and outline boundaries. Take charge of your own fate. Others could be sincere, but also "sincerely misinformed." Pisces is represented.

Sunday, April 14 (Moon in Taurus)   This could be your money day, even though it's Sunday. People make decisions behind the scenes which directly affect you. You'll be given more power, responsibility, and money. Don't go hat in hand—exude confidence.

Monday, April 15 (Moon in Taurus to Gemini 4:55 p.m.)   You enjoyed a Sunday night dinner—today you'll be rid of many doubts and fears. People look to you for direction and motivation, and you can gain by recommending a degree of meditation. Aries and Libra play sensational roles and have these letters in their names—I and R.

Tuesday, April 16 (Moon in Gemini)   Despite the odds, you win! Avoid self-deception. See people, places, and relationships in a realistic light. Be wary of Pisces and Leo—they could really feel affection, but motivation is another question. Your lucky number is 1.

Wednesday, April 17 (Moon in Gemini) Your credo could be "Give a little and get a lot!" Money owed you will be paid. Make intelligent concessions without giving up your principles. Questions about partnership and marriage will loom large. There's a broiled lobster dinner tonight!

Thursday, April 18 (Moon in Gemini to Cancer 1:59 a.m.) You might be asking, "Is this déjà vu?" Today's scenario features familiar faces and places. Diversify; highlight versatility and intellectual curiosity. Avoid scattering your forces. Ask questions, and insist on answers, not evasions. A Sagittarian is in the picture.

Friday, April 19 (Moon in Cancer) Be with people who are on your side and will give you a "square deal." Taurus, Leo, and Scorpio figure prominently. They will have these letters or initials in their names— D, M, V. Some persons attempt to trip you up, but you foil them.

Saturday, April 20 (Moon in Cancer to Leo 8:19 a.m.) A flirtation or sexual escapade is featured. Maintain emotional control; know when to say, "Enough is enough!" Be analytical and do your own investigation. You could meet someone destined to play a major role in your life. Have luck with number 5.

Sunday, April 21 (Moon in Leo) Be with family, if possible. Settle financial differences. A valuable lost article will be found. Someone who gives you tips should be told, "Give yourself tips. You look as if you need it!" Taurus and Libra will play fascinating roles.

Monday, April 22 (Moon in Leo to Virgo 11:33 a.m.) You have been through a period of confusion. Today, you see people and relationships in a "mysterious" way. This means you perceive a combination of the practical and mystical. Base actions on instincts and your heart. Pisces plays an outstanding role.

Tuesday, April 23 (Moon in Virgo) Suddenly you "snap out of it!" This means today's circumstances enable you to take a practical view and to do something about it. Capricorn and another Cancer help you put the finishing touches on a project. Have luck with number 8.

Wednesday, April 24 (Moon in Virgo to Libra 12:20 p.m.) Lucky lottery: 4, 5, 9, 15, 19, 42. Look beyond the immediate. Your potential is great, so take advantage of it by extra study and efforts. Aries and Libra play dramatic roles. A professional superior compliments you on recent work.

Thursday, April 25 (Moon in Libra) The emphasis is on property, real estate, and the ability to discern quality and to strike a hard bargain. Leo and Aquarius will play "terrific" roles. A practical Libran helps in your selection of values and priorities. March to your own rhythm!

Friday, April 26 (Moon in Libra to Scorpio 12:15 p.m.) You'll be asked to render a decision concerning cooperative efforts, partnership, and marriage. Strive to see both sides, to be fair, and to permit past experience to color your judgment. Another Cancer will seem hostile, but that is only temporary.

Saturday, April 27 (Moon in Scorpio) A very social Saturday! The full moon in Scorpio, in your fifth house, means your creative juices stir. You exude personal magnetism, an aura of sensuality and sex appeal.

A Scorpio is attracted and says so in no uncertain terms. Have luck with number 3.

Sunday, April 28 (Moon in Scorpio to Sagittarius 1:13 p.m.) People might expect more from you than you are willing to give. Let your own feelings be known—there are numerous details to be attended to, so check your priority list. For this Sunday, to gain friends and allies, be quiet within.

Monday, April 29 (Moon in Sagittarius) Pressure is relieved; you might actually miss the spirit of competitiveness. Accept a change of pace as positive. Dig deep for information and do basic research. On a personal level, you know once and for all that your love is not unrequited. Virgo is represented.

Tuesday, April 30 (Moon in Sagittarius to Capricorn 5:02 p.m.) On this last day of April, the moon is in Sagittarius, your sixth house. Focus on new understandings with coworkers and determination to follow health rules. Attention also revolves around your home, family, and insurance payments. Music is featured.

MAY 2002

Wednesday, May 1 (Moon in Capricorn) If not careful, you get "involved." Sexual attraction is part of today's scenario. Protect yourself in emotional clinches. Take note of dreams; tonight's could be a lulu! Gemini, Virgo, and Sagittarius will play fascinating roles. Have luck with number 5.

Thursday, May 2 (Moon in Capricorn) The emphasis is on your ability to cooperate with those whose ideas you do not share. The opposition lends spice. Focus on partnership, legal affairs, public relations, and marriage. A meaningful day; one you won't soon forget! Libra is in the picture.

Friday, May 3 (Moon in Capricorn to Aquarius 12:44 a.m.)   Within 24 hours you'll have solved a major dilemma. Ride with the tide; maintain confidence and emotional equilibrium. You will be surprised by people who become allies, but also encouraged. Pisces and Virgo play unusual roles, emerge from emotional shells.

Saturday, May 4 (Moon in Aquarius)   You get down to "brass tacks." This means face the music, see places, people as they are and not merely as you wish they could be. Capricorn and another Cancer figure in this scenario. Focus on promotion and production. A relationship gets too hot not to cool down.

Sunday, May 5 (Moon in Aquarius to Pisces 11:45 a.m.)   Look beyond the obvious— predict your future and make it come true! The Aquarian moon has to do in your case with eighth house matters— accounting, the occult, a willingness to dig deep for information. Aries plays a top role.

Monday, May 6 (Moon in Pisces)   Clear away emotional debris—be open to innovation and originality. Display derring-do. Some people confide, "You have opened me to new, thrilling experiences." A Leo does have your best interests at heart, but may be clumsy in displaying it.

Tuesday, May 7 (Moon in Pisces)   You've been through this before—could it be déjà vu? Today's scenario features familiar places, faces. The spotlight is on close relationships that include marriage. Not a restful day, but there's plenty of excitement, much to ponder. Another Cancer is involved.

Wednesday, May 8 (Moon in Pisces to Aries 12:21 a.m.)
Racing luck—all tracks: post position special—number 3
in the third and fifth races. Wishes are due to be fulfilled
no later than one month from now. Be sure you know
what you want and how to ask for it. A Sagittarian
is involved.

Thursday, May 9 (Moon in Aries)   The moon in
the top part of your chart coincides with "rubbing
shoulders with big wigs!" Don't go hat in hand. Exude
confidence—realize you have plenty of appeal, and
that includes "sex appeal." Taurus, Leo, and Scorpio
figure in this scenario.

***Friday, May 10 (Moon in Aries to Taurus 12:30
p.m.)***   You will have plenty of "wiggle room." Explore, experiment, discover—you could "discover"
someone destined to play a major role in your life.
Gemini, Virgo, and Sagittarius figure prominently and
could have these initials in their names—E, N, W.

Saturday, May 11 (Moon in Taurus)   A family
member confesses, "I'm so confused!" Be sympathetic, but don't become the "umpire." If you forgo
this advice, you will end up in the middle and be
blamed for trouble that occurs. Your intuitive intellect
is honed to razor sharpness.

***Sunday, May 12 (Moon in Taurus to Gemini 11:02
p.m.)***   Spiritual values surface. The new moon in
Taurus, your eleventh house, means you get what you
ask for, so please also request what you really need.
The financial picture is brighter than you originally
assumed. Pisces and Virgo figure prominently.

Monday, May 13 (Moon in Gemini)   Within 24
hours, you will be tested and challenged. Do some basic

research, solve a puzzle, and speak frankly to Taurus and Scorpio. Focus on pressure, responsibility, and a major financial transaction. Capricorn, seeking to impress, puts forth grandiose concepts.

Tuesday, May 14 (Moon in Gemini) Finish what you start. Look behind the scenes. You don't have to be neurotic to sense that you are being followed. Be your own person; respond to instincts and your heart. Aries will play a "secret role." In matters of speculation, stick with number 9. Wear the color red.

Wednesday, May 15 (Moon in Gemini to Cancer 7:32 a.m.) Your cycle is moving up, so get ready for new experiences and possibly a "new love." Focus on independence of thought and action. Strive for originality, freshness, and avoid what has been done before ad nauseum. Lucky lottery: 1, 11, 14, 18, 22, 33.

Thursday, May 16 (Moon in Cancer) The moon in your sign equates to a time when you will be at the right place at a special moment. Trust yourself! Imprint style. Don't follow others. Your timing is exquisite—people will ask, "How did you know?" Respond: "I just did—that's all I know!"

Friday, May 17 (Moon in Cancer to Leo 1:50 p.m.) Your personality "vibrates." You exude magnetic appeal, including sex appeal. Welcome the new. Put aside old concepts. Realize there are more things in Heaven and Earth than might fit your philosophy. Gemini and Sagittarius figure in today's exciting scenario.

Saturday, May 18 (Moon in Leo) On this Saturday, you could win a contest! The moon activates your money house, so you locate lost articles almost effortlessly. Some people, very jealous, ask you point blank,

"Why do you have all the luck?" Respond: "The harder I work, the luckier I get!"

Sunday, May 19 (Moon in Leo to Virgo 6:00 p.m.) On this Sunday, as luck will have it, you locate a lost article in the same place that you last saw it. Furthermore, you learn about investments, the stock market, and how to get the most for your money. Gemini and Virgo will play dynamic roles.

Monday, May 20 (Moon in Virgo) On this Monday, you receive a "surprise call" from a relative, very likely a Virgo. Don't look for hidden motives. Enjoy the call and the promise of company in the near future. You will be "counting your blessings." Have luck with number 6.

Tuesday, May 21 (Moon in Virgo to Libra 8:17 p.m.) On this Tuesday, you will be amazed that others are responding to questions and other requests made two weeks ago. Don't make a federal case of it. Ride with the tide. Do not ask too many questions! Pisces will play a "mysterious" role.

Wednesday, May 22 (Moon in Libra) You get results today. You no longer are mystified by what you give and receive. You gain new understanding of "to get a smile, give a smile!" People who were difficult to get along with could now become your friends. Your lucky number is 8.

Thursday, May 23 (Moon in Libra to Scorpio 9:37 p.m.) Racing luck—all tracks. Post position special—numbers 3, 6, and 9 will be in Winner's Circle in the third, sixth, and ninth races. Aries jockeys will fare well and could win photo finishes. On a personal level, let go of a burden not really your own.

Friday, May 24 (Moon in Scorpio) Nothing happens halfway—it will be all or nothing. A love relationship is controversial, exciting, will drain your energy, but you would not miss it for all the world. Leo and Aquarius play meaningful roles and have these letters in their names—A, S, J.

Saturday, May 25 (Moon in Scorpio to Sagittarius 11:21 p.m.) You'll receive proposals—career, business, and marriage. A Scorpio hints, "You cannot really succeed without my help!" Be diplomatic, but respond, "Thanks but no, thanks—I do intend to do this on my own!" Lucky lottery: 7, 9, 12, 13, 18, 51.

Sunday, May 26 (Moon in Sagittarius) On this Sunday, get together with someone who shares your basic interests, perhaps a coworker. It could be a day of discovery, humor, and the ability to laugh at your own foibles. You'll learn more about fashion, how to wear clothes, and how to look your best.

Monday, May 27 (Moon in Sagittarius) What appeared to be a "big problem" will turn out to be "easily solved." Put aside preconceived notions; tear down in order to rebuild. Let others know you are here to stay and you won't be "bullied" into leaving before the task is completed.

Tuesday, May 28 (Moon in Sagittarius to Capricorn 2:54 a.m.) Within 24 hours, questions loom large concerning legal rights, your reputation, public relations, and marital status. Today, be analytical. Find out the "why" of things. Read, write, teach, and help others to understand themselves. Gemini is represented.

Wednesday, May 29 (Moon in Capricorn) A family member who recently confided "confusion" will now help you resolve your own dilemma. Focus on decorating, remodeling, and beautifying your home surroundings. A "grandfather clock" could be part of this scenario. Have luck with number 6.

Thursday, May 30 (Moon in Capricorn to Aquarius 9:35 a.m.)   On this Thursday, take time to be aware of why you are here and what to do about it. Regard kindly those who offer to fill in, to help, to run your errands. Maintain an aura of independence mixed with intrigue. Pisces plays an important role.

Friday, May 31 (Moon in Aquarius)   This is your power play day! Dig deep for information. You will be surprised at what you find out about money and partners. Check for computer errors. Look beyond the immediate. Be your own person, despite the temptation to let others be responsible.

JUNE 2002

Saturday, June 1 (Moon in Aquarius to Pisces 7:36 p.m.)   You find out where previous errors occurred, most likely computer. Stay close to home and family, if possible. A Libra is eager to tell you something; it is a confidential matter. Focus on diplomacy and intelligent concessions. Have luck with number 6.

Sunday, June 2 (Moon in Pisces)   Don't be in too much of a hurry! What appears on the surface is not necessarily the truth. Remember the saying "All that glitters is not gold!" Pisces and Virgo figure in this scenario—you face a challenge and will succeed. Have luck with number 7!

Monday, June 3 (Moon in Pisces)   A lively discussion takes place regarding motion pictures and actors.

Be patient; give your opinion and let it go at that. Aries extends a dinner invitation. It is okay to accept. A Capricorn talks business and career—listen carefully!

Tuesday, June 4 (Moon in Pisces to Aries 7:50 a.m.) Within 24 hours, news is received concerning your career and a current project. You have been doing the "right thing," despite skepticism expressed by a "little person." Look beyond the immediate; open lines of communication. A foreign agent involved.

Wednesday, June 5 (Moon in Aries) Take the initiative. Let associates, including superiors, know that you are a person who is bright and who has creative ideas. On a personal level, a Leo flatters and thrills you. Lucky lottery: 1, 5, 11, 14, 22, 50.

Thursday, June 6 (Moon in Aries to Taurus 8:05 p.m.) Racing luck—all tracks: post position special—number 6 p.p. in the fifth race. Focus on cooperative efforts, partnership, and marriage. Your opinion is sought in connection with food and beverages. Another Cancer native will be involved.

Friday, June 7 (Moon in Taurus) Keep resolutions concerning physical activity and nutrition. You'll be involved today in talks about fashion. Be aware of design and sales potential. Gemini and Sagittarius will play leading roles, and have these letters in their names— C, L, U.

Saturday, June 8 (Moon in Taurus) Be positive that a supporting structure is solid. Do not tempt fate! You not long ago had a narrow escape from injury. Don't repeat that mistake! An insurance policy requires review. Taurus, Leo, and Scorpio will play memorable roles.

Sunday, June 9 (Moon in Taurus to Gemini 6:28 a.m.)   Get ready for change, travel, and a variety of experiences. The Taurus moon in your eleventh house means that some of your most dynamic wishes will be fulfilled. You'll be lucky; this could be the start of a winning streak. Additional funding is received.

Monday, June 10 (Moon in Gemini)   Focus on security, being with people whose aims and goals are similar to your own. Don't look for or invite trouble. A passionate Scorpio challenges you to a verbal duel. The new moon in Gemini in your twelfth house encourages secrets and sly moves.

Tuesday, June 11 (Moon in Gemini to Cancer 2:13 p.m.)   You have more admirers than you originally anticipated. Some people have been "under cover." Others are emerging from emotional shells. By speaking up, exposing likes and dislikes, you earn respect. Despite temporary embarrassment, you do right thing.

Wednesday, June 12 (Moon in Cancer)   At the track: post position special—number 8 p.p. in the fourth and eighth races. An older person is impressed with your acumen. Discussion ensues concerning numbers and astrology. Be discreet, don't tell all, let people play a "guessing game."

Thursday, June 13 (Moon in Cancer to Leo 7:38 p.m.)   The moon in your sign tells of circumstances turning in your favor, even as you read these words. The color purple figures prominently. You'll be dealing with a verbose individual. Get promises on paper. "A verbal agreement is not worth the paper it's written on," declared Samuel Goldwyn.

Friday, June 14 (Moon in Leo)   The money picture is bright. You locate a lost article. You feel as if:

"Everything is going my way!" Focus on partnership, cooperative efforts, and special collections. Leo and Aquarius play fascinating roles and have these letters in their names—A, S, J.

Saturday, June 15 (Moon in Leo to Virgo 11:22 p.m.) Proposals are received—business, career, partnership, and marriage. Be near water, if possible. Come to an agreement with an older Cancer, notably your mother. You are going places, so go with an easy mind! Capricorn and another Cancer help in establishing business.

Sunday, June 16 (Moon in Virgo) Experiment, explore, discover—share information by writing and teaching. Laugh at your own foibles. You are a very special person—today you learn this is true. Gemini and Sagittarius will play amazing roles.

Monday, June 17 (Moon in Virgo) Be willing to reestablish contact with a Taurus or Scorpio. Don't permit pride to deter your progress—pride goeth before a fall. This can be a "makeover day"—try something different, be daring, and display your pioneering spirit.

Tuesday, June 18 (Moon in Virgo to Libra 2:10 a.m.) There's plenty of activity, mostly "busywork." Relatives take advantage, you may find yourself running errands. A short trip is part of this scenario. Avoid getting stuck in traffic. A relationship that was "lost" will regain its spark. Virgo is in this picture.

Wednesday, June 19 (Moon in Libra) A family member cooperates in decorating and remodeling. The value of property is enhanced as a result. The moon in Libra promotes fashion, luxury items, and music.

Taurus, Libra, and Scorpio play unusual roles. Have luck with number 6.

Thursday, June 20 (Moon in Libra to Scorpio 4:41 am.)   You might be asking, "Is this déjà vu?" Today's scenario presents familiar places and faces. You might be saying, "I've heard that song before!" Another Cancer wants to tell you something—listen and learn! Pisces figures in this scenario.

Friday, June 21 (Moon in Scorpio)   The moon in Scorpio is in your fifth house—that section of your horoscope equates to excitement, adventure, creativity, and sex appeal. A Libra individual declares, "I tried to catch up to you, but you are really something!" Your lucky number is 8.

Saturday, June 22 (Moon in Scorpio to Sagittarius 7:41 a.m.)   On this Saturday, you make an important decision—to take a trip, to temporarily separate from your family. This scenario features children, challenge, and a variety of sensations. An important opportunity awaits; don't go hat in hand. Exude confidence, tell what you can do.

Sunday, June 23 (Moon in Sagittarius)   You'll feel good about a recent decision—vitality makes a comeback. Spiritual values surface. The moon in your sixth house translates into "Health is good!" A coworker could become a friend and might participate in an original project that requires high intelligence.

Monday, June 24 (Moon in Sagittarius to Capricorn 12:01 p.m.)   The full moon in your sixth house in Sagittarius translates into a journey in connection with work. Focus also on partnership, cooperative efforts, and your marital status. Capricorn and another Cancer will play astounding roles. Be kind and diplomatic.

Tuesday, June 25 (Moon in Capricorn)   You might be saying, "Something mystical is going on here!" The lunar position accents publicity, special appearances, and your partnership and marital status. A legal agreement is presented; study it carefully. Gemini and Sagittarius figure in this exciting scenario.

Wednesday, June 26 (Moon in Capricorn to Aquarius 6:35 p.m.)   Racing luck—all tracks: post position special—number 4 p.p. in the fourth race. A Scorpio jockey could suffer injuries or win a photo finish. Be aware of these letters in the names of potential winning jockeys and horses—D, M, V. You'll receive compliments.

Thursday, June 27 (Moon in Aquarius)   Delve deep into a "mystery." What you discover is apt to relate to investments and accounting. Don't hesitate to express your opinions, to act on instincts and inner feelings. In the stock market, choose stock associated with entertainment. Have luck with number 5.

Friday, June 28 (Moon in Aquarius)   Attention revolves around innovative arrangements in connection with your home. Seek harmony. Music plays a role. Be cooperative, but not weak. Someone who cares very much for you will put feelings into words. Be receptive, not obsequious.

Saturday, June 29 (Moon in Aquarius to Pisces 4:02 a.m.)   Face the fact that you have been, in some ways, falling victim to self-deception. There's no real harm done if you revise some opinions. Someone who talks about "taking a cruise" has no idea about costs and expenses. Know it, and respond accordingly.

Sunday, June 30 (Moon in Pisces)   Strength returns. Act on ideas and inspiration. On a personal level, you get assurance that your love is not unrequited. Those who thought you were a lost cause will sit up and take notice, admitting they were wrong. A Capricorn figures prominently.

JULY 2002

Monday, July 1 (Moon in Pisces to Aries 3:48 p.m.)   You will feel right at home, despite "mysterious happenings." A Pisces family member talks about poltergeists, and the survival of personality after bodily death. Be neither a believer nor a skeptic—salute, and keep the peace. A dream could be prophetic!

Tuesday, July 2 (Moon in Aries)   There's much talk today about investments, stock market, and bonds. Maintain an aura of responsibility—you could be called upon to make a "financial decision." Capricorn and another Cancer figure in this dynamic scenario. Have luck with number 8.

Wednesday, July 3 (Moon in Aries)   Finish what was started three months ago. The moon position highlights your career, success, and promotion. Don't be overly excited, nor should you be nonchalant either. Events happen to your liking. Aries and Libra will play leading roles.

Thursday, July 4 (Moon in Aries to Taurus 4:15 a.m.) Holiday preparations pay off—the day features fireworks, history, and pride. Before the holiday is finished, you'll know more about the Declaration of Independence and who wrote it. A Leo livens up the festivities, and plays a top role.

Friday, July 5 (Moon in Taurus)   Family members get together on an agreement regarding investments and property. Overcome a tendency to brood—substitute meditation. You'll be told by Scorpio that you are attractive, dynamic, and sexy. Focus on home, direction, where you are going from here and on what date.

Saturday, July 6 (Moon in Taurus to Gemini 2:59 p.m.)   On this Saturday, you find ways to entertain others and yourself. Imitating a quiz program might be "just right." Keep resolutions about exercise, diet, and nutrition. You are looking good; keep it that way! Lucky lottery: 1, 12, 13, 15, 18, 50.

Sunday, July 7 (Moon in Gemini)   Much that happens will be behind the scenes. Gemini does lots of talking, is on the borderline of threatening. Maintain your own emotional equilibrium. You instinctively will know what to take seriously. Taurus, Leo, and Scorpio will also figure in this scenario.

Monday, July 8 (Moon in Gemini to Cancer 10:34 p.m.)   Your cycle is moving up, despite minor setbacks. Within twenty-four hours, circumstances will turn in your favor. Strive to solve a mystery, especially the mystery of someone who one day talks about love and the next talks about going away. Gain by reading.

Tuesday, July 9 (Moon in Cancer)   On this Tuesday, get together with a family member who recently has been discouraged. Point out that by tomorrow circumstances will favor effort. Let music be part of your life tonight. Taurus, Libra, and Scorpio will play major roles today.

Wednesday, July 10 (Moon in Cancer to Leo 3:06 a.m.)   On this Wednesday there will be new activities. Circumstances take a dramatic change in your favor. Define terms, outline boundaries, and deal gingerly with Pisces and Virgo. Lucky lottery: 4, 7, 12, 18, 19, 36.

Thursday, July 11 (Moon in Leo)   You finally know where you are going and why. You emit personal magnetism, sensuality, and sex appeal. People ask, "What has come over you?" Respond: "I just feel good and am in the mood for love!" Focus on production, promotion, and responsibility. The pressure is on, but you'll be up to it.

Friday, July 12 (Moon in Leo)   The moon in Leo represents your "money sector." You locate lost valuables. You'll also display a knack for winning. Accent advertising, publicity, and showmanship—you will attract many things, especially romance. Aries and Libra figure in this scenario.

Saturday, July 13 (Moon in Leo to Virgo 5:39 a.m.)   On this Saturday the 13th, you'll be lucky in money and love. Some people claim you get all the breaks and have no time for those who remain poor. Explain: "The harder I work, the luckier I get!" Leo and Aquarius help make this a colorful day.

Sunday, July 14 (Moon in Virgo)   Family, prayer, and meditation are featured. A Virgo relative arrives unannounced. Be understanding and kind—help alleviate some of the loneliness felt by this Virgo. The spotlight is on where and how you live, the sale or purchase of property. Another Cancer plays a role.

Monday, July 15 (Moon in Virgo to Libra 7:38 a.m.)   On this Monday, you embark on a short trip to satisfy the demands of a relative. Don't try too hard to please—be yourself, refuse to get involved in a wild-goose chase. You receive a present, short of payment for your understanding. Gemini is in the picture.

Tuesday, July 16 (Moon in Libra)   Check the details. Be sure of property values. You will encounter fast-talking salespeople. Be amused, withhold judgment. Taurus, Leo, and Scorpio will be part of this scenario. Read between the lines; solve a mathematical puzzle.

Wednesday, July 17 (Moon in Libra to Scorpio 10:12 a.m.)   Be ready for change, travel, and a variety of sensations. The moon position emphasizes basic issues, values, and the ability to break away from restricting influences. The spotlight is on words, reading and writing, sending messages, and opening lines of communication. Your lucky number is 5.

Thursday, July 18 (Moon in Scorpio)   The Scorpio moon relates to your fifth house. This means your creative juices stir. You could also be madly in love and make plans for a change of residence. The moon in your fifth sector has also to do with children. Aries and Libra make known their presence.

Friday, July 19 (Moon in Scorpio to Sagittarius 2:01 p.m.)   You wonder, "Was the work I did on this house worthwhile?" The answer is a positive "yes." Your imagination and creative force requires an outlet. When this day is finished, you will know that you are on the right track. Pisces will play a dramatic role.

Saturday, July 20 (Moon in Sagittarius)   You get things done. The lunar position accents work and health. Maintain your emotional equilibrium. A steady pace is important. You will have more responsibility, but also more money. Capricorn and another Cancer play extraordinary roles. Have luck with number 8.

Sunday, July 21 (Moon in Sagittarius to Capricorn 7:27 p.m.) Finish what you start; don't ignore details. You will receive a compliment on your knowledge of food and recipes. Look beyond the immediate; maintain a universal outlook. Pay close attention to dreams. Tonight's could be "sensational." An Aries declares, "I'm with you!"

Monday, July 22 (Moon in Capricorn) Those who attempt to block your progress will be in for a rude awakening. Do what must be done, and do it efficiently. Oddly enough, persons who were against you could become your staunch allies. Money worries soon will become a "thing of the past." Leo plays a top role.

Tuesday, July 23 (Moon in Capricorn) Consultations and conversations take place about marriage. Give your opinion; make crystal clear that you do not regard yourself as an expert. Focus on legal matters, your reputation, and marital status. Another Cancer reinforces your beliefs. "You are the best!"

Wednesday, July 24 (Moon in Capricorn to Aquarius 2:39 a.m.) Lucky lottery: 7, 11, 12, 18, 22, 49. The full moon position highlights mystery, intrigue, and the "Playground of the occult." You are gaining recognition and will be asked to arrange a social setting. Gemini and Sagittarius will heed your commands—don't be shy!

Thursday, July 25 (Moon in Aquarius) A computer error is possible—check the figures in your bank balance. Have faith in yourself, not computers. Be ready for change, travel, and a variety of experiences. A romantic interlude is fine, but know when to say, "Enough is enough!" Taurus and Scorpio are involved.

Friday, July 26 (Moon in Aquarius to Pisces 12:04 p.m.)   Within 24 hours, you will learn more about the "immediate future." This could involve publishing, advertising, writing, and travel. There has been a log-jam, but it is being removed. You are well thought of; the key is to think well of yourself. Gemini figures prominently.

Saturday, July 27 (Moon in Pisces)   A journey is planned in connection with business and family. Music plays a role. You will be sensitive to sound, and could be involved in an engineering project. Taurus and Libra will work on your behalf—show appreciation without being obsequious. Have luck with number 6.

Sunday, July 28 (Moon in Pisces to Aries 11:38 p.m.)   Spiritual values surface—you'll gain self-knowledge. Pay attention to your inner feelings. You will not be led astray if you follow your instincts and your heart. Pisces or Virgo could corner you with a dubious scheme. Say, "Thanks, but no thanks!"

Monday, July 29 (Moon in Aries)   As the moon leaves Pisces, you will have a break in your career, possibly a promotion. People will be envious, claim you are lucky. Respond: "The harder I work, the luckier I get!" An Aries will show you the ropes. Capricorn is also in the picture.

Tuesday, July 30 (Moon in Aries)   On this Tuesday, you will feel, "I have arrived." Exude confidence; be generous, but let others know you are "strong." Aries and Libra will play major roles and could have these letters or initials in their names: I and R. A relative awaits your arrival in a distant land.

Wednesday, July 31 (Moon in Aries to Taurus 12:15 p.m.)   You have a new outlook. You might be telling yourself, "This is one Wednesday different from any other I've experienced." Put forth original ideas, formats, and concepts. Wear bright colors, and make personal appearances. Take a chance on romance! Your lucky number is 1.

AUGUST 2002

Thursday, August 1 (Moon in Taurus)　　On this first day of August, organize priorities. Your numerical cycle is 8, which equates to Saturn, and combines with your moon significator. You will recall this day as "bittersweet." You'll have more money, authority, and will be watched as one who is on the rise.

Friday, August 2 (Moon in Taurus to Gemini 11:44 p.m.)　　Finish what you start, look beyond the immediate, open lines of communication. You'll be relieved when a long-distance call verifies your views. At the track: post position special—number 8 p.p. in the first race. Libra is in the picture.

Saturday, August 3 (Moon in Gemini)　　On this Saturday, grab hold of your dreams. You can make your wishes come true. Behind the scenes, Gemini is maneuvering, mostly for your good. Elements of timing and luck ride with you. Take the initiative. Don't wait to be told what to do; do what your heart tells you.

Sunday, August 4 (Moon in Gemini)　　It is almost as if you had "double vision." You have the choice of two directions, can actually see "twins." Focus on tradition, motivation, and meditation. A family member is directly involved and wants to be considered a partner.

Monday, August 5 (Moon in Gemini to Cancer 8:00 a.m.)   What a Monday! Social activities accelerate. A secret is revealed to your advantage. Your cycle moves up; circumstances are beginning to turn in your favor. Accent diversity and versatility, but avoid scattering your forces. A Sagittarian will play an extraordinary role.

Tuesday, August 6 (Moon in Cancer)   On this Tuesday, the moon is in your sign—which means your high cycle. You exude confidence, enthusiasm, and sex appeal. Circumstances, even as you read these lines, are moving in your favor. Be selective and choose the best. Genuine bargains are available.

Wednesday, August 7 (Moon in Cancer to Leo 12:25 p.m.)   Racing luck—all tracks: post position special—number 3 p.p. in the seventh race. The emphasis is on reading and writing, publishing and advertising. You could be the "talk of the town"! Virgo and Gemini will figure in today's fascinating scenario.

Thursday, August 8 (Moon in Leo)   The new moon in Leo is in your second house—that section of your horoscope is identified with your ability to locate lost articles and to increase your income. A family member encourages you and says words you love to hear. Taurus and Libra will play distinctive roles.

Friday, August 9 (Moon in Leo to Virgo 2:02 p.m.)   See people and relationships as they are, not merely as you wish they could be. Protect your money. Someone will present you with a get-rich-quick scheme—steer clear of it! Number 7 and Neptune are involved, which means fight a tendency to see only the rosy picture.

Saturday, August 10 (Moon in Virgo)   What had been hidden from view will be obtainable. A Virgo relative plays an important role and deserves credit. A short trip is necessary to obtain a legal document. Avoid riding with a heavy drinker. Capricorn and another Cancer figure prominently.

Sunday, August 11 (Moon in Virgo to Libra 2:37 p.m.)   On this Sunday, you could have a "mystical experience." Number 11 and Uranus are involved—you can readily explain what happens, but it might be more romantic to "guess." Aries and Libra play "magnificent" roles.

Monday, August 12 (Moon in Libra)   Shake off emotional lethargy. The moon in your fourth house has to do with the sale or purchase of property. You are on solid ground in a possible real estate transaction. Make a fresh start in a new direction; exercise independence of thought and action.

Tuesday, August 13 (Moon in Libra to Scorpio 4:00 p.m.)   Keep your options open. Repair work could be required in connection with property. You are not driving a "hard bargain;" you are making intelligent requests. Know it, and respond accordingly to those who attempt to intimidate. Capricorn plays a role.

Wednesday, August 14 (Moon in Scorpio)   Your popularity increases. The Scorpio moon relates to your creativity and sex appeal. Follow your heart. You could be on the precipice of love and fortune. There can be confusion, but you are the one to view your priorities in a realistic light. Have luck with number 3.

Thursday, August 15 (Moon in Scorpio to Sagittarius 7:25 p.m.)   At the track: post position special— number 4 p.p. in the fourth race. Others call upon you to solve problems, including crossword and mathematical games. You'll be told, "Rewriting is necessary!" Taurus, Leo, and Scorpio figure in this scenario.

Friday, August 16 (Moon in Sagittarius) You almost had it "just right." Patience is truly a virtue. A family member seeks harmony, but one might never know it! There will be music, writing, and showmanship. Don't pull punches! You learn much by making note of dreams.

Saturday, August 17 (Moon in Sagittarius) Lucky lottery: 5, 12, 13, 17, 26, 44. Your attention revolves around home and an ability to beautify your surroundings. Be gentle, diplomatic, but not weak. You are in the spotlight. More people observe and report. Taurus and Libra play main roles.

Sunday, August 18 (Moon in Sagittarius to Capricorn 1:15 a.m.) On this Sunday, spiritual values become obvious. Within 24 hours, concern will be about legal affairs, public relations, and your marital status. It is hoped that this foreknowledge will enable you to know what to say and do. Pisces and Virgo figure in this intriguing scenario.

Monday, August 19 (Moon in Capricorn) It is not business as usual; it will be a concentrated effort, with more responsibility and a chance for financial gain. A Capricorn will play a major role, and will help with concerns about your reputation, public relations, and marriage. Your lucky number is 8.

Tuesday, August 20 (Moon in Capricorn to Aquarius 9:16 a.m.) You are challenged to present your views openly and candidly. Your seventh house is involved, meaning controversy, partnership, and marriage. Maintain a universal outlook. Be sympathetic to the underdog, without being naive. Aries and Libra are represented.

Wednesday, August 21 (Moon in Aquarius) You might be asking, "Is this déjà vu?" Today's scenario features familiar places and faces. Someone tells an anecdote: you could swear you heard it before. Strive to exercise independence, originality, and freedom of thought. Lucky lottery: 1, 10, 19, 37, 38, 50.

Thursday, August 22 (Moon in Aquarius to Pisces 7:10 p.m.) The full moon in Aquarius is in your eighth sector. This puts the pressure on accounting, the budget, what you owe, and what you will be paid. The focus is also on direction, motivation, meditation, and your marital status. Another Cancer confides the loss of a valuable.

Friday, August 23 (Moon in Pisces) On this Friday, you study faraway places with the intention of a possible journey. Blend spirituality with materialism. Gemini and Sagittarius will play memorable roles. There are social invitations galore! Have luck with number 3.

Saturday, August 24 (Moon in Pisces) You'll be told your work is excellent, but some revisions are required. Taurus and Scorpio are likely to be involved and will have these letters or initials in their names— D, M, V. You will be tested on your extrasensory perception.

Sunday, August 25 (Moon in Pisces to Aries 6:47 a.m.) Your career is due to get a boost. Meantime, don't neglect personal obligations. Focus on change, travel, and variety. It will be necessary to write. Your dream last night could have prophetic value. Gemini, Virgo, and Sagittarius are in the picture.

Monday, August 26 (Moon in Aries)   Attention revolves around home, family, and insurance payments. Someone in a position of authority requests a conference. You could be dealing with an Aries who means well, but whose tone is sharp. Your climb to the top is accelerated.

Tuesday, August 27 (Moon in Aries to Taurus 7:30 p.m.)   Go slow and play the waiting game. In recent days, you have advanced quickly. Today, slow your pace. You are due to make friends and influence people. Avoid self-deception; see people and relationships as they are and not merely as you wish they could be.

Wednesday, August 28 (Moon in Taurus)   On this day, you'll have a streak of "good luck." This applies especially if you stick with numbers 8, 11, and 22. You will know that your love is not unrequited. You will feel fulfilled and happier as a result.

Thursday, August 29 (Moon in Taurus)   Be aware of foreign affairs, money exchange, and games of luck and skill. You might be asking yourself, "Is this really me?" Much that happens can be labeled "fantastic." Aries and Libra help you in solving a financial dilemma. Roadblocks are removed. There's smooth sailing ahead if you so permit.

Friday, August 30 (Moon in Taurus to Gemini 7:44 a.m.)   Don't get in your own way—stress originality, independence, and derring-do. Imprint style, grab hold of "luck," and don't give up the ship. You recently, this week, had proof that you can be lucky and ultimately you are a winner. A Leo figures prominently.

Saturday, August 31 (Moon in Gemini)   On this Saturday, with the moon in Gemini, you learn secrets and could visit one confined to home or hospital. Your cycle moves up, so get ready for a "smashing victory." Luck or not, you display amazing ability. Your fortunate number is 2.

SEPTEMBER 2002

Sunday, September 1 (Moon in Gemini to Cancer 5:13 p.m.)   The first day of this month is one you will remember. You learn secrets. A Gemini becomes your friend, and you make a fresh start in a new direction. Finish what you start; look beyond the immediate. Travel plans impinge themselves upon your mind.

Monday, September 2 (Moon in Cancer)   What you failed to finish 24 hours ago can be completed by tonight. A relationship that "sputtered" will be back on track. Leo and Aquarius figure in this scenario and are likely to have these letters or initials in their names—A, S, J.

Tuesday, September 3 (Moon in Cancer to Leo 10:34 p.m.)   Questions about joint efforts and marriage loom large. You will be wondering, "Why am I here, where do I fit in?" The answers become available if you look within and face the music. Capricorn and another Cancer figure in this scenario.

Wednesday, September 4 (Moon in Leo)   You receive "bright indications" that your financial picture will improve, since the moon is in Leo, your "house of money." A product requires more advertising and showmanship. Emphasize humor and versatility, and give full rein to your intellectual curiosity. Your lucky number is 3.

Thursday, September 5 (Moon in Leo)   At the track—post position special—number 4 p.p. in the fifth race. On a personal level, express feelings concerning love and passion. Money comes your way like a bolt out of the blue. Check details, read the fine print, and don't be afraid to suggest a "computer error."

Friday, September 6 (Moon in Leo to Virgo 12:14 a.m.) Your restlessness and creativity find outlets—be ready for change, travel, and a variety of experiences. Investigate, discover, communicate. Gemini, Virgo, and Sagittarius play memorable roles, and have these letters or initials in their names—E, N, W.

Saturday, September 7 (Moon in Virgo to Libra 11:56 p.m.) The new moon in Virgo coincides with requests and surprises involving relatives. You'll be asked to participate in a short trip. Be sure you don't get involved in a wild-goose chase. Attention also revolves around your home, family, and questions about a possible reunion with a "past love."

Sunday, September 8 (Moon in Libra) Don't confuse spiritual values with self-deception. You will be tested and questioned—it is best to leave people playing guessing games. This means don't confess, confide, or tell all. Pisces and Virgo play what could become "sensational" roles.

Monday, September 9 (Moon in Libra to Scorpio 9:48 p.m.) This could be your power play day. Property value and real estate enter the picture. You'll be dealing with a wise Capricorn who will help you if you also help yourself. Another Cancer is also in the picture, and will prove loyal. Have luck with number 8.

Tuesday, September 10 (Moon in Scorpio) Desire to travel is very much on your mind, but responsibilities at home negate that desire. The focus is on property, home, real estate, and details which are "unraveling."

A transaction will be completed. A Libra will have much to do with it.

Wednesday, September 11 (Moon in Scorpio)   Out of the welter of confusion will emerge enlightenment. Almost in a flash, you will know what to do and will take direct action. There's no time to procrastinate. Make a fresh start in a new direction and be receptive to a different kind of love. Have luck with number 1.

Thursday, September 12 (Moon in Scorpio to Sagittarius 1:44 a.m.)   Racing luck—all tracks: post position special—number 2 p.p. in the sixth race. The emphasis will be on cooperative efforts, City Hall activities, and your marital status. Maintain creative control. Refuse to give up something of value for nothing in return.

Friday, September 13 (Moon in Sagittarius)   You will not be unlucky! The elements of timing and luck ride with you, despite it being Friday the 13th! In fact, this could be the start of a winning streak. Gemini and Sagittarius will play meaningful roles and have these letters or initials in their names—C, L, U.

Saturday, September 14 (Moon in Sagittarius to Capricorn 6:47 a.m.)   On this Saturday, protect your arms and hands from injury—this means special precautions. This could be your "makeover day." Rebuild, rewrite, and revise. This applies also to your personal life. Deal gingerly with Taurus and Scorpio. Publish!

Sunday, September 15 (Moon in Capricorn)   Surprises are due. A member of the opposite sex declares, "I am very attracted to you and at times I can hardly keep my hands off you!" Focus on communication, and finding the "right words." Gemini, Virgo, and

Sagittarius play serious roles and have these initials in their names: E, N, W.

Monday, September 16 (Moon in Capricorn to Aquarius 2:54 p.m.) A family member comes to your aid at the "last minute." A legal document is involved, along with public relations, your reputation, partnership, and marriage. Attention revolves around your home, security, music, and sound. Libra and Aries refuse to let you escape your past.

Tuesday, September 17 (Moon in Aquarius) Lie low; play the waiting game. You don't have the complete story. It's not a matter of deception, but you do best by holding off on a major decision. See people, places, and relationships as they exist, not merely as you wish they could be. Avoid self-deception!

Wednesday, September 18 (Moon in Aquarius) Lucky lottery: 2, 8, 11, 12, 14, 18. Pounce on an opportunity relating to a "big financial deal." It will be obvious you did not fall off a turnip truck. People express admiration; many want you to be "on our side." Capricorn and another Cancer figure in this scenario.

Thursday, September 19 (Moon in Aquarius to Pisces 1:17 a.m.) Mistakes are corrected. You get credit for being observant. This should be a lesson: Don't leave everything to computers. A mysterious physical attraction will be "explained" by Aries. You will be called in for consultation; don't go hat in hand.

Friday, September 20 (Moon in Pisces) State terms; don't back down. You are in the driver's seat! Imprint style, let others know, "I know what I am doing and I am sticking to what I know!" Leo and Aquarius figure prominently and will have these letters in their names: A, S, J. Your lucky number is 1.

Saturday, September 21 (Moon in Pisces to Aries 1:10 p.m.)   Open lines of communication. You could be invited to travel overseas! People want to be with you. Some vie for the "honor" of wining and dining you. Be your natural self; show appreciation, without being obsequious. A marriage question looms large.

Sunday, September 22 (Moon in Aries)   On this Sunday, your self-esteem grows—you are given special greetings by those who, at one time or another, appeared to ignore you. Your popularity increases; you could be placed in charge of entertainment for a company or charitable organization.

Monday, September 23 (Moon in Aries)   You will have more responsibility. You will be aware of it, almost as soon as you open your eyes this Monday. Focus on twists and turns, complications, and mathematical puzzles. Take it in stride—you are not expected to know everything at once.

Tuesday, September 24 (Moon in Aries to Taurus 1:53 a.m.)   You are "released" from a burden you should not have volunteered to carry in the first place. The spotlight is on freedom of thought and action. You could travel, write, and flirt. What begins as a mild relationship gets warm, and could get too hot not to cool down.

Wednesday, September 25 (Moon in Taurus)   Focus on money, home, and the security of your family. You'll be told, "Let's get down to brass tacks!" Respond: "That is perfectly all right with me, so let's get to the bottom of this!" You'll be sensitive to sound, music, and subtle hints. Your lucky number is 6.

Thursday, September 26 (Moon in Taurus to Gemini 2:25 p.m.)   You can afford to play the waiting game!

Don't be bullied, rushed, or cajoled into making snap decisions. Take the overall view, then make a "pronouncement." Remember: Don't give up something of value for nothing in return. Virgo plays a dynamic role.

Friday, September 27 (Moon in Gemini)   On this Friday, there are numerous opportunities—pick and choose! Something is occurring, even as you read these words, behind the scenes. Gemini plays the role of director. Let it be known that you are knowledgeable. Another Cancer is in the picture.

Saturday, September 28 (Moon in Gemini)   On this Saturday, you will feel generous, very worthwhile. Your outlook will be universal. Nothing will approach narrowmindedness. Keep an open mind without being naive. Aries and Libra persons will play dramatic roles. Have luck with number 9.

Sunday, September 29 (Moon in Gemini to Cancer 12:59 a.m.)   Your cycle is moving up. Circumstances are turning in your favor. Gemini confesses to a secret, something you already knew. Look beyond the immediate; you are going to receive a tempting offer—in career or romance. Leo will figure prominently.

Monday, September 30 (Moon in Cancer)   On this last day of September, with the moon in your sign, expect surprises, compliments, and cash. Another Cancer plays an instrumental role and will prove to be your valuable ally. Wear the color sea green, and make personal appearances. Capricorn is in the picture.

OCTOBER 2002

Tuesday, October 1 (Moon in Cancer to Leo 7:56 a.m.)   You will be provided with information about a "fascinating future." Look beyond the immediate: it appears everything has been set up for you to succeed. Take the initiative; make a fresh start; be receptive to romance. Leo will play a dramatic role.

Wednesday, October 2 (Moon in Leo)   It might appear as if something has been taken away—if so, it will be quickly replaced. Line up your assets; be familiar with profit-and-loss columns. Another Cancer becomes "chummy." This includes a dinner invitation during which recipes will be traded.

Thursday, October 3 (Moon in Leo to Virgo 10:50 a.m.)   Everything begins to "fit." Don't get in your own way! Examine, investigate, and make inquiries—depending upon your intensity, answers will be received. Gemini and Sagittarius figure in this dynamic scenario. Have luck with number 3.

Friday, October 4 (Moon in Virgo)   Don't permit yourself to be discouraged by a pileup of details. Confront red tape, do what must be done, and don't permit it to disturb your sleep tonight. Taurus, Leo, and Scorpio are likely to be involved and have these letters or initials in their names—D, M, V.

Saturday, October 5 (Moon in Virgo to Libra 10:50 a.m.)   Take special care in traffic; people experience "road rage." A promise has not actually been broken, so don't equate delay with defeat. Read, write, do some research, and be knowledgeable about your subjects. Lucky lottery: 7, 14, 16, 28, 32, 51.

Sunday, October 6 (Moon in Libra)   The new moon highlights where you live, the sturdiness of a project, and a balance between extremes. Someone who once played an important role in your life will make a reappearance. Taurus, Libra, and Scorpio figure in this dynamic scenario. Have luck with number 6.

Monday, October 7 (Moon in Libra to Scorpio 9:57 a.m.) During meditation and much contemplation, you receive answers to questions such as, "Why am I here?" You also have a lesson repeated: "The wise person controls his or her destiny—astrology points the way!" See people, places, and relationships as they are, not merely as you wish they could be.

Tuesday, October 8 (Moon in Scorpio) Nothing happens halfway today! If you start something, finish it. A physical attraction is highlighted; what begins as "playful" will become serious and hot. If you don't want to get burned, don't play the game. Capricorn and another Cancer will figure in this fascinating scenario.

Wednesday, October 9 (Moon in Scorpio to Sagittarius 10:21 a.m.) Racing luck—all tracks: post position special—number 1 p.p. in the eighth race. Focus on wisdom and understanding, blended with passion. You will know the right thing to do. The question is, "Will you do it?" Aries and Libra are in this picture.

Thursday, October 10 (Moon in Sagittarius) You've waited for this kind of day! It is a Thursday during which you can "show off" your talent and product. Emphasize innovativeness, originality, and your pioneering spirit. Leo and Aquarius will play dramatic roles—you'll benefit as a result.

Friday, October 11 (Moon in Sagittarius to Capricorn 1:45 p.m.) Your family is confused about your direction and motivation. Do what you can, without appearing "haughty." Use your intuitive intellect—maintain an aura of mystery and intrigue. An

Aquarian will play a preposterous role. Have luck with number 2.

Saturday, October 12 (Moon in Capricorn) Luck rides with you; you could win a contest. The moon in your seventh house means you will be confronted by those who wish to test your knowledge. The spotlight is also on cooperative efforts, legal agreements, and your partnership and marriage. Your fortunate number is 3.

Sunday, October 13 (Moon in Capricorn to Aquarius 8:51 p.m.) Lie low; play the waiting game. There are many details which must be "untangled." Be willing to tear down in order to rebuild. A Scorpio might attempt to "take over." Proofreading is necessary and could save embarrassment and money.

Monday, October 14 (Moon in Aquarius) Get ready for change, travel, variety, and a request for accounting. Within 24 hours, expect a solution to a financial puzzle. Be sure computers are in order. A romantic relationship is anything but steady. Adjustments may be necessary, especially when dealing with a stubborn Taurus.

Tuesday, October 15 (Moon in Aquarius) Someone close to your family indicates, "I would like to be closer to you!" The emphasis is on what happens at home, a domestic situation, color coordination, music, and decorations. Aries and Libra will play outstanding roles.

Wednesday, October 16 (Moon in Aquarius to Pisces 8:51 p.m.) At the track—post position special: number 1 p.p. in the sixth race. Define terms, perfect techniques, don't be deceived by outward appearances. All that glitters is not gold. Pisces and Virgo will play outstanding roles.

Thursday, October 17 (Moon in Pisces) What you have been waiting for will arrive tonight. Be sure to take note of your dreams—they could be guideposts to your future. People you are familiar with will prove loyal, including Capricorn and Cancer. Have luck with number 8.

Friday, October 18 (Moon in Pisces to Aries 7:12 p.m.) Travel plans are verified. Maintain a universal outlook; deal gingerly with Aries and Libra. People are drawn to you with their questions and problems, some of them quite intimate. Do your best. The Golden Rule is the word: The more you help others, the more your own dilemmas dissolve.

Saturday, October 19 (Moon in Aries) Take charge! Your cycle is such that your personality impresses and conquers. Don't follow others; do your own thing. Welcome a different kind of love. Leo and Aquarius will play dramatic roles, and help you achieve your goal. Lucky lottery: 1, 10, 12, 16, 18, 24.

Sunday, October 20 (Moon in Aries) Someone at the top wants to confer with you. Do not arrive hat in hand. Express confidence; be charming, but not obsequious. Put forth concepts that will include home and marriage. Capricorn and another Cancer figure in this "fantastic" scenario.

Monday, October 21 (Moon in Aries to Taurus 7:55 a.m.) The full moon at the top of your horoscope once again emphasizes leadership and promotion. Those who originally planned to oppose you are now having second thoughts. There are questions about emotional and financial security. You'll be asked to leave home for period of three weeks.

Tuesday, October 22 (Moon in Taurus)   What at first appeared to be a setback will turn out to be much in your favor. The transitting moon in your eleventh house means you gain allies, win friends, and influence people. You could raise funding for a unique project. Take a chance on romance!

Wednesday, October 23 (Moon in Taurus to Gemini 8:16 p.m.)   Benefits pile up. You can hardly believe this is happening to you. The number 5 numerical cycle, plus the moon in your eleventh house, is a winning combination. Members of the opposite sex will find you especially attractive. Have luck with number 5.

Thursday, October 24 (Moon in Gemini)   There's music in your life; dance to your own tune. You go through a minor setback, but your cycle moves up and you will succeed in the long run. Attention revolves around the sale or purchase of a home, your family, and marital status. An Aries will speak up on your behalf.

Friday, October 25 (Moon in Gemini)   You will hear these words: "Don't change horses in midstream!" Those who claim they have better ways could be talking out of both sides of their mouths. Put succinctly: You are on a roll! A lesser person may be jealous; that is too bad.

Saturday, October 26 (Moon in Gemini to Cancer 7:09 a.m.)   At the track: post position special—number 4 p.p. in the eighth race. Focus on teaching, sharing knowledge, and being subjected to challenges. You'll surprise even yourself with the answers, which are simple and accurate and at times funny. Capricorn is in the picture.

Sunday, October 27—Daylight Saving Time Ends (Moon in Cancer)   On this Sunday, your spiritual values surface. The moon is in your sign; people are drawn to you; you exude personal magnetism and sex appeal. Finish what you start. Let go of a burden not your own in the first place. Aries and Libra edge into this scenario, wishing you well.

Monday, October 28 (Moon in Cancer to Leo 2:18 p.m.)   This is the time for a new start, romance, creativity, and style. Make a fresh start; wear sea green. Personal contacts will be of much importance. Someone of the opposite sex declares, "I can hardly keep my hands off you!" An Aquarian is involved.

Tuesday, October 29 (Moon in Leo)   There's much confusion, but you ultimately get the money. Stick to your principles. Maintain creative control. A question persists about whether you are being unorthodox. Answer: "Yes, I am, and I intend to be even more unorthodox!" Another Cancer is in this picture.

Wednesday, October 30 (Moon in Leo to Virgo 6:58 p.m.)   Money comes your way, so line up priorities. Those who once said they would have nothing to do with you are now pleading, "Give us another chance!" Gemini and Sagittarius will grab the spotlight. Lucky lottery: 3, 16, 19, 40, 42, 51.

Thursday, October 31 (Moon in Virgo)   Plans change. Stress versatility and intelligence. A Virgo relative wants more attention and lets you know it. Ride with the tide. You continue to be in charge of your own destiny. The weather proves to be a puzzle—possibly very windy.

Friday, November 1 (Moon in Virgo to Libra 8:27 p.m.)   Maintain a new attitude of optimism. Your ears must be burning. People are talking about you. A Virgo relative acts as your representative, whether you like it or not. A short trip is necessary. Don't turn it into a wild-goose chase! Insist on your turn!

Saturday, November 2 (Moon in Libra)   All that glitters is not gold! You will be praised; you will be popular; big promises will be made to you. Get it in writing! Gemini and Sagittarius play major roles. Diversify and show that you can laugh at your own foibles. Have luck with number 3.

Sunday, November 3 (Moon in Libra to Scorpio 8:09 p.m.)   Obstacles are overcome. Libra proves to be your valuable ally. Someone "at the top" respects you, and seeks your counsel. Take notes about ideas, concepts. A dream tonight, properly interpreted, proves enlightening. By proofreading, you discover an error that would have been serious.

Monday, November 4 (Moon in Scorpio)   The new moon relates to your house of creativity and romance. In Scorpio, the lunar position stimulates your creative juices. Someone you care about will be receptive to your advances. Gemini, Virgo, and Sagittarius play memorable roles. Your lucky number is 5.

Tuesday, November 5 (Moon in Scorpio to Sagittarius 8:01 p.m.)   At the track—post position special—number 6 p.p. in the fourth and eighth races. You emit personal magnetism; your sales ability reaches new heights. Someone of the opposite sex comments on your "sex appeal." Write your views!

Wednesday, November 6 (Moon in Sagittarius)   Lucky lottery: 7, 9, 12, 18, 33, 41. Define meanings, outline boundaries, and let people know you will go only so far. Pisces and Virgo play meaningful roles, and could get in the way of progress. Take an independent course; also take a chance on romance.

Thursday, November 7 (Moon in Sagittarius to Capricorn 10:00 p.m.)   What 24 hours ago was considered a deficit will now be transformed into an asset. Your general health report is good; proceed toward your ultimate goal. A coworker admires you and says so. Capricorn and another Cancer will play outstanding roles.

Friday, November 8 (Moon in Capricorn)   Finish what you start; be aware of legal angles. The moon position accents your reputation, public relations, partnership, and marriage. Stress universal appeal. Dealing with a foreign nation is a distinct possibility. Aries is represented.

Saturday, November 9 (Moon in Capricorn)   You will encounter people who are congenial. Some could be overly enthusiastic. Heed your own counsel; highlight independence of thought and action. Imprint style; do not follow others. An apparent lonely road will not remain so—there will be plenty of people and excitement. Your lucky number is 1.

Sunday, November 10 (Moon in Capricorn to Aquarius 3:27 a.m.)   Your efforts turn to unorthodox subjects. If it interests you, it will also interest others. If true to yourself, you cannot go wrong. Proceed accordingly. Another Cancer native is in the picture and will lend support. Those who once shunned you now appeal, "Let us in on it!"

Monday, November 11 (Moon in Aquarius)   Money comes from a surprise source—be positive that everything is on the up-and-up. Diversify, examine various aspects of a project. On a personal level, keep recent resolutions about exercise, diet, and nutrition. Social promotion!

Tuesday, November 12 (Moon in Aquarius to Pisces 12:41 p.m.)   Within 24 hours, you will be in charge of your own destiny. Make travel plans, look beyond the immediate, and do what you can to learn more about a foreign language. Exchange rates are important for you to know; don't be kept in ignorance. Scorpio is involved.

Wednesday, November 13 (Moon in Pisces)   You have more freedom of thought and action. Be in communication with representatives of foreign lands. You are on the verge of an international deal. Look to fame and fortune—they are not so far away! Get close to the ambassador of a place you intend to visit.

Thursday, November 14 (Moon in Pisces to Aries 12:37 a.m.)   A family member, currently far away, will be "in touch." The spotlight is on your ability to dance to your own tune. Those who discourage you are victims of the "green-eyed monster." Jealousy is the only vice for which one receives no pleasure in return.

Friday, November 15 (Moon in Aries)   At the track: number 1 p.p. in the seventh race. The Aries moon represents for you promotion, production, and added responsibility. Be generous, not extravagant. Gather strength, and prepare for a weekend that will include mystery, intrigue, and the necessity for making decisions.

Saturday, November 16 (Moon in Aries)   Someone who talks a big game may have nothing to show for it. Know it, and protect yourself accordingly. Refuse to be inveigled into a wild-goose chase. Your dream tonight could be fantastic—it might be a guidepost to the future. Lucky lottery: 1, 8, 10, 12, 18, 22.

Sunday, November 17 (Moon in Aries to Taurus 1:22 p.m.)   Within 24 hours, the moon position will be "just right" for coinciding with winning plays. You are due to win friends and influence people—in matters of speculation, tonight stick with number 9. Libra plays an important role.

Monday, November 18 (Moon in Taurus)   You get the proverbial second chance. The Taurus moon relates to your eleventh house—that section of your horoscope is associated with an ability to get your way. Your popularity increases; you might have an "army of friends." Leo is in this picture.

Tuesday, November 19 (Moon in Taurus)   Focus on trepidation in connection with signing an agreement. Don't be afraid to wait and to ask for "time out." You will be at the right place at a special moment almost effortlessly. Support will come from an unusual source—don't ask too many questions.

Wednesday, November 20 (Moon in Taurus to Gemini 1:23 a.m.)   The full moon, lunar eclipse falls in your eleventh house—people you depend upon may "disappear." By contrast, people who are practically strangers will "report" ready to fight for your cause. Gemini and Sagittarius will play outstanding roles.

Thursday, November 21 (Moon in Gemini)   Be willing to rewrite, revise, to tear down in order to rebuild. The Gemini moon represents your twelfth house—you will have dealings with institutions, perhaps even theaters. Secret efforts by Gemini will be revealed; you will be pleasantly surprised.

Friday, November 22 (Moon in Gemini to Cancer 11:46 a.m.)   The day is "just right" for making necessary changes. You gain information and will be better prepared for change, travel, and a variety of experiences. A Sagittarian declares, "There are secrets; you are being kept from essential knowledge."

Saturday, November 23 (Moon in Cancer)   Attention revolves around your home, security, and the protection of your property and family. The moon in your sign represents your high cycle—take the initiative; you will be at the right place at a special moment. Wear the color sea green, and make personal appearances, and imprint your style.

Sunday, November 24 (Moon in Cancer to Leo 8:01 p.m.)   A clandestine operation is exposed—to your advantage. Spiritual values dominate; you'll be dealing with people who are secretive, not necessarily evil, but reluctant to let you know them completely. Pisces plays a major role.

Monday, November 25 (Moon in Leo)   A power play—money you have had coming to you will be paid. Let others know you are not without allies. When this point is made, events transpire to help you emotionally and financially. You could run for public office and win!

Tuesday, November 26 (Moon in Leo)   By planning ahead, you almost ensure success. You locate lost articles. Your investment know-how will prove profitable. Focus on entertainment stock, highlight showmanship, and color coordination. Aries and Libra will play "distinguished" roles.

Wednesday, November 27 (Moon in Leo to Virgo 1:40 a.m.)   Make a fresh start in a new direction. Focus on trips, visits, and children. Emphasize your willingness to make intelligent concessions. Don't abandon your principles, but avoid appearing fanatical. How about that recent dream! Lucky lottery: 1, 11, 12, 18, 22, 46.

Thursday, November 28 (Moon in Virgo)   Thanksgiving! This year, this holiday, you will admit to yourself: "I don't have much of anything, but I do have lots to be thankful for!" Another Cancer plays a key role, will help you, and will join in on the festivities. Your lucky number is 2.

Friday, November 29 (Moon in Virgo to Libra 4:53 a.m.)   Refuse to be discouraged by an aura of confusion. People tend to change their minds, if not their policies. Focus on work methods, employment, and your ability to solve difficult mathematical problems. Libra, Sagittarius, and Gemini figure in this scenario.

Saturday, November 30 (Moon in Libra)   On this last day of the month, check details, and be aware of possible computer errors. Be confident. You have winning ways, which others are beginning to notice. A Libran declares, "I wish I had known you long ago, and if I had, I feel I would be happier and wealthier!"

DECEMBER 2002

Sunday, December 1 (Moon in Libra to Scorpio 6:14 a.m.)   You could be celebrating on this first day of December. There's plenty of laughter and communication from those whom you truly admire. Gemini and Sagittarius will play outstanding roles. In matters of speculation, stick with number 3. Good luck!

Monday, December 2 (Moon in Scorpio)   At the track: post position special—number 4 p.p. in the fourth race. Throughout the day, attend to details, check for computer errors. Arrange priorities, take charge of your own destiny. Taurus, Leo, and Scorpio will play outstanding roles.

Tuesday, December 3 (Moon in Scorpio to Sagittarius 6:57 a.m.)   Your creative juices stir; you'll attract people who previously seemed to ignore you. Focus on reading, writing, and teaching. Whether you intend to or not, you will take a chance on romance. Deal with advertisers, publishers, and publicity people. You're going places!

Wednesday, December 4 (Moon in Sagittarius)   The new moon, solar eclipse falls in Sagittarius, your sixth house. Translated, expect "fireworks" in connection with your health and employment. A family member tells you things which prove "stunning." It's not all bad, but very surprising. Libra is involved.

Thursday, December 5 (Moon in Sagittarius to Capricorn 8:38 a.m.)   Hold back, pull no punches, and play the waiting game. There are facts which are yet to be revealed. Decisions should be based on information that will be made available within 24 hours. Pisces and Virgo play key roles, will figure prominently.

Friday, December 6 (Moon in Capricorn)   The spotlight is on your reputation. credibility, legal affairs, and public relations. The question of your marital status will loom large. See people, places, and relationships in a realistic light. Avoid deceiving yourself. Capricorn plays an unorthodox role.

Saturday, December 7 (Moon in Capricorn to Aquarius 12:54 p.m.)   Some bitterness remains, as you remember Pearl Harbor Day. Look beyond the immediate; maintain a universal outlook. You might find yourself heavily involved with "world affairs." Aries and Libra play fascinating roles, and have these letters in their names: I and R.

Sunday, December 8 (Moon in Aquarius)   A wish is fulfilled! Take the initiative. Make a fresh start in a new direction. You exude personal magnetism, an aura of sensuality and sex appeal. Your vigor returns; confidence replaces doubt. Leo and Aquarius figure in this unusual scenario. Have luck with number 1.

Monday, December 9 (Moon in Aquarius to Pisces 8:46 p.m.)   Factors pile up to indicate interest in "restaurant management." Seek delay, without appearing to be "stalling." You are needed; others let you know it. Capricorn and another Cancer play creative roles. Have luck with number 2.

Tuesday, December 10 (Moon in Pisces)   The moon is "getting ready" to enter Pisces. That will happen tomorrow, representing a high cycle for you. Tonight, settle differences with a member of the opposite sex who of late has been taking you for granted. A Gemini figures prominently.

Wednesday, December 11 (Moon in Pisces)   Circumstances are turning in your favor—focus on travel, inspiration, creativity, and romance. By a careful reading of proofs, you discover subtle mistakes that, had they not been discovered, would have been costly and embarrassing.

Thursday, December 12 (Moon in Pisces to Aries 7:57 a.m.) The emphasis is on travel, publishing, and making known your views. Someone in another land wants to "tell you something." An opportunity exists to find a representative for your talents and products. You are alert and dynamic; vigor makes a comeback. Virgo is involved.

Friday, December 13 (Moon in Aries) While many people will consider this an unlucky day, for you it will be pleasant and you will be lucky in financial affairs. Beautify your surroundings, especially in the home. A family member talks about "singing lessons." Aries plays the top role.

Saturday, December 14 (Moon in Aries to Taurus 8:42 p.m.) Focus on career, business, production, and promotion. Warning: Remove fire hazards, and avoid carelessness in connection with combustibles. Pisces and Virgo command part of scenario and could have these letters and initials in their names: G, P, Y.

Sunday, December 15 (Moon in Taurus) Although it is Sunday, you'll be called upon for your expertise in a unique project. The pressure is on; you will be up to it. Capricorn and another Cancer figure prominently. What you do today will relate to how much money you'll earn in the near future.

Monday, December 16 (Moon in Taurus to Gemini 8:41 a.m.) The Taurus moon relates to your eleventh house—in turn, that is associated with your ability to win friends and influence people. Put succinctly, it is lucky. You could obtain funding for an unusual project. Your popularity is on the rise; Libra will play a fascinating role.

Tuesday, December 17 (Moon in Gemini)   Shiny objects are part of this scenario, including jewelry. A gift is received; be gracious and grateful, not obsequious. Imprint style; display your pioneering spirit. Leo and Aquarius will grab the spotlight. Color coordination and publicity play meaningful roles.

Wednesday, December 18 (Moon in Gemini)   On this Wednesday, you have luck by sticking with number 2. You'll be dealing with Capricorn and another Cancer. The Gemini moon relates to secrets, institutions, hospitals, and theater. Dining out tonight could feature broiled lobster.

Thursday, December 19 (Moon in Gemini to Cancer 6:29 p.m.)   You could "invent a game." The full moon in your twelfth house represents mystery, intrigue, and romance. A Gemini will be here, there, everywhere, and will command attention. A Sagittarian attempts to exercise control, and might prove successful.

Friday, December 20 (Moon in Cancer)   Be willing to tear down in order to rebuild, write and read, learn and teach. In your high cycle, get ready to advance fast. Display confidence; others will be duly impressed. Avoid being with those who take you for granted. Have luck with number 4.

Saturday, December 21 (Moon in Cancer)   What an exciting Saturday! The moon is in your sign, and your numerical cycle is 5. The spotlight is on change and a variety of sensations. Someone of the opposite sex comments, "You are sexy indeed, and I have trouble keeping my hands off you!" Get a publishing project started tonight.

Sunday, December 22 (Moon in Cancer to Leo 1:47 a.m.) Invite a literary agent to your home. Blend business with pleasure. You have much to offer; know it and be confident. Deal with diet and ways to overcome being obese. You are a very special person, and others sense it. Taurus plays a role.

Monday, December 23 (Moon in Leo) Contrast! You are pulled in two directions simultaneously. One direction leads to mystery, intrigue, and uncertainty. The other direction represents inspiration and emotional involvement. Your choice will be simple: Expose emotions to valid realistic feelings.

Tuesday, December 24 (Moon in Leo to Virgo 7:04 a.m.) Christmas Eve! The Leo moon, the number 8 numerical cycle, plus other factors will make this a Christmas Eve you won't soon forget. Focus on showmanship and expense. You receive a gift that could cause embarrassment because of the obvious expense, much more than you anticipated.

Wednesday, December 25 (Moon in Virgo) On this Christmas Day, spiritual values will be much in evidence. You'll be finished with a project; your critical faculties will be honed to razor-Sharpness. Make it clear that the Three Wise Men were astrologers. Libra plays a "magical" role.

Thursday, December 26 (Moon in Virgo to Libra 10:52 a.m.) You are due to make a fresh start, to have a health checkup, to resolve to take better care of yourself. Imprint style, display pioneering spirit, and express your views in a dynamic, forceful way. Refuse to be intimidated by one who "knows it all."

Friday, December 27 (Moon in Libra) The spotlight will be on security, coming down to earth, and building confidence because you will know "inside" what is happening and what to do about it. Another Cancer extends the hand of friendship, assuring, "I will be there when you need me!"

Saturday, December 28 (Moon in Libra to Scorpio 1:40 p.m.)   On this Saturday, pressure is relieved. You will have fun. A lively discussion with a Sagittarian combines business with pleasure. Remember resolutions about diet and nutrition. People consult you about travel, social affairs, and political and charitable activities.

Sunday, December 29 (Moon in Scorpio)   Out of a period of confusion will arise knowledge and spiritual strength. Be willing to rewrite, revise, and rebuild. The question of architecture becomes a subject of interest. Basic research is necessary; you could be asked to debate, so be sure of factual information.

Monday, December 30 (Moon in Scorpio to Sagittarius 4:00 p.m.)   You'll be told, "You are an excellent companion." The Scorpio moon is in your fifth house—obviously, you'll be more than a "companion." Focus on creativity, personal magnetism, and sex appeal. You could get involved, so know when to say, "Enough is enough!"

Tuesday, December 31 (Moon in Sagittarius)   New Year's Eve! Celebrate at home, if possible. Go slow on adult beverages. Avoid driving with a heavy drinker. A family member wants reassurance that "I am really loved!" Many resolutions are made, most of them sincere. Libra plays a fascinating role.

HAPPY NEW YEAR!

ABOUT THE AUTHOR

Born on August 5, 1926, in Philadelphia, Sydney Omarr was the only person ever given full-time duty in the U.S. Army as an astrologer. He also is regarded as the most erudite astrologer of our time and the best known, through his syndicated column (300 newspapers) and his radio and television programs (he was Merv Griffin's "resident astrologer"). Omarr has been called the most "knowledgeable astrologer since Evangeline Adams." His forecasts of Nixon's downfall, the end of World War II in mid-August of 1945, the assassination of John F. Kennedy, Roosevelt's election to the fourth term and his death in office . . . these and many others are on the record and quoted enough to be considered "legendary."

ABOUT THIS SERIES

This is one of a series of twelve
Day-by-Day Astrological Guides
for the signs of 2002
by Sydney Omarr.